Hiking Washington

A Guide to the State's Greatest Hiking Adventures

Revised Edition

Oliver Lazenby

FALCONGUIDES

GUILFORD, CONNECTICUT
HELENA, MONTANA

AN IMPRINT OF ROWMAN & LITTLEFIELD

FalconGuides is an imprint of Rowman & Littlefield.
Falcon, FalconGuides, and Outfit Your Mind are registered trademarks of Rowman & Littlefield.

Photos by Oliver Lazenby unless otherwise noted

Maps: Daniel Lloyd © Rowman & Littlefield

Distributed by NATIONAL BOOK NETWORK

Library of Congress Cataloging-in-Publication data is available on file.
ISBN 978-0-7627-8188-1
Printed in the United States of America

Contents

The Hikes

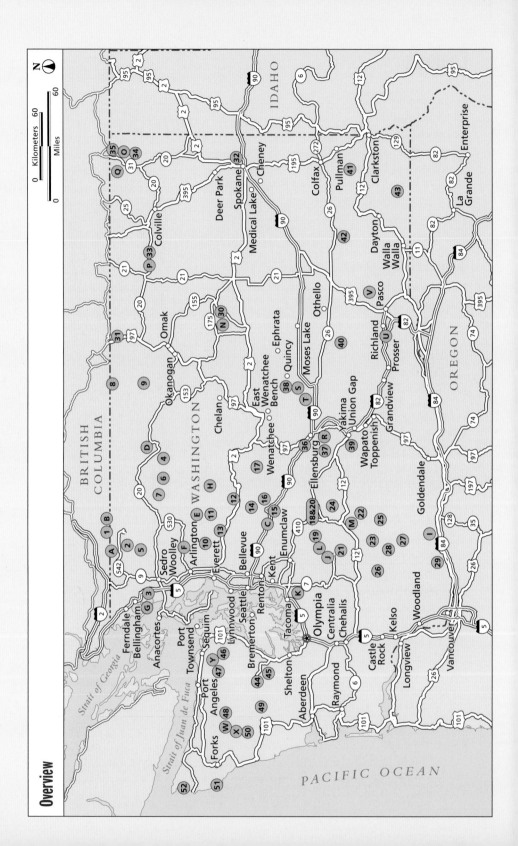

Overview

N

Kilometers 0 — 60

Miles 0 — 60

BRITISH COLUMBIA

WASHINGTON

IDAHO

OREGON

PACIFIC OCEAN

Strait of Georgia

Strait of Juan de Fuca

Ferndale
Bellingham
Anacortes
Port Townsend
Sequim
Port Angeles
Forks
Lynnwood
Seattle
Bellevue
Bremerton
Shelton
Tacoma
Renton
Kent
Olympia
Centralia
Chehalis
Aberdeen
Raymond
Castle Rock
Kelso
Longview
Woodland
Vancouver

Sedro Woolley
Arlington
Everett

Okanogan
Omak
Chelan
Wenatchee
East Wenatchee Bench
Ellensburg
Enumclaw
Yakima
Union Gap
Wapato
Toppenish
Grandview
Goldendale

Colville
Deer Park
Spokane
Medical Lake
Cheney
Quincy
Ephrata
Moses Lake
Othello
Prosser
Richland
Pasco
Grandview

Colfax
Pullman
Clarkston
La Grande
Enterprise
Dayton
Walla Walla

Honorable Mentions

Northeast Washington 137

Honorable Mentions

Southeast Washington... 167

Honorable Mentions

HELP US KEEP THIS GUIDE UP TO DATE

Every effort has been made by the author and editors to make this guide as accurate and useful as possible. However, many things can change after a guide is published—trails are rerouted, regulations change, techniques evolve, facilities come under new management, etc.

We would appreciate hearing from you concerning your experiences with this guide and how you feel it could be improved and kept up to date. While we may not be able to respond to all comments and suggestions, we'll take them to heart, and we'll also make certain to share them with the author. Please send your comments and suggestions to the following address:
  GPP
  Reader Response/Editorial Department
  PO Box 480
  Guilford, CT 06437
Or you may e-mail us at: editorial@GlobePequot.com

Thanks for your input, and happy trails!

Acknowledgments

A lot of special people helped with the writing and research of this book. I'd like to thank my friends and family for encouragement, for companionship on the trail and on the road, and for the space on your couches and in your guest rooms.

Ron Johnson contributed beautiful photos, and his whole beautiful family hiked with me on several occasions. My parents helped by being the mother and father of my passion for beautiful places, among innumerable other things. Thanks, Annie Keegan, for being my first editor and reading the entire book in its earliest stages. And thanks to the rest of my editors for their careful job. I'd also like to thank Joanna Markell and other friends and coworkers at the *Daily Record* for allowing me the flexibility to work on this book.

Many individuals from the parks and land management agencies through which these trails pass provided invaluable information and feedback. And most important, thanks to the people who work to preserve the amazing and diverse landscapes in Washington.

About the Author

Freelance writer Oliver Lazenby specializes in stories about adventure and the environment. He recently retired from his job as a newspaper reporter in Ellensburg to hit the road in his red station wagon and hike as much as possible. He has lived all over Washington, but currently his only permanent address is his website: oliverlazenby .wordpress.com.

INTRODUCTION

I've hiked a lot in Washington. With each new trip—whether it's a 30-mile trek or a 2-mile stroll on a local rail trail—my sense of wonder at the landscape grows. The fluttering in my chest on the way to a beautiful spot isn't dulled by frequent exposure to beauty, it grows stronger.

Many of Washington's different ecosystems and landscapes are exceptional. The Olympic Peninsula has one of the largest protected landscapes, and the wildest coastline in the continental United States. The Cascades may not be impressive in elevation alone—much of the range is lower than the lowest point in Colorado—but the state has more than half of all the glaciers in the lower 48. The geology of the eastern, drier side of Washington is dominated by shrub-steppe terrain that was once part of the largest grassland in North America.

Volcanoes are prominent in the current landscape, and they also shaped the flatlands of Eastern Washington. Lava flow after lava flow piled up in the Columbia Basin in the Miocene and Pliocene epochs. During the end of the last ice age, some of the largest floods the world has ever seen poured out of Glacial Lake Missoula and carved deep canyons and potholes in the basin. The result left impressive canyons, coulees, and scablands all over the southeastern part of the state and left a path for the present-day Columbia River—another of Washington's natural treasures and one of very few rivers to cut through a major mountain range.

There are a lot of amazing things to see here. The state's beauty is as varied as it is grand. Where else can you ski snowfields in August and surf ocean waves in the same day, explore inland sand dunes one day and ancient forests the next? The staggering variety in terrain can be explored with hikes of all lengths. Often the state's treasures are only a mile from a paved-trailhead, or even just outside city limits.

The large protected areas in the Cascades and Olympics make it possible walk until you're days from the nearest road. The state's mountain ranges are also seemingly at the perfect climate and latitude to be a petri dish for culturing eye-popping scenery. Huge snowfall and mild summers create glaciers. When you see the Cascades or Olympics in summer under a clear blue sky, the white glaciers complete them—a reminder of the long wet winters and improbable elevation of the mountains in our backyard. Flowers bloom just below massive glaciers. Wild coastline, pockets of desert wilderness, and wet and dry slopes offer different terrain and vegetation.

And while Washington is cold and snowy enough for our mountains to be framed by glaciers, summer thaws the mountain soil enough to allow a great variety and number of wildflowers to blossom in every color imaginable. This is a treat that our neighbors to the north don't experience, at least not to the same degree.

If that's not enough, wild mountains are surrounded by ocean and lonely desert. To truly appreciate Washington State's beauty, you must experience the variety. Explore the deserts that are parched and dry thanks to the height of the Cascades.

Wander the beaches and gaze offshore, where the storms that blanket our mountains begin.

The Internet has plenty of resources to help plan a hike, so why write a guidebook? There are a couple reasons I thought this book would be a good idea. The first is the most simple: It's nice to have something to bring on the trail—or at least to help you find the trail. More important, there are many outstanding trails in our state, so it's helpful to have a collection of hikes picked by a selective author to show off the state's variety. I tried to pick hikes that explore the most beautiful places in the state, while also trying to spread them throughout the state's varied terrain. Some hikes in this book are simple strolls just beyond a paved parking lot. Others are long treks over high passes or beyond raging streams. That's the attraction of Washington—beauty and adventure lurk deep in the mountain ranges, but also just beyond city limits.

Weather

Like everything else in the state, the weather is highly variable. The mountains and the west side of the state are overcast and drizzly for most of the year. Luckily, the prime hiking season and the best weather coincide. Summer in Washington can be dry for weeks or even months at a time. In the mountains, though, be prepared for rain even if it's not in the forecast, and expect chilly nighttime temperatures even in summer. Big mountains, and especially the volcanoes, can create their own weather. Most Washington hikers don't leave home without a rain jacket, no matter the season or the forecast.

In general, the closer you are to the coast, the more likely it is to rain. You can use the mountain ranges to your advantage, however. Frequently the weather on the east slopes of the Cascades and Olympics will be much drier than the west slopes. Snow in the Cascades and Olympics melts later than almost anywhere else in the lower 48. Some years you can hike high in the mountains in mid-June; other years you'll encounter snow patches in the high country through August. If you're unsure of the amount of snow in the mountains, call a ranger station. Luckily for Washington residents, the mountains are often visible from far away, and you can get a fairly good idea of how snowy the mountains are just by looking at them.

The snow that ends the hiking season is also fickle. Sometimes the mountains stay summery into October; other years, snow storms blanket the mountains in the beginning of October.

Flora and Fauna

The mighty Douglas fir is everywhere in Western Washington. These trees grow big, especially on the west side of the Olympics. Western red cedar and western hemlock are also common. In the mountains, subalpine fir and mountain hemlock join the Douglas firs. Pine trees march up the east slope of the mountains. Lodgepole, white, and ponderosa pines grow throughout Eastern Washington.

Other trees of interest include western larches and quaking aspens. Larches are treasured by Washington hikers. In fall their needles turn a brilliant gold before falling off. The needles are in their prime for one short week, known as "golden week" by their devotees. Larches are most common on the east slopes of the North Cascades, but they also thrive in the Kettle River Range, and a few spare larches grow in the Selkirk Mountains. Deciduous quaking aspens, which grow in some lowland valleys east of the mountains, also produce brilliant fall colors.

Shrub-steppe desert covers much of Southeast Washington. It's a fragile cold-desert ecosystem that's characterized by sagebrush and grasses. Wildflowers are prolific here in spring, including similar species as the alpine meadows but also a host of colorful species unique to these deserts. Washington even has a couple species of native cactus that grow in the shrub-steppe, including hedgehog and prickly pear.

Anywhere you go in Washington, you'll find deer. Elk roam much of the state as well. Black bears and mountain goats are common in alpine meadows in summer. In recent years, some rare megafauna have shown signs of recovering. The state's first confirmed gray wolf pack appeared in 2008. Today nine wolf packs roam the state, mostly in the northeast corner, with a few in the North and Central Cascades. Moose are also spreading south and west from the northeast, and about fifty grizzly bears currently live in the Washington Selkirks. After a half decade without a confirmed sighting in the North Cascades, a hiker photographed a grizzly bear south of the North Cascades Highway in 2011.

Wilderness Restrictions and Regulations

More than 40 percent of the land in Washington is publicly owned. The majority of that is managed by the USDA Forest Service in the form of national forests or wilderness areas. This is where the majority of the hikes in this book are located. To park on forest service land, you'll need to purchase a Northwest Forest Pass, which is good for a year. Washington State has three national parks: North Cascades, Mount Rainier, and Olympic National Parks. Some areas in these parks require that you purchase a day pass. In July 2011 Washington State began requiring an annual Discover Pass to park at state parks, Washington Department of Natural Resources land, and Washington Department of Fish and Wildlife managed land. There are very few trailheads in this book that don't require a pass. Check with the appropriate government agency for current pricing.

Hikers are abundant in Washington. In most cases land managers have reacted to the potential wilderness overpopulation with reasonable regulations. National parks require permits for backcountry camping, and several quota areas exist in the parks. Be especially careful when planning backpacking trips in Olympic National Park, where nearly all the popular overnight destinations are quota areas that require a permit. In Olympic National Park, 50 percent of the campsites at quota areas can be reserved; the rest are given out on a first-come, first-served basis. You have to show up at a ranger station to get these spots.

How to Use This Guide

Each regional section begins with an introduction that gives you a sweeping look at the lay of the land. After this general overview, specific hikes within that region are described. You'll learn about the terrain and what surprises each route has to offer.

To aid in quick decision making, each hike chapter begins with a hike summary. These short summaries give you a taste of the hiking adventure to follow. You'll learn about the trail terrain and what the route has to offer. Next you'll find the quick, nitty-gritty details of the hike: where the trailhead is located, total hike length, approximate hiking time, difficulty rating, type of trail terrain, best hiking season, what other trail users you may encounter, trail schedules, whether a fee is required, and trail contacts (for updates on trail conditions). The "Finding the trailhead" section gives you dependable directions from a nearby city or town right down to where you'll want to park your car. The hike description is the meat of the chapter; here you'll get a detailed and honest, personally researched impression of the trail. Mileage cues in "Miles and Directions" identify all turns and trail name changes, as well as points of interest. The "Hike Information" section at the end of each hike is a hodge-podge of information. Here you'll find local information resources through which you can learn more about the area, where to stay, where to eat, and what else to see while you're hiking in the area.

Route maps show all the accessible roads and trails, points of interest, water features, towns, landmarks, and geographical features along the hike. They also distinguish trails from roads. The selected route is highlighted, and directional arrows point the way.

Trail Finder

Best Hikes for Backpackers

5 Park Butte—Railroad Grade Moraine

8 Horseshoe Basin

11 Gothic Basin

27 Indian Heaven Loop

44 Flapjack Lakes

48 High Divide Loop

Best Short Hikes

9 Tiffany Mountain

14 Mirror Lake

20 Naches Peak Loop

21 High Rock Lookout

38 Ancient Lakes

42 Palouse Falls

45 Mount Ellinor

Best Hikes for Lake Lovers

15 Mirror Lake

16 Rachel and Rampart Lakes

17 Lake Ingalls

24 Twin Sisters Lakes and Tumac Mountain

44 Flapjack Lakes

48 High Divide Loop

Best Hikes for Peak-baggers

1 Yellow Aster Butte

7 Hidden Lake Lookout

9 Tiffany Mountain

10 Mount Pilchuck

12 Beckler Peak

19 Burroughs Mountain: Second Burroughs Loop

21 High Rock Lookout

35 Shedroof Mountain

43 Oregon Butte

45 Mount Ellinor

49 Pete's Creek to Colonel Bob Peak

Best Snow-free Winter Hikes

3 Oyster Dome

13 Wallace Falls

28 Lewis River

30 Northrup Canyon

Map Legend

Municiple

≡90≡	Interstate Highway
≡97≡	U.S. Highway
≡20≡	State Road
≡CR 12≡	Local/Forest Road
= = = =	Unpaved Road
┣━┿━┫	Railroad
— ·· — ·	State Boundary
▬▬▬▬	National Forest/Park
————	Wilderness/State Park

Trails

▬ ▬ ▬ ▬	Featured Trail
- - - -	Trail
··········	Off-Route Hike

Water Features

⬭	Body of Water
▱	Glacier
⸚⸚⸚	Marsh
∼∼	River/Creek
∼∕∖	Intermittent Stream
≋	Waterfall
⟲	Spring

Symbols

▭	Bench
◣	Boat Ramp
⏝	Bridge
■	Building/Point of Interest
⛺	Campground
❗	Gate
🅿	Parking
⤬	Pass
▲	Peak/Elevation
🛆	Picnic Area
👫	Ranger Station/Park Office
🚻	Restroom
📷	Scenic View
20	Trailhead
🏛	Tower/Lookout
○	Town

Land Features

•—·—•—·—•	Power Line
≈≈≈	Lava

North Cascades

I n the northern reaches of Washington's Cascades, the range grows wider and the mountains get steeper and icier. The North Cascades have the highest concentration of glaciers in the continental United States. These glaciers carved and chiseled the tall peaks into endless spires, horns, and minarets. From one of the North Cascades' many summits, the range appears to be a sea of pointed summits protruding through snow and ice. These peaks attract climbers from all over the planet. Some of the most impressive terrain in this region is in North Cascades National Park. Here the high country is composed of towering bare-rock peaks that often have crevassed glaciers hanging from their shoulders. In addition to the national park, several wilderness areas and national recreation areas protect this region.

Record amounts of snow helped create those glaciers. The Mount Baker Ski Area on Mount Shuksan broke the world snowfall record in 1999, when 95 feet of snow fell on the mountain. Unfortunately, these glaciers have shrunk dramatically in the last century. Some, like Lyall Glacier near Rainy Pass, have melted entirely, leaving a lake at the bottom of a bare rock slope.

In general, the Cascade Range gets wider toward Canada. Long-distance hikers can find plenty of places to walk until they're days from the nearest road. The Boundary Trail crosses the northern end of the range from the Pasayten Wilderness to Ross Lake in 107 miles of strenuous hiking.

Glacier Peak and Mount Baker, the regions two volcanoes, are the tallest peaks in the North Cascades. The round domes are surrounded by subranges of sharp peaks, such as the Picket Range near Mount Baker and the Monte Cristo group of peaks on the Mountain Loop Highway. At the south end of the region, between Snoqualmie and Stevens Passes, the Alpine Lakes Wilderness covers 394,000 acres of mountains, meadows, and lakes. Instead of glaciers, this wilderness is packed with sparkling lakes and pools. Expect company on hikes in the southern parts of the North Cascades—fantastic trails are little more than an hour from Seattle.

The Pasayten Wilderness, in the northeast corner of the North Cascades, is a sprawling wonderland of grassy tundra and rounded, 8,000-foot-tall mountains. Unlike most of the range, the peaks here are easy to climb, and mixed forests of pines and firs cover the valleys. The Wenatchee Mountains are another anomaly in the North Cascades because they run east to west. This subrange includes the Stuart Range and the Enchantment Lakes. The range is composed mostly of the Mount Stuart Batholith, which is a huge mass of uniform gray granite. The rock and dry weather make this range similar to California's Sierra Nevada.

While trails are officially open year-round in these mountains, the trails are generally covered with 6 feet of snow throughout the winter and are therefore unhikeable during that time.

1 Yellow Aster Butte

You'll see grand views and colorful flowers from every step of this trail, but the scenery peaks at the blueberry-covered summit. From here your eyes can wander the stunning naked cliffs of the American and Canadian Border Peaks, the glassy tarns in the meadow beneath the butte, or the icy masses of Mounts Baker and Shuksan. Thanks to its gentle grade and constant sensory stimulation, the trail to Yellow Aster Butte is one of the most pleasant hikes in the North Cascades.

Start: Trailhead on the left (north) side of FR 3065

Distance: 8.0 miles out and back

Hiking time: About 5 hours

Difficulty: Difficult due to elevation gain and sections of snowy trail

Trail surface: Dirt trail with patches of snow near the top

Elevation gain: 2,500 feet

Land status: National forest, federal wilderness area

Nearest town: Glacier

Best season: July through Oct

Other trail users: None

Canine compatibility: Leashed dogs allowed

Fees and permits: Northwest Forest Pass required to park at trailhead

Maps: USGS Mount Larrabee; Green Trails no. 14, Mt. Shuksan

Trail contacts: Mount Baker Ranger District; (360) 856-5700; www.fs.usda.gov/mbs

Other: No camping allowed on the trail; camp only in established sites at the lakes under the butte.

Finding the trailhead: From Deming go east on the Mount Baker Highway (WA 542) 33 miles to FR 3065 (signed TWIN LAKES ROAD). The road is behind the Department of Transportation's Shuksan maintenance facility. Continue north on FR 3065 for 4.3 miles until you reach the trailhead and a privy at a switchback. Parking is available on the road shoulder before and after the trailhead. GPS: N48 56.58' / W121 39.69'

The Hike

It's such a pleasure to hike near volcanoes. Views of Mount Baker, just 15 miles away, start less than 0.5 mile into this hike. Mount Shuksan, its neighbor to the east, soon joins it on the skyline, and the views only get better as you climb. The hike is 8.0 miles long, but those miles fly by thanks to stunning alpine scenery. The trail climbs continuously, but it never gets very steep. Maybe it's the refreshing berries along the way or the ample views and wildflowers, but the trail is a joy from start to finish.

As the name suggests, Yellow Aster Butte is surrounded by gardens of wildflowers. But you probably won't see yellow asters. Both purple asters and yellow daisies grow in clumps along the trail, so that's good enough. Yellow Aster Butte is home to gorgeous color all year long, whether it's the array of wildflowers that fill the meadows near the top of the butte, the blueberry and mountain ash displaying brilliant

A steep path leads the final stretch to Yellow Aster Butte's summit.

wine-colored foliage in fall, or the white and blue tarns in different stages of thawing below the butte.

A lawn of blueberries and heather grow atop the butte. From this vantage, the most impressive peaks are Mounts Baker and Shuksan to the south, the bare cliff faces of the American Border Peak, the Canadian Border Peak and Mount Larabee to the north, and Goat Mountain to the southeast. Tomyhoi Peak is the complicated mass of rock to the northwest with the waterfall roaring through a narrow gap in its rocks. Tomyhoi is a favorite among climbers, who access the mountain from the Yellow Aster Butte Trail.

The best views are from the top of the butte, but the euphoria of endless beauty surrounds the trail. Many hikers never reach the top of Yellow Aster Butte because there is so much to see and explore along the way. This hike is entirely without boring sections—no long switchbacks without views, no flat marches with unchanging scenery.

A dense, low jungle of fireweed, false hellebore, thimbleberry, and cow parsnip blanket the lower slopes of Yellow Aster Butte. After kicking up dust onto the brushy flowers, you'll hike through a patchy forest of silver and Douglas firs. As the trail climbs, the trees shrink and you begin traverses through meadows of asters, lupines, scarlet columbines, Indian paintbrush, monkey flowers, and bear grass that are soon joined by heather and blueberries at higher elevations. Color explodes from the vegetation all season long. Two miles below the summit, you reach a junction with the trail to Tomyhoi Lake. It goes right, climbing Gold Run Pass before descending 1,500 feet to the big lake. The meadow surrounding this junction or, better yet, the top of Gold Run Pass makes an excellent place to stop for photos, snacks, or lunch.

The blueberries at Yellow Aster Butte are bountiful and tasty. They start in the meadow below Gold Run Pass, and you can find them near the trail from here to the very top of the butte, where in fall they color the round butte in a deep, dark scarlet.

At nearly 4.0 miles from the trailhead, the trail splits. The left path goes toward the tarn-filled meadow below the butte. Here you'll find reflective tarns surrounded by snow and even more berry bushes and wildflowers. Campsites are plentiful here. A walk toward the cone-shaped peak to the south or toward Tomyhoi Peak will reveal more and more places to pitch a tent. Stay on the trail, as wandering boots have stamped parts of the meadow into oblivion in recent years.

The final spur to the butte is steep and direct, but it's worth the sweat for the 360-degree views. An informal trail goes between here and the slightly higher point to the north, but it's a trail more suited to goats than humans.

Miles and Directions

0.0   Start at the Yellow Aster Butte Trailhead off FR 3065. The trail starts behind a pit toilet at a bend in the road.

0.3   Views of Mount Baker begin.

1.5   Cross a boggy area and pass a campsite on the right.

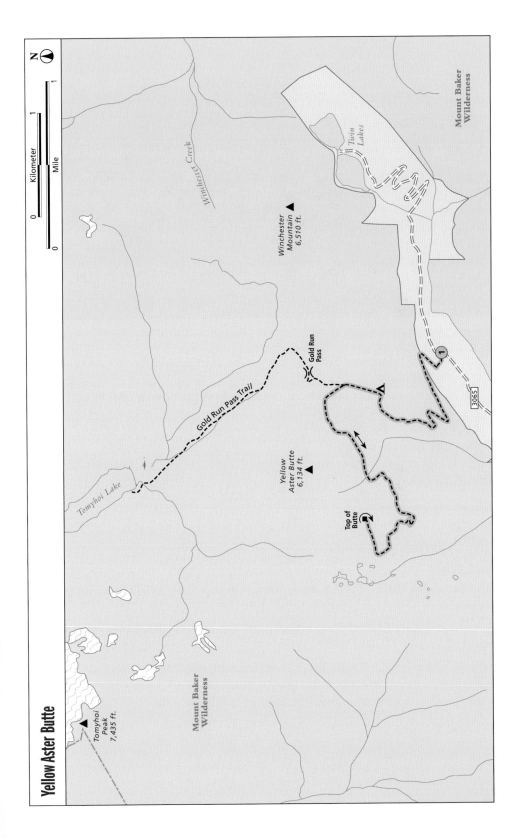

Yellow Aster Butte

Mount Baker Wilderness

Tomyhoi Peak
7,435 ft. ▲

Tomyhoi Lake

Winchester Creek

Gold Run Pass Trail

Gold Run Pass

Yellow Aster Butte
6,134 ft. ▲

Top of Butte ■

Winchester Mountain
6,510 ft. ▲

Twin Lakes

Mount Baker Wilderness

1

3065

Mount Baker Wilderness

N

0   1   Kilometer   1
0   Mile   1

Fall color dresses up Yellow Aster Butte

1.9 Bear left at the junction with the Gold Run Pass Trail, which climbs up to Gold Run Pass and Tomyhoi Lake.

3.8 Turn right (north) for the final climb up the butte, or go left (southwest) to reach the campsites at the lakes below Yellow Aster Butte.

4.0 Reach the summit of Yellow Aster Butte. Return the way you came.

8.0 Arrive back at the trailhead.

Hike Information

Local Information

Mt. Baker Foothills Chamber of Commerce, PO Box 866, Maple Falls 98266; (360) 599-1518; mtbakerchamber.org

Lodging

The Inn at Mt. Baker, 8174 Mt. Baker Hwy., Deming; (360) 599-1776; theinnatmt baker.com

USDA Forest Service Douglas Fir Campground; (360) 599-2714; www.fs.usda.gov/mbs

Restaurants

Graham's Restaurant, 9989 Mt. Baker Hwy., Glacier; (360) 599-3663

Milano's Restaurant, 9990 Mt. Baker Hwy., Glacier; (360) 599-2863

Casa Que Pasa, 1415 Railroad, Ave., Bellingham; (360) 756-8226

2 Skyline Divide

The views of Mount Baker from Skyline Divide are spectacular, but the vibrant color of the wildflowers outshines the volcano's icy glaciers. The divide is one long meadow packed with flowers. After the initial climb through old-growth forest with patches of lupines, the trail reaches the Skyline Divide. From here the trail swoops up and down on a tall, flowery ridge leading toward the foot of the Hadley Glacier.

Start: Parking lot at the end of FR 37
Distance: 8.8 miles out and back
Hiking time: About 2 hours to the divide; 5 hours to the trail's end
Difficulty: Moderate due to length
Trail surface: Dirt trail
Elevation gain: 1,500 feet to the divide; 2,200 feet to the end of the trail
Land status: National recreation area, federal wilderness area

Nearest town: Glacier
Best season: July through Oct
Other trail users: None
Canine compatibility: Leashed dogs allowed
Fees and permits: Northwest Forest Pass required to park at the trailhead
Maps: USGS Mount Baker; Green Trails no. 13, Mt. Baker
Trail contacts: Mount Baker Ranger District; (360) 856-5700; www.fs.usda.gov/mbs

Finding the trailhead: From Bellingham go east on the Mount Baker Highway (SR 542) 25 miles to the Glacier Public Service Center, just past the town of Glacier. At 0.7 mile past the Glacier Public Service Center, turn right onto Glacier Creek Road (FR 39). Immediately turn left onto FR 37 and follow this road for 12.6 miles. For the first 6 miles the road follows the North Fork Nooksack River. After that, it begins climbing steeply to the trailhead. GPS: N48 52.88' / W121 51.87'

The Hike

The Skyline Divide trail is a fantastic walk along an airy ridge, starting deep in the forest north of Mount Baker. The trail begins by contouring uphill through old-growth forest. The big, dense forest is a nice appetizer to the lofty ridge the trail leads to. The path is wide, uniform, and easy to follow as it parts the sea of mountain hemlocks and Douglas firs. After 1.0 mile or so, the trail breaks out of the stately trees into lush meadows of false hellebore, lupines, yellow daisies, and cow parsnip, punctuated by the occasional grove of stunted trees.

Two miles from the trailhead, you reach a broad ridgetop meadow where you're treated to excellent views of Mounts Baker and Shuksan. These are some of the best views along the ridge, and you can turn around here for a short hike. For a longer walk, keep going through fields of abundant

> Mount Baker is one of the snowiest places on Earth. In 1999 the Mount Baker Ski Area, on Mount Shuksan, set the world record for most snowfall in a single season with 95 feet of snow.

Mount Baker hidden by clouds at the end of the Skyline Divide Trail

flowers toward Mount Baker. You can keep trekking as far as you like. In fact, ascents of Mount Baker have been attempted from Skyline Divide up the Hadley Glacier. The big volcano is close enough that you can reach out and touch it. It is the second most glaciated mountain in the Cascades, behind Mount Rainier, and is home to ten main glaciers.

The trail dances through the sky on Mount Baker's north flank. The flowers and the volcano duel for your attention. In clear weather, this hike has some of the best views of Mount Baker you'll find anywhere. When overcast, you can look down through shifting clouds to year-round snow patches and mountain meadows and enjoy the flower show right at your feet. Bring bug spray, as the mosquitoes and flies are notoriously bad here.

Walking along the divide is almost like flying. The 6,000-foot-tall ridge falls away toward Deadhorse Creek to the east and Thompson Creek to the west. The ridge itself leads right up to the Hadley Glacier on Mount Baker's northern flank. Grouse roam the ridge along with you; so do occasional bears. Overhead, hawks soar and hunt.

On your way south from the first viewpoint atop the divide, there is just one important junction to watch for. The trail forks 3.3 miles from the trailhead. The

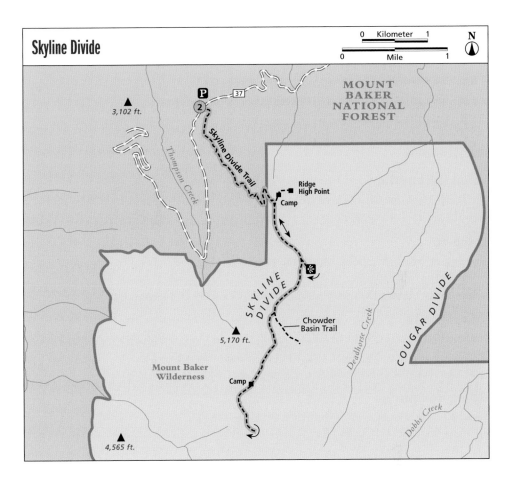

Skyline Divide

left (east) path appears much more popular, but it veers off the ridge and dead-ends in 1.0 mile or so at Deadhorse Creek. This is a fine place to camp and has water all summer, but for better views and flowers, go right. This junction tricks many hikers, because the main trail starts out steep and loose and is less appealing than the trail down to Deadhorse Creek. After the first scramble, the trail levels out and becomes easy to follow.

The ridge constantly meanders up and down, with 500-foot dips and climbs, until it reaches a high point (6,535 feet) on the ridge 4.4 miles from the trailhead. At evening on the divide, Bellingham Bay and Puget Sound glow as the sun sinks into the Olympic Mountains. Mount Baker reflects the pink light of sunset and sunrise.

Miles and Directions

0.0 Start at the trailhead on FR 37.

2.0 Come out of the trees and arrive at Skyline Divide. (*Option:* Turn around here for a 4.0-mile round-trip.)

2.6	Pass a trail on the left that leads to the top of a knoll.
3.3	Reach the junction with the trail to Chowder Basin. Go right up a short, steep hill to stay on the Skyline Divide Trail.
4.1	Pass a tent site in a sheltered saddle below a knoll.
4.4	Arrive at the top of a knoll at 6,535 feet. Return the way you came.
8.8	Arrive back at the trailhead.

Hike Information

Local Information

Mt. Baker Foothills Chamber of Commerce, PO Box 866, Maple Falls 98266; (360) 599-1518; mtbakerchamber.org

Lodging

The Inn at Mt. Baker, 8174 Mt. Baker Hwy., Deming; (360) 599-1776; theinnatmt baker.com

USDA Forest Service Douglas Fir Campground; (360) 599-2714; www.fs.usda.gov/mbs

Restaurants

Graham's Restaurant, 9989 Mt. Baker Hwy., Glacier; (360) 599-3663

Milano's Restaurant, 9990 Mt. Baker Hwy., Glacier; (360) 599-2863

Casa Que Pasa, 1415 Railroad, Ave., Bellingham, (360) 756-8226

Other Resources

Koma Kulshan: The Story of Mount Baker, by John C. Miles

3 Oyster Dome

Oyster Dome pokes its bald head above the beautiful lowland forests of the Chucka-nut Range between Bellingham and the Skagit Valley. The view of the San Juan Islands and Samish Bay from Oyster Dome are incredible. The shimmering water is dotted with infinite islands. Some are just big enough for a seagull to take a nap on; others are as tall as Oyster Dome's summit. The best part? You can hike this beautiful trail year-round.

Start: Trailhead on Chuckanut Drive
Distance: 6.2 miles out and back
Hiking time: About 3.5 hours
Difficulty: Moderate due to elevation gain and steep sections
Trail surface: Dirt trail
Elevation gain: 1,800 feet
Land status: Washington Department of Natural Resources
Nearest town: Burlington

Best season: Year-round; more pleasant when it's dry
Other trail users: None
Canine compatibility: Dog friendly
Fees and permits: Discover Pass required to park at trailhead
Map: USGS Bow
Trail contacts: Washington Department of Natural Resources, Northwest Region; (360) 856-3500; dnr.wa.gov

Finding the Trailhead: From Burlington drive 10 miles north on Chuckanut Drive (WA 11). The trailhead is on the right (east) between mileposts 10 and 11. Park on the shoulder across from the trailhead. From Bellingham go 10 miles south on Chuckanut Drive to reach the trailhead. GPS: N48 36.49' / W121 25.99'

The Hike

Oyster Dome is a fantastic year-round hike in an interesting area of lowland mountains, lush forests, and tranquil lakes. With ample trails and viewpoints, the Chuckanut Mountains offer plenty of exploring. The hike to Oyster Dome is the most scenic hike in the area and a good sample of the coastal Chuckanut Mountains, which stretch from Bellingham to the Skagit Valley.

Blanchard Mountain, the mountain Oyster Dome is on, rises right out of the salt water. This makes for unparalleled views of islands and water. The shimmering sound is dotted with more islands than you can count—some are massive and mountainous, while others are solitary points of rock just big enough to pull a canoe onto. To the southeast, the snowcapped Olympic Mountains cradle the shimmering water and provide a backdrop to the islands. From atop the bald dome, the Chuckanut Range stretches as far as you can see to the north, ending abruptly at the Skagit lowlands to the south.

Oyster Dome is slightly more than 2,000 feet above the water. The bare dome pokes out of a thick, moist second-growth forest with firs and cedars hiding the

Sandstone boulders and lush forest cover the Chuckanut Mountains

original forest's giant stumps. Snowberries, salal, sword fern, and vine maples make up the understory.

At the trailhead on Chuckanut Drive, you can breathe deeply of the salty air. Nearby Bellingham consistently ranks in the American Lung Association's list of cities with the cleanest air. The trail has a steep start and a steep finish, with some pleasant hiking on flatter ground in between. Get your fill of the salty sea breeze and warm your muscles by huffing up the switchbacks that start immediately on a wide, well-maintained trail. A quarter-mile later you will still be able to see Chuckanut Drive well below you. Just over 1.0 mile into the hike, trees are crowding into an old clear-cut where you get your first glimpse of the San Juan Islands and Puget Sound. A bench at 1.2 miles is a nice spot for a water break.

Soon you'll be meandering along the side of the hill on a relatively flat trail choked with jagged rocks, roots, and occasional little streams and patches of mud. At 2.8 miles you reach an intersection. Go left to continue toward Oyster Dome.

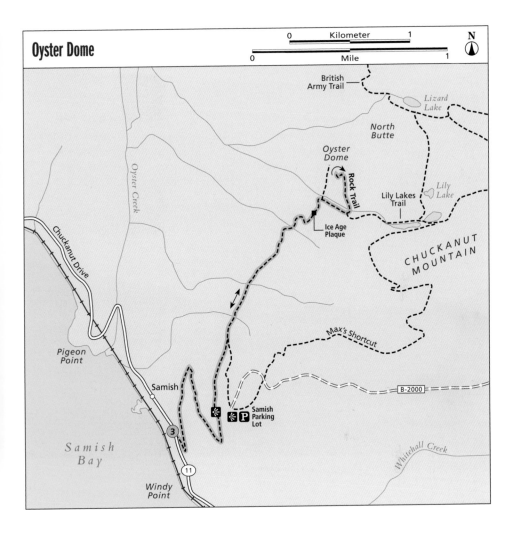

Lily Lake is to the right and makes a nice side trip. It's a calm lake surrounded by tall firs and cedars and is about 0.5 mile out of the way. The rest of the hike—about 0.3 mile—is brutally steep, but it pays off with breathtaking views.

Miles and Directions

0.0 Start at the Pacific Northwest Trailhead on Chuckanut Drive.

1.2 Reach a viewpoint with a bench.

1.6 Go left at the junction with the trail to the Samish Overlook parking lot.

2.8 Go left at the junction with the Lily Lakes Trail.

3.1 Reach the bare rock at the top of Oyster Dome. Return the way you came.

6.2 Arrive back at the trailhead.

The San Juan Islands from the top of Oyster Dome

Hike Information

Local Information

Burlington Chamber of Commerce, 520 E. Fairhaven Ave., Burlington 98233; (360) 757-0944; burlington-chamber.com

Local Events/Attractions

Skagit Valley Tulip Festival; April; (360) 428-5959

Lodging

Larrabee State Park Campground, 245 Chuckanut Drive, Bellingham; (360) 676-2093

Restaurants

Train Wreck Bar & Restaurant, 427 E. Fairhaven Ave., Burlington; (360) 755-0582
Boundary Bay Brewery, 1107 Railway Ave., Bellingham; (360) 647-5593

4 Maple Pass Loop

This loop hike starts at the top of Rainy Pass, near some of the most iconic features on the North Cascades Highway. The loop trail circles Lake Ann, a beautiful glacier-carved tarn, on a high ridge speckled with larches, flowers, and blueberries. The views are dominated by the towering hulks of Frisco, Corteo, and Black Peaks. Beyond the emerald oval of Lake Ann, a golden ridge spreads out between Cutthroat Peak and Golden Horn.

Start: Trailhead at the southwest corner of the Rainy Pass Picnic Area, at the top of Rainy Pass near milepost 158
Distance: 7.4-mile loop
Hiking time: About 4 hours
Difficulty: Moderate due to length and elevation gain
Trail surface: Dirt trail
Elevation gain: 2,100 feet
Land status: National forest, national park
Nearest town: Mazama
Best season: Late July to Oct
Other trail users: None
Canine compatibility: Leashed dogs allowed
Fees and permits: Northwest Forest Pass required to park at trailhead. Wilderness camping in North Cascades National Park requires a free permit. Permits are available at the Wilderness Information Center in Marblemount.
Maps: USGS *Washington Pass, Mount Arriva*; Green Trails *no. 49, Mount Logan,* and *no. 50, Washington Pass*
Trail contacts: Methow Valley Visitor Center, Okanogan-Wenatchee National Forest, 509-996-4000; North Cascades National Park; (360) 873-7200; nps.gov/noca
Other: Camping is not allowed within 0.25 mile of Lake Ann, Maple Pass, or Heather Pass due to fragile meadows that have been trampled and are slowly revegetating.

Finding the trailhead: From Mazama go west on WA 20 (North Cascades Highway) for 21 miles to milepost 158, at the top of Rainy Pass (Rainy Pass is 69 miles west of Concrete). Turn left (south) into the Rainy Pass Picnic Area, following signs. GPS: N48 30.91' / W120 44.14'

The Hike

The North Cascades is the best place in the state to hike if you like being high in the mountains surrounded by glaciers, peaks, lakes, and naked rock. From the highway, the most iconic views are near Rainy Pass and Washington Pass. At these two high passes, you'll also find trailheads for some of the most spectacular and convenient hiking in the North Cascades. From a trailhead at the top of Rainy Pass, a relatively short loop hike to Heather and Maple Passes meanders through rugged terrain with brilliant fall colors and panoramic views.

Because of lingering snow and radiant autumn color, Maple Pass is a great fall destination. If you go at the right time in October, you can watch golden larches slowly shed their needles onto steep slopes of crimson blueberry and huckleberry foliage. To

Larches frame Lake Ann on the Maple Pass Loop

the north, a pointy peak called Golden Horn mimics the color of the autumn larches.

Lakes, meadows, flowers, high peaks, and the ability to hike in a loop make this trail an excellent hike anytime during the season. That season, however, isn't very long—the ridge between Heather and Maple Passes typically doesn't shed its snow until August.

Most people hike the loop in a counterclockwise direction—the more gradual ascent route, which is also more open and scenic. Start by hiking up the dirt trail from the parking lot. The paved Rainy Lake Trail, which goes left (south) from the trailhead, is the return path. The trail climbs gradually through big firs and mountain hemlocks, traversing the occasional slide path choked with alders beaten sideways and dusty thimbleberries and elderberries. A junction at 1.3 miles leads to Lake Ann, a refreshing lake in a deep bowl. Lake Ann is a popular destination and turnaround spot for many hikers and for tourists traveling over WA 20, and you'll shed some of the crowds as you get beyond the lake. The trail above Lake Ann on the talus slope to the north is a beautiful vantage of the lake and its cute ovular island.

The trail continues up across steep, loose slopes through patchy blueberries. Spirea, paintbrush, gentians, and columbines grow along the trail. The occasional mountain ash lends its leaves and berries to the fall color show.

You climb through a few short switchbacks above the lake before reaching Heather Pass. The surrounding peaks—Black and Corteo—come into view. Across the Granite Creek Valley (WA 20) is Whistler Mountain and Cutthroat Peak. Golden Horn seems to glow beyond them. Oddly enough, Golden Horn and everything northwest of Heather Pass are not part of North Cascades National Park. That includes the granite monoliths of the Liberty Bell, Concord Tower, Lexington Tower, and the Early Winter Spires—some of the most awe-inspiring and iconic peaks in the North Cascades (or anywhere else). Take solace in the fact that the land south of you is protected and that an effort is under way to expand the park.

▶ **North Cascades National Park contains one-third of all the glaciers in the lower 48. The Cascades between I-90 and the Canadian border are home to about half the glacial mass in the lower 48.**

From Heather Pass the trail is an airy ridge walk with spectacular views on both sides of the trail. Horns, knife edges, jagged peaks, crags—there aren't enough words to describe these mountains. The beauty of the North Cascades spreads out all around as you amble past numerous viewpoints and dips in the trail. At Maple Pass, larches frame Lake Ann and views stretch out to the east.

The descent toward Rainy Lake is steep. It begins on a tall ridge that divides Lake Ann and Rainy Lake, crossing open slopes with tight switchbacks. You can see the trail zigging and zagging hundreds of feet below through wide-open gardens of heather and blueberries. Past the switchbacks, the trail ducks into the forest and continues quickly and directly for a couple more miles.

At 2.2 miles from Maple Pass and 7.0 miles from the beginning of the hike, turn left at a junction with the Rainy Lake Trail. This trail is paved and level. Sturdy wooden bridges cross several creeks, and educational plaques provide information

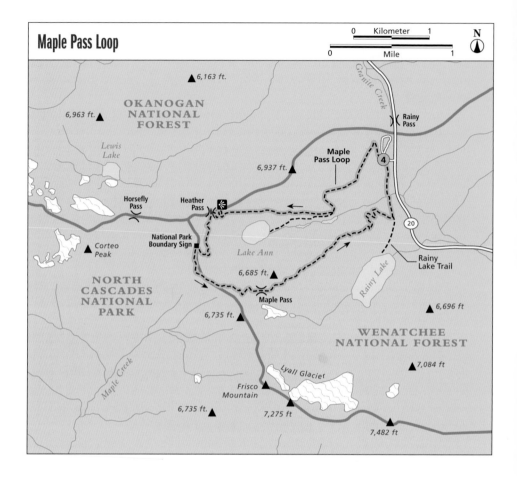

Maple Pass Loop

0 — Kilometer — 1
0 — Mile — 1

N

▲6,163 ft.

OKANOGAN
NATIONAL
FOREST

6,963 ft. ▲

Lewis Lake

Granite Creek

Rainy Pass

Maple
Pass Loop

6,937 ft. ▲

4

Horsefly
Pass

Heather
Pass

20

National Park
Boundary Sign

▲ Corteo
Peak

Lake Ann

Rainy
Lake Trail

6,685 ft. ▲

Rainy Lake

NORTH
CASCADES
NATIONAL
PARK

Maple Pass

▲ 6,696 ft

6,735 ft. ▲

WENATCHEE
NATIONAL FOREST

Maple Creek

Lyall Glacier

▲7,084 ft

Frisco
Mountain ▲

6,735 ft. ▲

7,275 ft ▲

7,482 ft ▲

about the surrounding old-growth forest. It's a civilized ending to a trail through such rugged terrain.

Miles and Directions

0.0   Start at the trailhead for the Lake Ann/Maple Pass loop trail. Take the trail to the right; you will return on the trail coming from the left.

1.3   At a junction with Lake Ann trail, go right toward Heather and Maple Passes.

2.3   Arrive at a viewpoint with views to Golden Horn, Whistler Mountain, and Cutthroat Peak.

4.1   Reach Heather Pass.

4.8   Arrive at Maple Pass.

7.0   Go left at the junction with the Rainy Lakes Trail.

7.4   Arrive back at the trailhead.

NORTH CASCADES NATIONAL PARK EXPANDING

Liberty Bell, Early Winter Spires, Golden Horn, and many other breathtaking sights near the North Cascades Highway are not in North Cascades National Park. A group of conservationists is led by former US Senator Dan Evans, famed climber Jim Wickwire, and several others are trying to get about 237,702 more acres of federal land included in the 501,458-acre park.

Currently North Cascades National Park is one of the least-visited national parks in the country, with about 20,000 visitors per year as of 2012. That's partly because the main road to access the park, the North Cascades Highway, is closed half the year. The proposal to expand the park includes creating low-elevation trails and campgrounds that would likely increase the number of park visitors.

Hike Information

Local Information

Winthrop Chamber of Commerce, PO Box 39, Winthrop 98862; (509) 996-2125; winthropwashington.com

Local Events/Attractions

Winthrop Rhythm and Blues Festival, Winthrop; usually mid-July; winthropbluesfestival.com

Methow Valley Rodeo, Winthrop; Memorial and Labor Day weekends; methowvalleyrodeo.com

Lodging

USDA Forest Service Klipchuck, on FR 300, one mile north of WA 20 at milepost 175 and Meadows Campgrounds, on FR 5400-500, 17 miles north of WA 20 near milepost 180; (509) 996-4003

Freestone Inn, 31 Early Winters Dr., Mazama; (509) 996-3906; freestoneinn.com

Mazama Country Inn, 15 Country Rd., Mazama; (509) 996-2681; mazamacountryinn.com

5 Park Butte–Railroad Grade Moraine

This beautiful parklike setting on the south flank of Mount Baker has a lot to explore. Wildflowers spill into creeks along the trail. An ancient dome of ice grinds into the andesitic rock of Mount Baker to the north of the lookout. Hanging glaciers cap the lustrous yellow of the Twin Sisters. Sit among wildflowers and tarns, climb to the summit of Park Butte, or ramble the Railroad Grade Moraine to the snout of Easton Glacier. If you tire of the crowds, take the long way home on the Scott Paul Trail.

Start: Parking lot at the end of FR 13
Distance: 7.4 miles out and back
Hiking time: About 4 hours
Difficulty: Moderate due to length
Trail surface: Dirt trail with creek crossings
Best season: July through Oct
Elevation gain: 2,100 feet to the lookout; 2,600 feet to the Easton Glacier
Land status: National recreation area
Nearest town: Concrete

Other trail users: Stock animals allowed Aug. 1 to Oct. 31
Canine compatibility: Leashed dogs allowed
Fees and permits: Northwest Forest Pass required to park at trailhead
Maps: USGS Baker Pass; Green Trails no. 54, Hamilton
Trail contacts: Mount Baker Ranger District; (360) 856-5700; www.fs.usda.gov/mbs

Finding the trailhead: From Burlington go east on WA 20 (North Cascades Highway) for 23 miles. Turn left onto Baker Lake Road, just past milepost 82. Continue for 12 miles and turn left at FR 12. In 3.5 miles turn right onto FR 13 (signed MOUNT BAKER NATIONAL RECREATION AREA). Follow this road for 5 miles until it ends at a large parking area at the trailhead. GPS: N48 42.40' / W121 48.70'

The Hike

Many of the flowery open meadows of Mount Rainier are called parks—Spray Park, Grand Park, Berkeley Park. They have a groomed look with their ample flowers, gentle terrain, pockets of tall trees, little lakes, ponds, creeks, and scenic mountains all around. Park Butte is Mount Baker's answer to the many parks of Rainier. Choose your own adventure from Morovitz Meadows below Park Butte: Climb to the lookout, inspect the glaciers of Baker, or take the long way home for solitude and even more meadows.

To get to Morovitz Meadow, walk the wooded trail 2.5 miles from the parking lot. After the trail crosses Sulphur Creek and passes a junction with the Scott Paul Trail, a boardwalk surrounded by exceptionally productive blueberry and huckleberry bushes spans the moist floor of Schreibers Meadow. The bulging berries are irresistible in late September. Farther afield are clumps of big trees, open meadows of heather, and numerous small ponds. Sulphur Creek is named for the sulfurous steam that hisses out of vents near the summit of Mount Baker, just 5.0 miles away.

A hiker high on the Railroad Grade Moraine

The trail meanders through these meadows toward Rocky Creek. Two rocky strips cut through the trees, washed out from the runoff of Easton Glacier, serve as the creekbed. The best place to cross the creek changes from year to year as the water changes course. It is usually not difficult, and sometimes a log bridge spans the trickle of water. Take note of the creek depth, as it grows during the day and can be higher in late afternoon. From the creek the trail begins climbing steeply through a tall forest rich in hemlocks and cedars.

After a series of switchbacks you enter Morovitz Meadow, where beauty and options for further exploring abound. The most popular option is to climb another 800 feet to enjoy 360-degree views at the fire lookout on Park Butte, where the glaciers of Baker and the golden slopes of the Twin Sisters Range stare you in the face. The trail to the lookout winds through more meadows and past Pocket Lake on the way to the lookout. The Black Buttes, two dark peaks immediately west of Mount Baker, are the remnants of the ancient Black Buttes volcano. This volcano formed about 500,000 years ago (Mount Baker is probably less than 30,000 years old), and

JOE MOROVITS, THE HERMIT OF BAKER LAKE

For Joe Morovits, Morovitz Meadow's namesake, carrying 100 pounds of food and supplies 32 miles from a settlement near Concrete was routine. Mighty Joe, "the hermit of Baker Lake," lived alone in a cabin near Morovitz Creek in 1891 and made the trip whenever he needed to replenish his bacon, flour, beans, dynamite, and other supplies. According to several historians, if his sack of commodities didn't weigh 100 pounds, he would load it with whiskey until it did. Joe's long gone, but he left a rich history of stories and folklore.

Morovits lived on salmon, wild game, a few vegetables that he grew, and the meager profits from his gold mining operation. In his spare time he explored the mountains, often guiding other mountain climbers up the southern slopes of Mount Baker. He became known for his brute strength, ingenuity, and wild glissades down the glaciers.

Morovits made his first ascent of Mount Baker in 1892 by way of the Rainbow Glacier. When the team of climbers he was guiding turned around at an icy face, Morovits wouldn't give up. He lumbered on toward the summit, using the butt of his rifle to cut steps in the steep ice.

Morovits came down from the mountain in 1918 after selling his claims. According to a 1963 article in *Sports Illustrated*, he had $175 to his name at the time. He disappeared shortly after.

some volcanologists think it was twice the size of Mount Baker. The sinister peaks look like a good place to dispose of any magical rings you may be carrying.

To inspect the glacier and get a look at a raw wasteland of fresh ground rock, climb the trail up the side of the Railroad Grade Moraine. The Railroad Grade Trail climbs steeply, with alpine meadows on one side and a slope of loose gravel and boulders on the other. The scarred moraine is constantly eroding, and few plants have arrived to stabilize the steep slope. Muddy water fresh off the Easton Glacier crashes through the middle of the loose moraine. From the end of the trail, you can gaze into deadly crevasses without ever stepping off the dirt path.

The third and most solitary option from here is to take the Scott Paul Trail back to the trailhead. The Park Butte Trail gets heavy use in summer, but not many of those users venture out of their way onto the Scott Paul Trail. This alternative return tour makes a big loop across the moraine, through more parklike terrain, and across the upper reaches of a handful of creeks choked with purple and pink lupines and monkey flowers. After about 3.0 miles of climbing and traversing from the junction with Trail 603, the Scott Paul Trail finally begins descending to the parking lot.

All three destinations are worth seeing. If you stay overnight at one of the many tent pads on the side of the Railroad Grade Trail, you can explore to your heart's

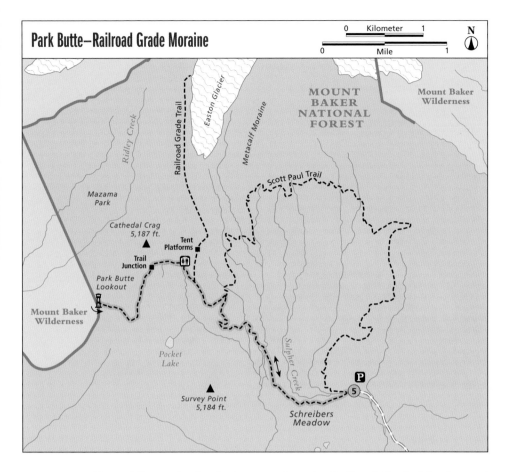

Park Butte–Railroad Grade Moraine

0   Kilometer   1

0   Mile   1

N

Railroad Grade Trail

Easton Glacier

Metacalf Moraine

MOUNT
BAKER
NATIONAL
FOREST

Mount Baker
Wilderness

Ridley Creek

Mazama
Park

Scott Paul Trail

Cathedal Crag
5,187 ft.

Tent
Platforms

Trail
Junction

Park Butte
Lookout

Mount Baker
Wilderness

Pocket
Lake

Sulpher Creek

Survey Point
5,184 ft.

Schreibers
Meadow

P

5

content. If you hike to the fire lookout, explore the Railroad Grade Moraine, and make a loop on the Scott Paul Trail, your round-trip will be nearly 16 miles.

Miles and Directions

0.0   Start at the parking lot at the end of Sulphur Creek Road (FR 13).

0.1   Bear left at the first junction with the Scott Paul Trail.

1.0   Cross Rocky Creek. The optimal crossing changes from year to year with the changing course of the creek.

2.0   Bear left at the second junction with the Scott Paul Trail.

2.5   Reach Upper Morovitz Meadows and a junction with the Railroad Grade Trail. Go left for Park Butte.

2.7   Pass a sign and trail leading to a pit toilet.

3.0   Go left at a fork in the trail. The path to the right goes to Mazama Park.

3.7   Reach the fire lookout on Park Butte. Return the way you came.

7.4   Arrive back at the parking lot.

Monkey flowers and lupine along a creek on the Scott Paul Trail

Hike Information

Local Information

Concrete Chamber of Commerce, PO Box 743, Concrete 98237; (360) 853-8784; concrete-wa.com

Local Events/Attractions

Skagit Eagle Festival, Concrete; weekends in January; skagiteaglefestival.com

Lodging

USDA Forest Service Panorama Point Campground; (360) 856-5700
Ovenell's Heritage Inn, 46276 Concrete Sauk Valley Rd., Concrete; (360) 853-8494; ovenells-inn.com/

Restaurants

Cascade Burgers, 45292 SR 20, Concrete; (360) 853-7580
Annie's Pizza Station, 44568 SR 20, Concrete; (360) 853-7227

Other Resources

Koma Kulshan: The Story of Mount Baker, by John C. Miles

6 Cascade Pass

Cascade Pass is a classic destination in North Cascades National Park. The 7.4-mile hike through old-growth forest leads to an incredible perch surrounded by sharp peaks, massive mountains, and crevassed hanging glaciers creeping toward cliff bands. From the top of this ancient route through the Cascades, you can explore in a variety of directions—or sit still and let your eyes do the exploring.

Start: Trailhead at the end of Cascade River Road
Distance: 7.4 miles out and back
Hiking time: About 4 hours
Difficulty: Moderate due to length
Trail surface: Dirt trail
Elevation gain: 1,800 feet
Land status: National park
Nearest town: Marblemount
Best season: Aug through Oct
Other trail users: None

Canine compatibility: Dogs not allowed
Fees and permits: Wilderness camping in North Cascades National Park requires a free permit, available at the Wilderness Information Center in Marblemount.
Maps: USGS Cascade Pass; Green Trails no. 80, Cascade Pass; North Cascades National Park map
Trail contacts: North Cascades National Park; (360) 873-4500; nps.gov/noca

Finding the trailhead: Drive west through Marblemount on WA 20 (North Cascades Highway). At the east end of town, continue across the bridge over the Cascade River onto Cascade River Road. Drive 23 miles to the end of the road. Most of the way is gravel, and it gets steep near the end. GPS: N48 28.06' / W121 03.55'

The Hike

At the center of an ancient path between Stehekin and Marblemount, and beneath complex, snowy peaks, Cascade Pass is one of the most awe-inspiring places in North Cascades National Park. Even the trailhead is breathtaking, with the dark cliffs and buttresses of Johannesburg Mountain jutting thousands of feet into the sky just across a small valley. It's one of the most scenic places accessible by road anywhere. Hanging glaciers cling high on Johannesburg's cliff faces, and chunks of ice occasionally break free and hiss their way down to the valley bottom in the afternoon sun. It's hard to find a hike of this length with a more high-alpine feel.

▶ Professor and historian W. D. Lyman said Cascade Pass was "a scene which surpasses anything the writer has ever witnessed in a course of extensive mountaineering. A scene which is the crowning work of this whole gallery of wonders, which not Yellowstone nor Yosemite can surpass."

At the pass you'll likely be greeted by howling winds, views of endless glaciers and peaks, and a sign pointing the way toward Stehekin. Either gaze down the long glaciated Cascade River valley toward Marblemount

HOW CASCADE PASS ALMOST BECAME A HIGHWAY

Nearly 10,000 years ago, indigenous peoples used Cascade Pass as a trade route between the coast and Eastern Washington. Stone tools and cooking hearths found on the pass date back 9,600 years. Much later, European explorers and prospectors used the route. Alexander Ross, a fur trader and explorer, may have crossed the pass as early as 1814, but his written description of his route is too vague to tell for certain. In 1890 John F. Stevens explored Cascade Pass as a possible route for the Great Northern Railway's road to Puget Sound.

He found the route impractical and discovered Stevens Pass shortly after. During the next half century, several groups surveyed Cascade Pass for a possible highway. Roads came close to the pass on both sides. Eventually the route across present-day WA 20 was discovered and the highway was built, ending the road-building near Cascade Pass.

or gaze down toward Pelton Basin, the long glaciated headwaters of the Stehekin River. Tall peaks hang over the valleys in both directions. Downhill, the heather and blueberries draped over the pass yield to narrow stream channels trickling through talus toward the deep valleys below. The tall ridge of Johannesburg leads west toward Mix-up Peak and Magic Mountain, similarly tall mountains with hanging glaciers. Across the Cascade River valley from Johannesburg, Sahale Mountain and Eldorado Peak—classic objectives for mountaineers—scrape the sky.

In the first 2.0 miles of hiking you will have peekaboo views of Johannesburg Mountain through dense trees. Chunks of ice falling from Johannesburg's hanging glaciers add to the excitement as they roar down the mountain. The trail climbs at a constant grade, switchbacking about thirty times before finally breaking out of the trees in a heather-filled meadow with views of Eldorado, Forbidden, and Mix-up Peaks and the ever-present Johannesburg Mountain.

Above the forest, the trail traverses past stunted trees and trickles of water until it crests Cascade Pass. Here you can gaze into the snowy, U-shaped valley of Pelton Basin, the ancient way through to Stehekin.

If you're not content to admire the views from the panoramic perch on Cascade Pass, there are plenty of options. Turn right for a short, steep jaunt up Mix-up Arm just south of the pass. The trail doesn't go far before petering out, but the views improve quickly. Even better, hike up the Sahale Arm to the Sahale Glacier. If you desire solitude, shed the crowds by hiking 1.0 mile up Sahale Arm and then descending for 1.0 mile toward Doubtful Lake. The pleasant tarn is surrounded by the exploratory probings of long-gone prospectors.

Camping is not allowed at the pass, but you'll find campsites in Pelton Basin, 1.0 mile down the trail toward Stehekin. Another option is to camp below the glacier at Sahale Camp, the highest official camp in the national park.

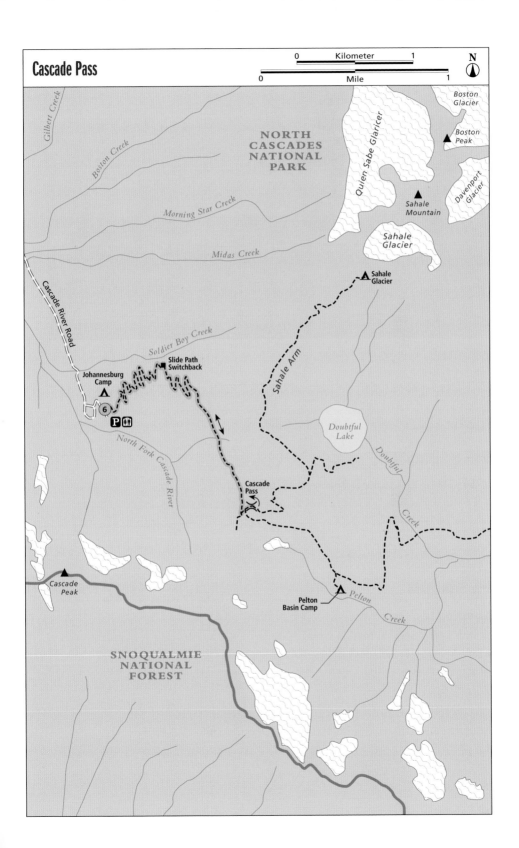

Cascade Pass

0 — Kilometer — 1

0 — Mile — 1

N

Gilbert Creek

Boston Creek

Morning Star Creek

Midas Creek

NORTH CASCADES NATIONAL PARK

Boston Glacier

Boston Peak

Quien Sabe Glacier

Davenport Glacier

Sahale Mountain

Sahale Glacier

Cascade River Road

Soldier Boy Creek

Slide Path Switchback

Johannesburg Camp

6

P

North Fork Cascade River

Sahale Glacier

Sahale Arm

Doubtful Lake

Doubtful Creek

Cascade Pass

Cascade Peak

Pelton Basin Camp

Pelton Creek

SNOQUALMIE NATIONAL FOREST

Johannesburg Mountain in the morning light

For the full Cascade Pass experience, backpackers can hike beyond Pelton Basin to High Bridge, 19 miles east of Cascade Pass. From here a shuttle bus takes hikers along the Stehekin River to the village of Stehekin.

Miles and Directions

0.0 Start at the Cascade Pass Trailhead and parking lot.

1.8 Switchback briefly through a treeless avalanche slide path with views of Johannesburg Mountain across the valley.

3.7 Reach Cascade Pass. Return the way you came.

7.4 Arrive back at the trailhead.

Hike Information

Lodging

USDA Forest Service Marble Creek Campgrounds; 8 miles east of Marblemount on Cascade River Road; (360) 856-5700

Skagit River Resort and Cabins, 58468 Clark Cabin Rd., Rockport; (360) 873-2250

Restaurants

Buffalo Run Restaurant, 60084 SR 20, Marblemount; (360) 873-2461

Marblemount Diner, 60147 SR 20, Marblemount; (360) 873-4503

7 Hidden Lake Lookout

The hike to the Hidden Lake Lookout is one of the prettiest day hikes anywhere. Big woods lead to wildflowers, open slopes, heather meadows, and finally snow patches and sheer granite slabs. Up and up you go, until the world falls away and you're surrounded by sky, snow, and stark-white rock. Here Hidden Lake reveals itself, its dark blue water lying just below in a basin of broken granite.

Start: Hidden Lake Trail 745 trailhead at the end of FR 1540
Distance: 9.0 miles out and back
Hiking time: About 5 hours
Difficulty: Difficult due to elevation gain and rock scrambles
Trail surface: Dirt trail with rock scrambles
Elevation gain: 3,100 feet
Land status: National forest, national park
Nearest town: Marblemount
Best season: Late July to Oct.
Other trail users: None
Canine compatibility: Leashed dogs are allowed on most of the hike, but not beyond the National Park boundary.

Fees and permits: Northwest Forest Pass required to park at the trailhead. Wilderness camping in North Cascades National Park requires a free permit. Permits are available at the Wilderness Information Center in Marblemount.
Maps: USGS Sonny Boy Lakes and Eldorado Peak; Green Trails no. 48, Diablo Dam, and no. 80, Cascade Pass
Trail contacts: Marblemount Ranger District; (360) 873-4590
Other: Camping is limited at Hidden Lake Peaks. This trail is best as a day hike.

Finding the trailhead: From WA 20 at Marblemount, go east on the Cascade River Road for 9.7 miles. Turn left onto FR 1540 (Sibley Creek Road) 1.7 miles after crossing Marble Creek. Follow FR 1540 for 4.2 miles until it ends at the trailhead and a parking lot. GPS: N48 30.85' / W121.12.32'

The Hike

Some call these mountains the American Alps. Others wonder why they don't call the Alps the North Cascades of Central Europe. Whatever you call them, the North Cascades are big, beautiful, and remote. The hike to the Hidden Lake Lookout may rank as one of the best hikes in either set of Alps.

The Hidden Lake Peaks are a pair of granite-topped mountains high above tree line and similar in height. The fire lookout is on top of the smaller of the two peaks. You can hike to both peaks, but the views are similar, and the taller one requires more off-trail scrambling.

The two Hidden Lake Peaks are far enough east to offer an excellent vantage into the heart of the North Cascades, where serrated peaks line the horizon. They are also just far enough west—near the flatlands—to give a sense of how tall these mountains

A hiker enjoys a short glissade down an early September snowfield

are and how far they rise from the valleys of the Cascade River and Marble Creek, which flank the mountains nearly 6,000 feet below the lookout.

From the lookout you can see Mounts Baker and Shuksan, the rugged Picket Range, and Bonanza Mountain—the tallest nonvolcanic peak in the state. The complicated mass of Snowking Mountain, just across the deep valley to the south, is remarkable for having such gargantuan glaciers at a modest elevation. Incredible amounts of snow fall on Snowking since it's so far west.

Several drastic changes in scenery take place as you ascend to Hidden Lake Peaks. The trail begins switchbacking through a moist forest of big trees and small streams as you work your way toward East Fork Sibley Creek. In just over 1.0 mile, the trail emerges from the forest, crosses the creek, and enters a lush open meadow of fireweed, paintbrush, spirea, and some head-high hellebore with huge, flat leaves. Only the rare tangle of yellow cedars or alders

▶ **Bonanza Peak, the tall granite point visible to the southwest from the Hidden Lake Lookout, is the tallest nonvolcanic mountain in the Cascades. Bonanza Peak was originally called North Star Mountain, and North Star Mountain, 2 miles away, was called Bonanza. The US Geologic Survey (USGS) switched the names in 1904.**

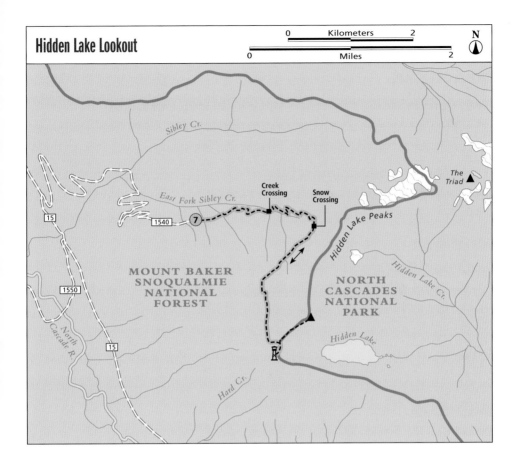

Hidden Lake Lookout

beaten sideways by avalanches shelters the trail from the sun. Bring sunscreen or a big hat.

At 2.5 miles another abrupt transition in trailside vegetation begins as the lush meadow gives way to a drier tundra of bright white granite rocks with a low covering of heather and blueberries. From here continue hiking under Sibley Pass and to the saddle between the two peaks. You will pass a couple cramped campsites in the 0.25 mile of trail below the saddle. Straight ahead is the cliffy white ridge below Hidden Lake Peaks.

In this top section of trail, rock faces shade little patches of snow that linger late into summer. You can avoid some snow by traveling up several slabs of nearly unbroken granite. The rock here is steep but provides a good grip on boot soles. As you crest the saddle between the two peaks, Hidden Lake is revealed. The glassy blue lake surface reflects the surrounding mountains, talus, snowfields, and sky.

The last 0.5 mile to the lookout tower is easier than it looks from below, but it's still airy and exposed in some places. It starts as a steep trail and ends with a scramble over huge boulders. At the tower you are greeted by an up-close view of Snowking

Mountain—the glacier-covered peak to the south. Explore the fire lookout, or use an exceptionally scenic pit toilet, the "Royal Throne," 100 feet south of the tower.

Miles and Directions

0.0 Start at the west end of the parking lot at the end of FR 1540, signed HIDDEN LAKE.

1.3 Cross East Fork Sibley Creek and enter an open meadow, leaving the forest behind.

2.5 Recross East Fork Sibley Creek. This crossing may be snowy.

3.8 Reach the saddle between the two Hidden Lake Peaks and enter North Cascades National Park. From here you can see Hidden Lake.

4.5 Arrive at the Hidden Lake Lookout. Return the way you came.

9.0 Arrive back at the trailhead.

Hike Information

Local Information

North Cascades Business Association and Visitor Center, PO Box 175, Marblemount 98267; (360) 873-4150; marblemount.com

North Cascades Institute; offers natural history seminars; (360) 854-2599; ncascades.org

Lodging

USDA Forest Service Marble Creek Campground; (360) 856-5700

Skagit River Resort and Cabins, 58468 Clark Cabin Rd., Rockport; (360) 873-2250

Restaurants

Buffalo Run Restaurant, 60084 SR 20, Marblemount; (360) 873-2461

Marblemount Diner, 60147 SR 20, Marblemount; (360) 873-4503

8 Horseshoe Basin

In the North Cascades, wilderness is usually rugged, choked with brush, and hard to travel through. Horseshoe Basin in the Pasayten Wilderness is the opposite. The expansive, rolling alpine tundra is easy to explore. Horseshoe Basin is a beautiful base camp for days of hiking over golden hills and mountains, to chilly lakes, and through groves of pines and larches. In fact, you almost need to stay a night or two to experience the quiet wilderness surrounding the basin.

Start: Iron Gate Trailhead at the end of FR 500
Distance: 12.4 miles out and back
Hiking time: About 6.5 hours
Difficulty: Difficult due to length
Trail surface: Dirt road and trail
Elevation gain: 1,150 feet
Land status: Federal wilderness area
Nearest town: Tonasket
Best season: June through Oct

Other trail users: Equestrians, pack animals
Canine compatibility: Leashed dogs allowed
Fees and permits: Northwest Forest Pass required to park at trailhead
Maps: USGS Horseshoe Basin; Green Trails no. 21, Horseshoe Basin
Trail contacts: Tonasket Ranger District, Tonasket; (509) 486-2186; www.fs.usda.gov/okawen

Finding the trailhead: From Tonasket go north on WA 7 for 5.5 miles and turn left (east) onto County Road 9437 (Okanogan CR 9437). Continue 10.5 miles to Loomis. From Loomis bear right to continue on CR 9425 and drive 2 miles to FR 39 (Toats Coulee Road). Continue 13.8 miles and turn right onto FR 500, signed IRON GATE ROAD. Follow this rough road 5.8 miles to the trailhead. GPS: N48 54.53' / W119 54.29'

The Hike

Go to Horseshoe Basin to see wildflowers, western larches, and golden hills basking in the sun of the far east Cascades. Stay a night or two to enjoy easy roaming in the basin and on the 8,000-foot peaks around it. The peaks in the area are all gentle and easy to walk up. From a base camp in the basin, inspect your map, pick a destination, and take off. Some favorite trips in the basin are the walk to glassy blue Smith Lake, at the foot of larch-covered Horseshoe Mountain, and the hike up Arnold and Armstrong Mountains and beyond to various Canadian border monuments.

The hike to Horseshoe Basin is doable as a day hike, but it's long. You could easily spend a second full day bagging peaks and sitting by lakes and a third day hiking out or looping back on the Windy Peak Trail and hiking to the summit of 8,334-foot Windy Peak on your way back to the trailhead. Windy Peak is ninety-second on the list of one hundred highest mountains in Washington State. The peak is an easy hike but is rarely visited, and the trail can be overgrown.

Another reason to spend a night at Horseshoe Basin is so that you can avoid hiking through miles of burned forest twice in one day. After walking slightly downhill

A burned but beautiful forest at the beginning of the Iron Gate Trail

from the trailhead for 1.0 mile through spruce and pine trees, the trail passes through almost 2.5 miles of charred forest from the 2006 Tripod Fire.

It's not the most exciting part of the hike, but don't expect the trek through fire country to be a desolate death march. Below the charred trees, a thick growth of fireweed is rejuvenating the soil. The pioneer plant, which is named for its abundance in recently burned areas, has colonized the entire burn and is slowly adding organic matter to support less-hardy plants. In summer, fireweed explodes with bright pink flowers. In fall the plants' leaves add vibrant yellow and dark red to the landscape.

Aside from enjoying the fireweed and other wildflowers, look closely for young pine trees. In the southern section of the burn, young lodgepole pines are springing to life everywhere. As you hike north toward Sunny Pass, the pines mysteriously diminish.

After 3.5 miles of mostly flat hiking, the trail begins climbing out of the burned forest toward Sunny Pass. You leave the dense burned forest behind and enter tundra

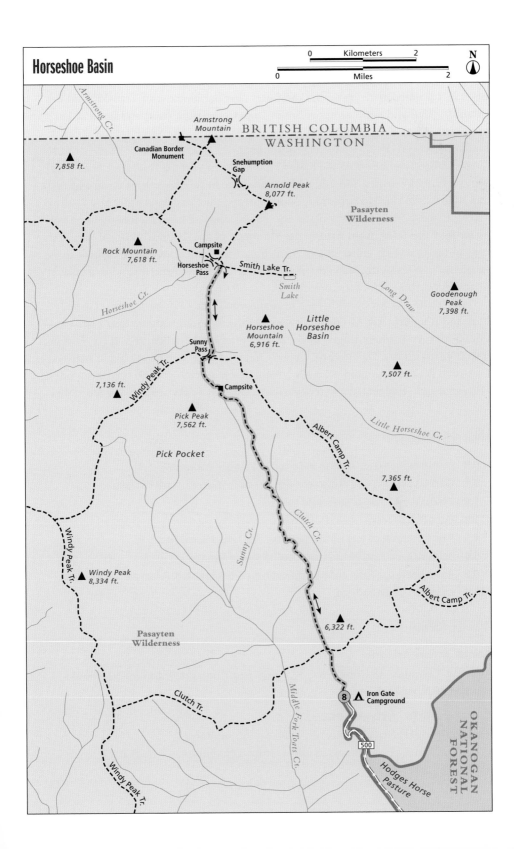

Horseshoe Basin

Kilometers
0 _____ 2

Miles
0 _____ 2

N

Armstrong Cr.

Armstrong
Mountain

BRITISH COLUMBIA
WASHINGTON

Canadian Border
Monument

Snehumption
Gap

Arnold Peak
8,077 ft.

Pasayten
Wilderness

7,858 ft.

Rock Mountain
7,618 ft.

Campsite

Horseshoe
Pass

Smith Lake Tr.

Smith
Lake

Long Draw

Goodenough
Peak
7,398 ft.

Horseshoe Cr.

Horseshoe
Mountain
6,916 ft.

Little
Horseshoe
Basin

7,507 ft.

Sunny
Pass

Windy Peak Tr.

Campsite

7,136 ft.

Pick Peak
7,562 ft.

Albert Camp Tr.

Little Horseshoe Cr.

7,365 ft.

Pick Pocket

Sunny Cr.

Clutch Cr.

Windy Peak Tr.

Windy Peak
8,334 ft.

Albert Camp Tr.

6,322 ft.

Pasayten
Wilderness

Clutch Tr.

Middle Fork Toats Cr.

8
Iron Gate
Campground

500

OKANOGAN NATIONAL FOREST

Windy Peak Tr.

Hodges Horse
Pasture

with sparse clumps of gnarled subalpine fir, spruce, and larch atop Sunny Pass. From the pass traverse the western slope of Horseshoe Mountain and reach Horseshoe Basin in 1.0 mile. There are several campsites near the junction of Trail 533 and the Boundary Trail and more camps at Smith Lake to the right (east) and Loudon Lake to the left (west). Year-round water is available at Smith Lake and Horseshoe Creek. Loudon Lake can dry up by the end of summer.

Day-hiking options from the basin abound. Go east on the Boundary Trail, travel west on Trail 340 toward Snowshoe Mountain, hike to Windy Peak, or do an easy off-trail walk up the ridge to Armstrong Mountain and the Canadian border. You'll know you're at the border when you see the obelisk-shaped border monuments. Look down into the forest from Armstrong Mountain at the 20-foot swath of clear-cut trees in the valleys on either side of Armstrong Mountain. This line of clearcut trees, called the "border swath," extends 5,525 miles across North America and is mandated by the International Border Commission.

Follow the swath east with your eyes and you'll see two sharp peaks: Cathedral Peak and Amphitheater Mountain. If you like the Pasayten country (you will), consider a journey to these jagged peaks in the heart of the wilderness. It's a 30-mile trek from Iron Gate Trailhead to Upper Cathedral Lake, which is nestled between Cathedral Peak and Amphitheater Mountain. Before glaciers gouged their steep sides, Cathedral and Amphitheater were wide domes like the peaks surrounding Horseshoe Basin.

Miles and Directions

0.0 Start at the Iron Gate Trailhead and enter the Pasayten Wilderness.
0.7 Continue hiking straight at junctions with the trail to Windy Pass and Trail 341.
1.0 Reach the beginning of the burned trees.
1.6 Cross Clutch Creek.
4.5 Pass a campsite on your left and begin climbing toward Sunny Pass.
5.0 Arrive at Sunny Pass, and contour under Horseshoe Mountain.
6.2 Reach Horseshoe Basin and a junction with the Smith Lake Trail. Return the way you came.
12.4 Arrive back at the trailhead.

Hike Information

Local Information

Tonasket Chamber of Commerce, PO Box 523, Tonasket 98855; (509) 486-4543; tonasketchamber.com

Local Events/Attractions

Tonasket Farmers Market, Tonasket; Thursdays in summer
Okanogan Family Faire, Tonasket; mid-October; okanoganfamilyfaire.net

THE TRIPOD FIRE: 175,000 SCORCHED ACRES

In 2006 the Tripod Fire burned 175,000 acres between Winthrop and Loomis, including sections of the trails to Horseshoe Basin and Tiffany Mountain. It was one of the largest fires in Washington in the past hundred years.

After several warmer-than-average summers, the population of mountain pine beetles and spruce bark beetles had swelled, leaving thousands of dead trees in their wake. On July 24, 2006, lighting sparked a fire in beetle-killed trees 6 miles northeast of Winthrop. The fire quickly spread and moved north, with Horseshoe Basin being the far northern end of the fire.

More than 2,000 firefighters battled the blaze during its peak in the first week of September. They focused on protecting the towns of Twisp, Winthrop, and Conconully. The fire burned and smoldered for more than three months until October 31, 2006. The burned trees south of Sunny Pass on the Horseshoe Basin Trail are an example of the unpredictable nature of fires. Healthy, living trees stand adjacent to swatches of blackened snags.

Lodging

Washington Department of Fish and Wildlife Palmer Lake Campground, Loomis; (360) 902-2515

Junction Motel, 23 W Sixth St., Tonasket; (509) 486-4421

Restaurants

Okanogan River Natural Foods Co-op, 21 W. Fourth St., Tonasket; (509) 486-4188

Tonasket Pizza Company, 15 W. Fourth St., Tonasket; (509) 486-4808

9 Tiffany Mountain

Sunshine, high-elevation, no crowds, beautiful scenery and a short distance make Tiffany Mountain an exceptional outing. The open grasslands on the lonely east side of the Cascades offer easy travel to tall peaks, and this round dome is a fine example. The trail winds up the gentle side of the mountain, but from the summit you can look down at the steep ridges on the northwest side of the mountain. The ridges cradle little lakes and are covered in pines and western larches.

Start: Trailhead at Freezeout Pass
Distance: 4.4 miles out and back
Hiking time: About 2.5 hours
Difficulty: Moderate due to elevation gain
Trail surface: Dirt trail
Elevation gain: 1,700 feet
Land status: National forest
Nearest town: Winthrop
Best season: June through Oct

Other trail users: Equestrians
Canine compatibility: Dog friendly
Fees and permits: Northwest Forest Pass required to park at trailhead
Maps: USGS Tiffany Mountain; Green Trails no. 53, Tiffany Mountain
Trail contacts: Methow Valley Ranger District; (509) 996-4000; www.fs.usda.gov/okawen
Other: No water along the trail

Finding the trailhead: From Winthrop go north on East Chewuch Road toward Pearrygin Lake State Park. In 6 miles, before crossing the Chewuch River, turn right onto FR 37. The pavement ends in 7.5 miles, and at 13 miles the gravel road comes to a junction with FR 39. Go left onto FR 39; in 3.2 miles park on the shoulder on the right (east) side of the road, just past a cattleguard. GPS: N48 39.77' / W119 57.97'

The Hike

Hikers come to Tiffany Mountain to bag a high peak, find some solitude, and enjoy the view. For the hiker who likes short, direct climbs to high peaks, Tiffany can't be beat. The only road in sight is the remote forest road you came in on, which winds into the distance between burned-out sticks. Even on weekends you won't run into many other hikers on this trail. Aside from FR 39, the mountains and wilderness are utterly uninterrupted as they stretch out before you and merge with the horizon.

The tall, round dome that is Tiffany Mountain reaches for the sun at 8,242 feet. From the summit, five broad ridges branch off and roll downhill into the creek valleys below. Western larches, whose needle-like leaves turn gold and fall off in autumn, cling to the north and west sides of every ridge. Glassy little lakes and ponds occupy the depressions between the ridges.

The terrain, like most of the Okanogan Cascades, is gentle and rolling, but the ridges crumble into talus at their steepest sections. Many of the peaks in this area are taller than peaks at the crest of the Cascades. The open terrain lends itself perfectly to hiking and exploring. You won't find the thick vegetation that clings to the subalpine

A colorful larch with Tiffany Mountain in the background

zones in the Cascades. Instead you will walk past wildflowers and golden grasses swaying in the high-elevation breeze.

The hike starts at Freezeout Pass at the Freezeout Ridge Trailhead, just north of a cattleguard. Park on the shoulder of the road, where there is room for about eight cars. That's usually enough space, as this hike is far from almost everywhere.

The trail follows Freezeout Ridge through trees burned in the 2006 Tripod Fire. The forest is regenerating and fireweed is crowding the burned slopes, providing color and vegetation to the otherwise barren landscape. Look closer and you can spot some young lodgepole pines reaching for light through the fireweed. The burned trees eventually give way to living spruce and lodgepole and whitebark pines that the flaming fingers of fire couldn't reach. All the while, the broad cone of Tiffany Mountain is visible ahead of you. It looks distant and massive but is surprisingly close.

A sea of purple lupines mingle with the golden grasses on this peaceful ridge. Snowshoe hares and marmots pop in and out from jumbled boulders. From the trail

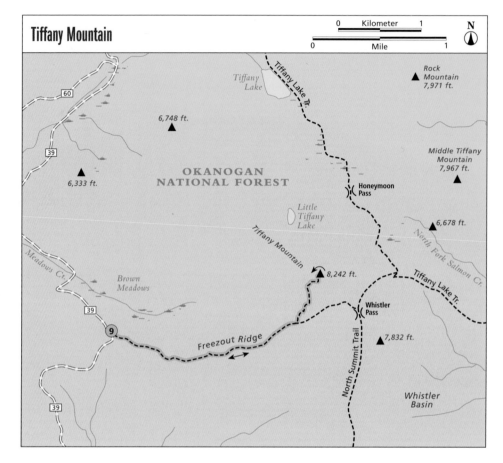

0 Kilometer 1

0 Mile 1

N

Rock Mountain 7,971 ft.

Tiffany Lake

Tiffany Lake Tr.

6,748 ft.

Middle Tiffany Mountain 7,967 ft.

OKANOGAN NATIONAL FOREST

Honeymoon Pass

6,333 ft.

Little Tiffany Lake

6,678 ft.

Tiffany Mountain

North Fork Salmon Cr.

Meadows Cr.

Brown Meadows

8,242 ft.

Tiffany Lake Tr.

Whistler Pass

9

Freezeout Ridge

7,832 ft.

North Summit Trail

Whistler Basin

you may see an assortment of birds, including golden eagles, mountain bluebirds, kestrels, and grouse.

A stripe of golden larches color the tree line on the north side of Freezeout Ridge in the fall. Wildflowers such as lupines, paintbrush, and daisies bloom on the ridge in summer. Right before Freezeout Ridge broadens and begins climbing more steeply, you reach a junction and a signpost for Whistler Pass Trail. Take a left and continue directly up Tiffany Mountain. From here the trail is like a climber's trail. It's direct and braided in places but easy to follow.

Sweat up the open slopes toward the rocky summit. Tiffany Mountain is gentle and rounded on the southwest side, which the trail ascends. First-timers at Tiffany Mountain usually prepare for a disappointing view, as the ridge on the way up is so broad. But cliffs fall away on the northeast side of the mountain, making for a spectacular view to the ridges and lakes below. The biggest lake beyond the loose east ridges is Tiffany Lake. Just beyond it, the Pasayten Wilderness stretches to the Canadian border. The mountains get increasingly more jagged to the west, and you can almost make out the sagebrush in the Okanogan Highlands to the east.

Miles and Directions

0.0 Start at the trailhead for Freezeout Ridge on FR 39.

0.8 After hiking through burned trees and brush, reach several stands of living trees.

1.5 Reach an open meadow above the initial forested ridge.

1.7 Go left at the signpost for Whistler Pass.

2.2 Reach the summit of Tiffany Mountain. Return the way you came.

4.4 Arrive back at the trailhead.

Hike Information

Local Information

Winthrop Chamber of Commerce, PO Box 32, Winthrop 98862; (509) 996-2125; winthropwashington.com

Local Events/Attractions

Winthrop Rhythm and Blues Festival; mid-July; winthropbluesfestival.com
Methow Valley Rodeo; Memorial and Labor Day weekends; methowvalleyrodeo.com

Lodging

Pearrygin Lake State Park Campground, Winthrop; parks.wa.gov
USDA Forest Service Chewuch and Falls Creek Campgrounds; 11 and 15 miles north of Winthrop on FR 51; (509) 996-4000; www.fs.usda.gov/okawen

Restaurants

Old Schoolhouse Brewery, 155 Riverside Ave., Winthrop; (509) 996-3183
Carlos1800 Mexican Grill & Cantina, 149 Riverside Ave., Winthrop; (509) 996-2245

10 Mount Pilchuck

This is one of the most popular trails in the state, and for good reason. It's a short hike to an incredible Cascades panorama. The trail leads through old-growth forest, heather slopes, granite boulders, and tall cliffs to a historic fire lookout. Mount Pilchuck rises from the far western edge of the Cascade Range, towering over the lowlands. Because of this location, the summit features unparalleled views of Puget Sound and the Olympic Mountains, as well as the snowy peaks of the Cascade Range.

Start: Trailhead for Mount Pilchuck Trail 700

Distance: 5.4 miles out and back

Hiking time: About 3 hours

Difficulty: Moderate due to elevation gain and a rocky scramble to the summit

Trail surface: Dirt and gravel trail

Elevation gain: 2,150 feet

Land status: National forest, Washington state park

Nearest town: Granite Falls

Best season: July through Oct

Other trail users: None

Canine compatibility: Dog friendly

Fees and permits: Northwest Forest Pass required to park at trailhead

Maps: USGS Verlot; Green Trails no. 109, Granite Falls; Darrington Ranger District map, available at the Verlot Public Service Center

Trail contacts: USDA Forest Service Verlot Public Service Center; (360) 691-7791; www .fs.usda.gov/mbs

Finding the trailhead: From Granite Falls go east on the Mountain Loop Highway for 15 miles. You'll pass the Verlot Public Service Center in 11 miles. Turn right onto FR 4020 and continue 7 miles to the parking lot and trailhead. The first 5 miles of this road are unpaved but well maintained. The last 2 miles to the trailhead are on pavement. GPS: N48 04.20' / W121 48.89'

The Hike

Mount Pilchuck is a rocky summit with a tower perched on top and spectacular 360-degree views of the North Cascades, the Olympic Mountains, and every volcano in the state. The views of the water to the west are spectacular because of Mount Pilchuck's location at the far western edge of the Cascades, just 18 miles from Everett. Puget Sound, the San Juan Islands, endless lakes and rivers, Seattle, and Everett are all visible from the tower.

Mount Pilchuck is a popular trail where you will encounter many friendly folks. Some of them might try to get to know you or have you take their photo in front of a volcano they can't name. First-time hikers may wander up to you and mutter something unintelligible, like "Wow, this is . . . mind blown away." But they're here for the same reason you are—a relatively short hike with expansive views in every direction. If you live in Western Washington and you're not sure why, come up here for a reminder. Endless mountains and valleys stretch in every direction, with the basin between the Cascades and Olympics filled with sparkling water.

The historic fire lookout's perch atop Mount Pilchuck

The summit block is a pile of house-size granite boulders. This is a first summit for many hikers, and it's easy to see why. You can come up to the top of Mount Pilchuck and feel as though you've seen the whole state. The lower forests, historic fire lookout, and talus fields are pretty enough sights to make this trail fun when clouds cover the sky, but you really should save it for a clear day.

The trail starts out in a pleasant forest of big conifers. The path is well built to withstand heavy traffic. In low-lying areas it's cribbed, nearly paved with rocks, and elevated above the level of the surrounding ground. Staircases of logs and rock help minimize erosion in some of the steepest sections. After about 0.5 mile of hiking, gaps in the trees treat you to occasional view of Mount Baker.

A mile and a half from the trailhead the forest begins to open up as the trail crosses slopes of talus. At the concrete base of an old ski lift you get the first views of the summit ridge, a cliff of naked granite.

At the summit the trail ends just below some giant boulders. To get to the lookout, you must scramble over the rocks to a ladder, which leads the final feet to the fire

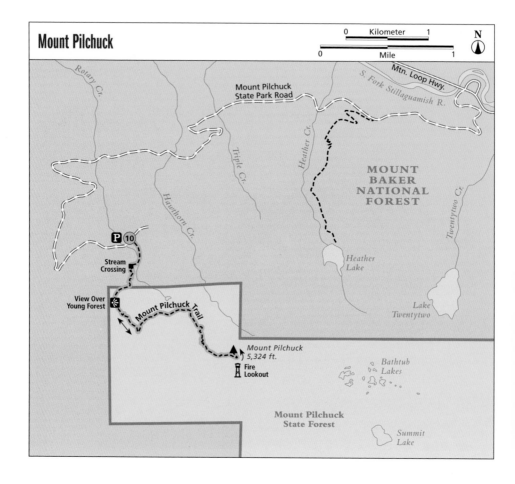

0   Kilometer   1

0   Mile   1

N

Rotary Cr.

Mount Pilchuck
State Park Road

S. Fork Stillaguamish R.

Mtn. Loop Hwy.

Triple Cr.

Heather Cr.

Hawthorn Cr.

MOUNT
BAKER
NATIONAL
FOREST

Twentytwo Cr.

P 10

Stream
Crossing

View Over
Young Forest

Mount Pilchuck Trail

Heather
Lake

Lake
Twentytwo

Mount Pilchuck
5,324 ft.

Fire
Lookout

Bathtub
Lakes

Mount Pilchuck
State Forest

Summit
Lake

lookout. This probably won't be possible for your dog or small child. At the summit, check out the historical pictures and view from the lookout tower, but also explore the surrounding rocks. Brave scramblers can roam all over the summit in search of a private spot or for the perfect photograph of the iconic lookout tower.

The lookout tower at the top is a mini-museum packed with historical information and photographs about the tower and the mountain. All four sides of the tower have panoramic diagrams that point out the names of the peaks you can see through the windows. If you don't know the Mountain Loop Highway or the North Cascades as well as you'd like, come up here for a lesson in peak names.

Before it was a popular hiking destination, Mount Pilchuck was the site of a ski area with an upper chairlift climbing to 4,300 feet, just below the ridge of rock at the summit. The ski area closed permanently in 1980 after several winters of below-average snow and few skiers. (It was one of the lowest elevation ski resorts in the state.)

Miles and Directions

0.0 Start at the parking lot for Mount Pilchuck Trail 700 off the Mount Pilchuck State Park Access Road.

0.3 Cross a creek.

1.7 Continue hiking past the concrete base of the upper ski lift.

2.7 Reach the summit, and scramble up boulders to the lookout tower. Return the way you came.

5.4 Arrive back at the trailhead.

Hike Information

Local Information
Granite Falls Chamber of Commerce, PO Box 28, Granite Falls 98252; (360) 691-7733; granitefallswa.com

Local Events/Attractions
Big Four Ice Caves, 15 miles east of the Verlot Public Service Center on the Mountain Loop Highway; (360) 691-7791

Lodging
USDA Forest Service Verlot and Turlo Campgrounds; across the Mountain Loop Highway from the Verlot Public Services Center; (360) 691-7791

Restaurants
Alfy's Pizza, 401 N. Granite Ave., Granite Falls; (360) 691-5411

Organizations
Everett Mountaineers (they maintain the Mount Pilchuck lookout); everettmountaineers.org

11 Gothic Basin

This narrow basin of dark, naked rock, little pools, and a deep lake is wedged between the towers and buttresses of two formidable mountains. The trail is steep and rough, but it traverses beautiful forests high above the headwaters of the Sauk River. The uphill grunt ends when the trail crosses a pass into the awe-inspiring basin. The towering peaks and otherworldly rock make Gothic Basin an unforgettable destination.

Start: Barlow Pass on the Monte Cristo Road
Distance: 9.4 miles out and back
Hiking time: About 4.5 hours
Difficulty: Difficult due to steep, rocky terrain
Trail surface: Dirt and rock trail
Best season: Aug through Oct
Elevation gain: 2,900 feet
Land status: National forest, state conservation area
Nearest town: Granite Falls
Other trail users: None

Canine compatibility: Dog friendly
Fees and permits: Northwest Forest Pass required to park at trailhead
Maps: *USGS Monte Cristo and Bedal; Green Trails no. 143, Monte Cristo; Darrington Ranger District* map, available at Verlot Public Service Center
Trail contacts: Verlot Public Service Center, USDA Forest Service; (360) 691-7791; www.fs.usda.gov/mbs

Finding the trailhead: From Granite Falls go east on the Mountain Loop Highway for 30 miles. At Barlow Pass, park on the shoulder on the right side of the road or the parking lot to the left. The trail begins at the gated dirt road on the right (south) side of the highway. GPS: N48 30.91' / W121 26.65'

The Hike

Chiseled spires loom high above a deep frozen lake that seldom melts. Pikas signal to one another with high-pitched calls, and marmots sniff the alpine breeze from dark rocky towers. Gothic Basin awaits. This narrow, glacier-scraped basin sits between the three towers of Gothic Peak on one side and the equally jagged Del Campo Peak on the other. The year-round snowfield on Gothic Pass melts into Foggy Lake, a deep, fishless alpine lake beneath the peaks. A small stream flows out of the lake, pooling up in several ponds in the basin before plummeting steeply down the slope to Weden Creek.

It's easy to imagine that Gothic Basin got its name because the rugged terrain and steep peaks resemble gothic architecture. But it was actually named for William Gothic, an early prospector in the Monte Cristo area. The Monte Cristo townsite, which is just a few miles below Gothic Basin on the South Fork of the Sauk River, was home to 2,000 people at its peak in the 1890s. It was a base for miners, who extracted millions of dollars' worth of gold and silver from the mountains. Now it's one of Washington State's best ghost towns.

The three summits of Gothic Peak rise above Foggy Lake.

Don't underestimate the difficulty or length of the trail—2,900 feet of elevation in 4.7 miles may not sound excessive, but only the first 1.0 mile or so is on a flat road; the rest of the distance is brutally steep. You'll be climbing tight switchbacks that start out as firm, tacky dirt. Later on, the trail begins to resemble a creekbed. In the final 1.0 mile, angular rocks slices through the U-shaped, boulder-strewn trail.

Start out by walking past the gate at the Monte Cristo Road at Barlow Pass. The flat road runs parallel to the Sauk River for 1.0 mile. This is easy walking, with occasional views of the river. Several old mining trails take off to the right of the road, relics of a time when men and mules carried gold off the mountain. Stay on the road until it ends and a trail begins winding uphill. Soon you will reach a privy and a junction where you can go left to the Monte Cristo townsite or right for Gothic Basin.

After this junction the climb begins and doesn't let up. The trail winds through dense Douglas fir, cedar, spruce, and hemlock. Breaks in the trees show an occasional glimpse of Sheep Mountain, but views are rare. There's a brief break from climbing 3.0 miles from the trailhead, but your legs don't get much of a rest as you lumber

MONTE CRISTO TOWNSITE

For a side trip after hiking to Gothic Basin, go south at the junction with the Gothic Basin/ Weden Creek Trailhead near the South Fork Sauk and hike about 3.0 miles to the Monte Cristo townsite. The town was established in the late 1880s after Joseph Pearsall found samples of silver and gold in the Sauk River. Pearsall and his friend Frank Peabody, along with two investors, named the town Monte Cristo because they hoped it would make them as rich as the Count of Monte Cristo.

The area did prove to be rich in silver and gold. It produced millions of dollars in gold and silver ore, and the scale of the mining soon outgrew the power of human backs. By 1892 an investment company backed by John D. Rockefeller had bought most of the mines and built a railway—the Everett and Monte Cristo Railway—into the townsite.

Floods frequently damaged the railroad, which followed the turbulent South Fork Still- aguamish River through Lower Robe Canyon. By 1899 profit from the mines was declining and the railroad repairs were sucking up the investors' money. Rockefeller decided to rebuild and then sell the railroad, and Northern Pacific took over in 1903.

Soon after, when mining operations for silver and gold were no longer profitable, Monte Cristo became a resort for hunters, hikers, and other outdoor enthusiasts. Business dwin- dled, and by 1933 Monte Cristo was a ghost town. Today all that's left of the residences, shops, stables, churches, and infrastructure of Monte Cristo is a railroad turntable and a couple of neglected structures.

across steep terrain, creeks, talus, and early-season snowfields. Even when conditions are good, sections of loose trail and large boulders can be challenging. At 3.6 miles a waterfall splashes down several rocky steps. There are rumors of a mine shaft nearby.

After contouring across this hill, you will resume climbing. This final climb to the basin isn't as steep as the section below the falls, but the trail surface is worse. V-shaped ditches of jagged rock and boulders make up parts of the trail, and you'll need to use all four limbs in a few places. Just when you think your legs can't handle any more, you are forced to maneuver underneath several big fallen trees. This is especially gru- eling with an overnight pack. Finally the trail enters a notch and the dark, rocky basin spreads out in front of you. You reach this notch in just over 4.0 miles, but it's another 0.5 mile of steep scrambling before you reach the outlet of Foggy Lake.

From the notch, a couple campsites are wedged between trees to the left (south). Several more are at the outlet of the lake and at the lake itself. From Foggy Lake, a trail toward Del Campo Peak leads to a viewpoint to the east, where you can see Silvertip Peak, Foggy Peak, and Sheep Mountain. The peaks above Foggy Lake are popular with climbers, who scramble up all sides.

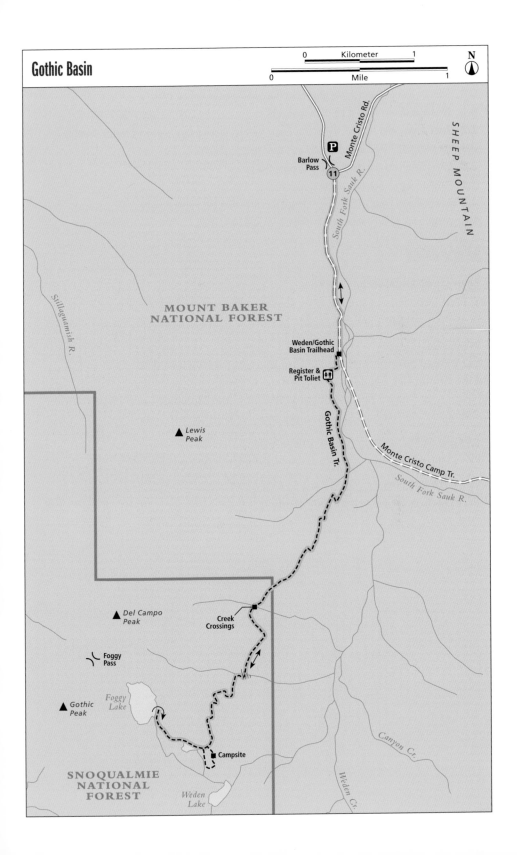

Gothic Basin

0   Kilometer   1

0   Mile   1

N

SHEEP MOUNTAIN

Monte Cristo Rd.

P

Barlow
Pass

11

South Fork Sauk R.

MOUNT BAKER
NATIONAL FOREST

Stillaguamish R.

Weden/Gothic
Basin Trailhead

Register &
Pit Toliet

▲ Lewis
Peak

Gothic Basin Tr.

Monte Cristo Camp Tr.

South Fork Sauk R.

▲ Del Campo
Peak

Creek
Crossings

⌣ Foggy
Pass

Foggy
Lake

▲ Gothic
Peak

Campsite

SNOQUALMIE
NATIONAL
FOREST

Weden
Lake

Weden Cr.

Canyon Cr.

Miles and Directions

0.0 Start down the gated gravel road from the parking lot at Barlow Pass.

0.7 Pass several old mining trails on your right.

1.2 Pass a privy and start on the Gothic Basin/Weden Creek Trail; pass a self-registration box.

3.0 Cross through an avalanche gully and past several streams.

3.6 Cross a stream just below a scenic waterfall.

4.3 Pass through a notch and into Gothic Basin.

4.7 Reach Foggy Lake, at the top of Gothic Basin. Return the way you came.

9.4 Arrive back at the trailhead and parking lot at Barlow Pass.

Hike Information

Local Events/Attractions

Big Four Ice Caves, 15 miles east of the Verlot Public Service Center on the Mountain Loop Highway; (360) 691-7791

Lodging

USDA Forest Service Red Bridge, 7 miles east of the Verlot Public Services Center on the Mountain Loop Highway; (360) 691-7791

USDA Forest Service Verlot Campgrounds, across the Mountain Loop Highway from the Verlot Public Services Center; (360) 691-7791

Restaurants

Alfy's Pizza, 401 N. Granite Ave., Granite Falls; (360) 691-5411

Other Resources

Hiking Washington's History, by Judy Bentley

12 Beckler Peak

A brand new, well-built trail leads up to Beckler Peak through an impressive mature forest. The peak is a high viewpoint into the Wild Sky Wilderness north of Stevens Pass. The 360-degree views and rocky summit lend the peak an alpine flavor. On top of all that, the trailhead is relatively easy to get to and it's just a 7.6-mile-round trip for the grand view.

Start: Trailhead at the Jennifer Dunn parking lot on FR 6066
Distance: 7.6 miles out and back
Hiking time: About 4.5 hours
Difficulty: Moderate due to length and elevation gain
Trail surface: Dirt trail
Elevation gain: 2,250 feet
Land status: National forest
Nearest town: Skykomish
Best season: Mid-June to Oct

Other trail users: None
Canine compatibility: Dogs allowed
Fees and permits: Northwest Forest Pass required to park at trailhead
Maps: Green Trails no. 176S, Alpine Lakes Stevens Pass; Skykomish Ranger District map
Trail contacts: Mount Baker-Snoqualmie National Forest, Skykomish Ranger District, Skykomish; (360) 677-2414; www.fs.usda .gov/detail/mbs/

Finding the trailhead: From US 2 continue east 3.4 miles past Skykomish (47.6 miles west of Leavenworth) and turn left (north) onto FR 6066. A sign on US 2 indicates the road. Continue on FR 6066, bearing right at a fork in 1.8 miles. The parking lot and trailhead are in 6.9 miles. GPS: N47 43.44' / W121 16.01'

The Hike

This new trail, opened by the forest service in 2011, is edge wilderness at its finest. Beckler Peak's location on the western edge of the Cascades makes it easy to get to for people in Western Washington cities. The trail is thoughtfully constructed, and the peak's elevation and prominence reward hikers with views of some of the most inspiring peaks in the Central Cascades. The vertical faces of Mount Index loom over the Skykomish River west of Beckler Peak. Del Campo and the Monte Cristo group of peaks tower over the Mountain Loop Highway north of Beckler Peak. To the west you'll get surprisingly good views of glacier-laden Mount Daniels and the pointed spires and steep snowfields of Lemah Mountain and Chickamin, Chimney, and Overcoat Peaks.

On the horizon, the white domes of Mount Baker and Glacier Peak rise above the other Cascades. Immediately north of Beckler Peak is the Wild Sky Wilderness— a 106,577-acre wilderness area designated in 2008. This makes it the first new wilderness area in the United States since the Washington State Wilderness Act of 1984.

A hiker admires a dense clump of Mountain Hemlocks

The trail climbs the peak's west side at the perfect grade. It begins on an old logging road that contours gently upward through a second-growth forest of young trees, thick bushes, and occasional wildflowers. The well-built trail crosses several small creeks as it undulates with the hillside in the first couple miles. Volunteers from the Washington Trails Association repaired several stretches of the old road at the beginning of the trail in 2013.

After hiking about 1.5 miles, you will pass through a small clear-cut that's growing up with a jungle of alders and young firs with fresh green tips. Here there's a view of the Skykomish Valley and several patches of wildflowers, including lupines, wild roses, and Columbia lilies.

This is the end of the second-growth forest. A mature forest of silver fir, subalpine fir, and mountain hemlock tower over the open understory surrounding the rest of the trail. A smattering of small white wildflowers including queen's cup, false Solomon's seal, and bunchberry grow on the ground among the thick tree trunks. The grade never gets too steep as the trail switchbacks through the forest. Just below the summit, at 3.4 miles, quartz boulders pepper the hillside. A set of rocky steps and

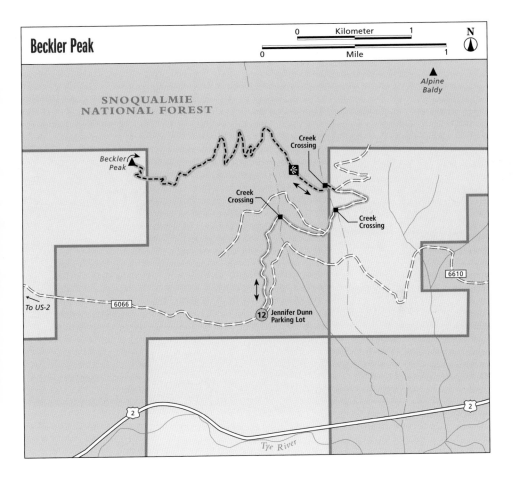

Beckler Peak

0   Kilometer   1

0   Mile   1

N

SNOQUALMIE
NATIONAL FOREST

Alpine
Baldy

Beckler
Peak

Creek
Crossing

Creek
Crossing

Creek
Crossing

6610

To US-2

6066

12 Jennifer Dunn
Parking Lot

2

2

Tye River

finally a short scramble put you on top of the world. The summit is airy and rocky, without a whole lot of room for hikers.

From here you can see the glory of the Central Cascades, as well as the craggy west and central summits of Beckler Peak. Both are remarkably close in height to the east summit at the end of the trail.

Miles and Directions

0.0 Start hiking up a gentle old logging road at the Jennifer Dunn parking lot and trailhead.

1.1 Hop over a small creek.

1.6 Cross another small creek.

1.9 Pass through an avalanche path with views of Mount Daniel and other snowy peaks on the crest of the Cascades.

3.8 Reach the summit of Beckler Peak. Return the way you came.

7.6 Arrive back at the Jennifer Dunn parking lot and trailhead.

Big trees on the trail to Beckler Peak

Hike Information

Local Information

Sky Valley Chamber of Commerce Visitor's Center, PO Box 46, Sultan 98294; (360) 793-0983; skyvalleychamber.com

Local Events/Attractions

Index Arts Festival, Index; usually held the first Saturday in August; indexartsfestival.org

Lodging

Cabins and two tent sites at Wallace Falls State Park (at the Wallace Falls Trailhead), Gold Bar; (360) 793-0420; parks.wa.gov

Bush House Historic Inn, 308 Fifth St., Index; (425) 298-7642; bushhouseinn.com

13 Wallace Falls

The Wallace River tumbles over waterfall after waterfall as it cuts through the lush landscape of Wallace Falls State Park. The park's network of trails makes an excellent off-season outing, and the views amaze even when the region is socked in with thick fog, as it so often is. The trail is flat and easy on the way to the best waterfall in the park, but it gets steeper on the way to the upper falls.

Start: Trailhead at Wallace Falls State Park
Distance: 5.5 miles out and back
Hiking time: About 3 hours
Difficulty: Easy to the lower and middle falls; moderate to the upper falls due to length and elevation changes
Trail surface: Dirt trail
Elevation gain: 200 feet to the middle falls; 1,100 feet to the upper falls viewpoint
Land status: State park

Nearest town: Gold Bar
Best season: Year-round
Other trail users: None
Canine compatibility: Leashed dogs allowed
Fees and permits: Discover Pass required to park at trailhead
Maps: *Green Trails no. 142, Index;* wallacefalls .org/trail_map/wallace_falls_trail_map.pdf
Trail contacts: Washington State Parks; (360) 793-0420; parks.wa.gov

Finding the trailhead: From Monroe drive east on US 2 for 12.5 miles to the town of Gold Bar. Turn left onto First Street, following signs for Wallace Falls State Park. Take the second right onto May Creek Road (which becomes Ley Road) and continue 1.2 miles to the parking lot in the state park. The trailhead is at the east end of the parking lot. GPS: N47 52.01' / W121 40.71'

The Hike

A network of popular trails tunnel into the woods just outside Gold Bar. Why are they so popular? They lead to a high concentration of amazing waterfalls. It's a gentle walk to the first two waterfalls, and people of all ages make the pilgrimage. Need another reason to go? You can hike the low-elevation trails year-round. Not even the heavy rains that blanket the mountains in thick fog for half the year can obscure the up-close views of the forested falls.

Hiking in Wallace Falls State Park is easy thanks to the relatively flat terrain and maps, kiosks, and signs throughout the area that keep even novice hikers from getting lost. The area was once heavily logged, and the beginning of the trail is the grade of a now-defunct railroad that hauled the timber to mills.

Begin the stroll to the waterfalls by walking underneath humming power lines on the railroad grade. Just before entering the dense woods, savor a view toward the tall stone faces of Mounts Baring, Index, and Persis, farther up the Skykomish Valley. These are the last mountains you'll see on this hike. From here on out the hike is all about the waterworks. Leave the railroad grade and enter the forest on the Woody Trail at 0.4 mile.

A bridge over the North Fork Wallace River

The trail runs parallel to the Wallace River. Several paths that access the river in the first 1.0 mile of the hike reveal rapids and pools of cold water choked with logs and surrounded by mossy forest. The trail is sturdy and graveled. A second-growth forest rich in western red cedars surrounds the Wallace River.

You reach the first falls at 1.8 miles and the middle falls shortly after, at 2.1 miles. The middle falls is the gem of the hike. A thin ribbon of water takes a 265-foot plunge into a rocky pool. Spray splashes up onto tall cedars and feeds moss and lichen growing on the rocks surrounding the rocky stream channel just downstream. You can watch the current flow through the turbulent channel and disappear into the forest toward the lower falls.

The hike is gentle on the way to the middle falls, which is just a few hundred feet higher than the parking lot. This is a turnaround point for young and old hikers, as the section of trail to the upper falls climbs steeply. The trail gains 900 feet in 0.6 mile on the way to the upper falls viewpoint. Hikers who press on will leave much of the crowd behind. From a viewpoint you can gaze through the emerald woods and view two majestic waterfalls with a single plunge pool in between the free-falling water.

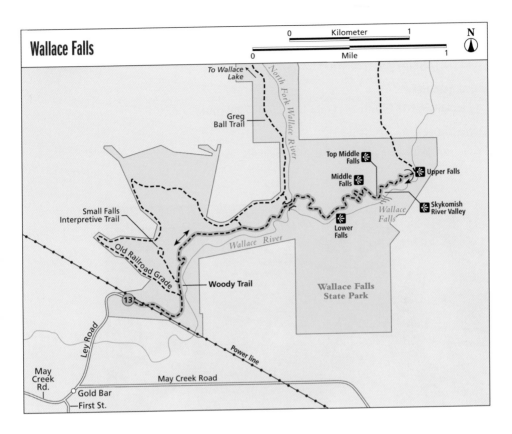

Miles and Directions

0.0 Start on the gravel road at the Wallace Falls Trailhead.

0.4 Turn right onto the Woody Trail, leaving the gravel railroad grade.

0.5 Go right at a junction with the Small Falls Interpretive Trail.

1.4 Go right at a junction with the Greg Ball Trail; then cross the North Fork Wallace River on a bridge.

1.8 Reach the lower falls and a shelter with several picnic tables.

2.1 Arrive at the middle falls.

2.75 Reach the upper falls viewpoint, just past a viewpoint of the valley between the middle and upper falls. Return the way you came.

5.5 Arrive back at the parking lot.

Hike Information

Local Events/Attractions

Gold Dust Days Heritage Festival, Gold Bar; last weekend in July; golddustdays.org

Lodging

Cabins and two tent sites at Wallace Falls State Park (at the Wallace Falls Trailhead), Gold Bar; (360) 793-0420; parks.wa.gov

Restaurants

La Hacienda, 101 Ninth St., Gold Bar; (360) 793-1096

Organizations

Friends of Wallace Falls State Park; wallacefalls.org

The trail passes beneath this bizarre western red cedar.

14 Kendall Katwalk

This hike passes through some of the most beautiful mountain terrain in the easily accessible Snoqualmie Pass area. It's all on the Pacific Crest Trail (PCT), which sticks to the high country and crosses incredibly steep slopes in places. One such slope is the 70-degree rock slab that the Kendall Katwalk crosses. To make a safe path across this slab, trail builders used dynamite to blast away a long rock shelf.

Start: Pacific Crest Trailhead north of the Summit at Snoqualmie ski area
Distance: 12 miles out and back
Hiking time: About 6 hours
Difficulty: Difficult due to length
Trail surface: Wide dirt path with a rocky traverse through talus
Best season: Mid-July to Oct
Other trail users: Equestrians, pack animals
Canine compatibility: Leashed dogs allowed

Fees and permits: Northwest Forest Pass required to park at trailhead
Nearest town: North Bend
Land status: Federal wilderness area
Maps: USGS Snoqualmie Pass; Green Trails no. 206, Bandera
Trail contacts: Mount Baker-Snoqualmie National Forest, North Bend Ranger District; (425) 888-1421

Finding the trailhead: From Seattle drive 52 miles east on I-90 to exit 52. Turn left at the bottom of the off-ramp and go under the freeway. In 0.1 mile take the first right onto a dirt road, following signs for the Pacific Crest Trail. The road splits into two parking areas. The lot to the right is closer, but either one works. GPS: N47 25.67' / W121 24.82'

The Hike

This entire hike is on the Pacific Crest Trail, and it's about as rugged and remote-feeling an area as you can find on a day trip near I-90. The trail starts at the top of Snoqualmie Pass and goes north for 6.0 beautiful miles, leaving the freeway far behind and probing into the Alpine Lakes Wilderness Area. The Katwalk itself is a unique feature—a narrow, man-made shelf blasted into a 70-degree granite cliff. The view from the Katwalk is among the best views near Snoqualmie Pass. From the Katwalk and the craggy upper sections of Kendall Peak—which the trail traverses—the freeway is out of sight and earshot, allowing hikers to experience the wilderness to the north in its silent, car-less glory. Combine that with views of distant peaks like Mount Stuart, which rears its head to the left of Alta Mountain, and this

▷ Commonwealth Basin, the deep valley to the west below this section of the PCT, was the birthplace of one of the glaciers that carved the valley through which I-90 now runs. The other glacier originated atop Source Lake. The two glaciers merged just south of Guye Peak and then split off, one portion heading into present-day Kittitas County and carving the Yakima River valley to the east and the other carving out the South Fork Snoqualmie River valley to the west.

A hiker crossing the Kendall Katwalk

area feels expansive and wild. Along the way, dense patches of flowers between talus slopes burst to life after the snow finally melts.

The Kendall Katwalk was blasted into the granite knife edge in the late 1970s as part of rerouting a section of the PCT. The PCT, which stretches from Mexico to Canada, started as a series of regional trails. Washington's section was called the Cascade Crest Trail. Apparently the engineers of the PCT weren't impressed by the Cascade Crest Trail, which went over Red Pass and down to the Middle Fork Snoqualmie River valley, bypassing the highcountry north of the Katwalk. The trail was rerouted in the 1970s to bring it up to PCT standards. It now traverses a series of airy, steep slopes with spectacular views and incredible heights. Since the trail builders couldn't find a route around it, they blasted a trail through the slab with dynamite—and the Katwalk was born.

Most folks do the Katwalk as a day hike. The trek to the Katwalk and back makes for a long day, but the trail climbs gently the whole way and gains less elevation than the trails to many nearby peaks. Ridge, Gravel, and Alaska Lakes are just beyond the Katwalk for an even longer day or overnight destination.

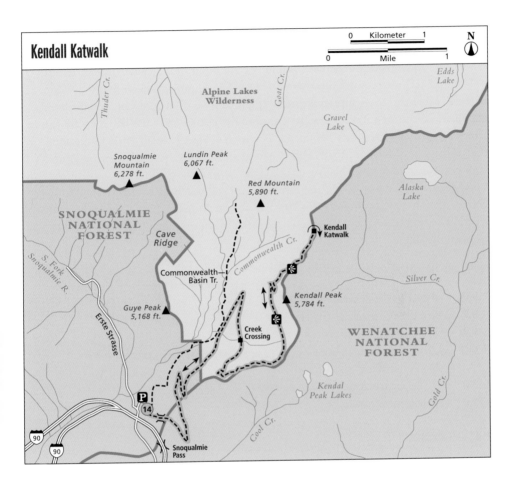

From the parking lot, follow the PCT as it switchbacks and contours through a forest of hemlocks and firs. The wide and well-maintained path crosses back and forth over several streams. The trail climbs steadily through this section but never gets steep. The tall evergreen trees conceal the surrounding peaks for the first 2.0 miles until Guye Peak, an imposing rocky spire with 2,000-foot-tall rock faces, appears to your left.

From here you leave the biggest of the trees behind, cross several talus meadows, and lose a few hundred feet in elevation only to climb back up. Red Mountain looms at the end of the Commonwealth Valley, Mount Rainier in the distant south. The trail skirts the south flank of Kendall Peak in an area called the Kendall Gardens. Here a lush mixture of Indian paintbrush, scarlet columbine, yarrow, and monkshood bloom among lady ferns. Above the gardens, the talus and cliff faces of Kendall Peak provide a home for marmots and garter snakes. Other flowers along the trail include phlox, lupine, Columbia lilies, penstemon, bleeding heart, queen's cup, monkey flowers, and thimbleberries.

Several patches of snow can cover the ridge south of the Katwalk into early August. The ridge leads to a flat area with sitting stones just below the Katwalk. You can sit here and look out over the Commonwealth Basin and the peaks that surround it. The iron-rich rock of the Red Mountain sits on a throne at the end of the valley, in stark contrast to the white rock and deep green trees of neighboring Snoqualmie Mountain to the west. Take a few steps around the corner and onto the Katwalk for a different set of views. Alta Mountain, Rampart Ridge, Kendall Peak, Chickamin Ridge, the top of Mount Stuart, Hibox Mountain, and a variety of other peaks and high points rise in the distance.

Option: On the way down, you can make a small loop back to the parking lot by going right at the Commonwealth Basin Trail, which descends to Commonwealth Creek. The trail is steep and overgrown, but it's a pleasure to watch the creek tumble through the forest.

Miles and Directions

0.0 Start from the Pacific Crest Trail parking lot.

0.2 Cross a creek on a wooden bridge.

3.4 Cross a creek.

5.0 Reach an alpine meadow below Kendall Peak. Mount Rainier comes into view to the south.

6.0 Reach the Katwalk. Return the way you came.

12.0 Arrive back at the parking lot.

Hike Information

Local Information

Snoqualmie Valley Chamber of Commerce, 38767 SE River St., Snoqualmie 98065; (425) 888-6362; snovalley.org

Local Events/Attractions

The Festival at Mount Si, North Bend; second weekend in August

Restaurants

Snoqualmie Brewery and Taproom, 8032 Falls Ave. SE, Snoqualmie; (425) 831-2357
Scott's Dairy Freeze, 234 E. North Bend Way, North Bend; (425) 888-2301

15 Mirror Lake

Tall trees, a sharp peak, and a flowery waterfall surround this gem of a lake just 1 mile from the trailhead. Mirror Lake is a popular destination for the first-time backpacker because it's a short hike with a destination as beautiful as dozens of more popular lakes in the Alpine Lakes Wilderness north of Snoqualmie Pass.

Start: Trailhead on FR 5480
Distance: 3.0 miles out and back
Hiking time: About 1.5 hours
Difficulty: Easy
Trail surface: Dirt trail
Best season: July through Oct
Nearest town: Cle Elum
Other trail users: None

Canine compatibility: Dogs allowed
Fees and permits: Northwest Forest Pass required to park at trailhead
Map: *Green Trails no. 207, Snoqualmie Pass*
Trail contacts: Okanogon-Wenatchee National Forest, Cle Elum Ranger District; (509) 852-1100; www.fs.usda.gov/okawen

Finding the trailhead: From Snoqualmie Pass drive east for 10 miles on I-90 to exit 62. Turn right at the bottom of the off-ramp, drive over the Yakima River, pass Stampede Gravel, and turn right onto FR 5480, 1.1 miles from the exit. Reach an intersection at 5.2 miles from I-90 and take a soft right to continue on FR 5480. This intersection is confusing, but you'll soon see Lost Lake; if you are on the right (north) side of the lake, you'll know you're on the correct road. From here the road begins climbing along the right (north) side of Lost Lake. At 7.1 miles from I-90, park on the wide shoulder on the left side of the road, or continue up a rougher section of road for 0.3 mile to the upper parking lot. GPS: N47 20.760' / W121 25.467'

The Hike

A herculean trek through virgin wilderness this is not. But it is a peaceful nook where you can enjoy the woods without a strenuous hike. If a short hike to an alpine lake is what you're looking for, look no farther than Mirror Lake. Even though it's close to the trailhead, Mirror Lake is every bit as beautiful as many other lakes in the nearby Alpine Lakes Wilderness.

The hike to this peaceful lake is a gentle stroll through a moss-draped forest of big trees, sparse understory, and pools of clear water. Several campsites along both Mirror and Cottonwood lake make this a great first backpacking trip that is doable with kids, dogs, and lots of gear. Just beyond the lake, the trail leaves the old-growth and enters a clearcut that extends toward a patchwork of trees and more clearcuts on the horizon. A trail winds down through a young forest alongside a waterfall at the lake outlet. The stream cascades down toward Twilight Lake. The young trees on this open hillside allow plenty of sunlight to reach a garden of crimson columbines, Columbia lilies, paintbrush, bear grass, asters, and lupines. The scene here looks like an impressionist

Mirror Lake beneath Tinkham Peak

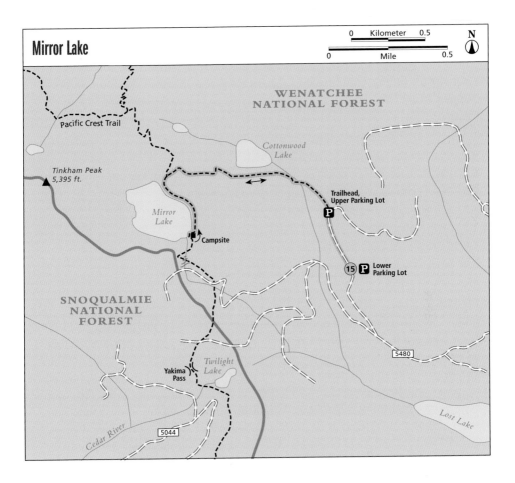

0   Kilometer   0.5

0   Mile   0.5

N

WENATCHEE
NATIONAL FOREST

Pacific Crest Trail

Cottonwood
Lake

Tinkham Peak
5,395 ft.

Mirror
Lake

Trailhead,
Upper Parking Lot

P

Campsite

15 P Lower
       Parking Lot

SNOQUALMIE
NATIONAL
FOREST

5480

Twilight
Lake

Yakima
Pass

Lost Lake

Cedar River   5044

painting—the view down to Yakima Pass is a smudgy palette of green with dots of red, orange, yellow, and purple in the foreground.

While tranquil, high-alpine lakes are plentiful near Snoqualmie Pass, nice hikes are rare in this heavily logged area south of I-90. Much of the north side of I-90 at Snoqualmie Pass is blessed with wilderness status, as the Alpine Lakes Wilderness stretches nearly to the interstate in some areas. The south side of I-90 does not enjoy this protection. It is USDA Forest Service land and is heavily logged. On the path to Mirror Lake, however, you'll walk through a forest of big firs spared the cables and saws. Amid these trees you can gaze into the glassy water of the lake and contemplate the reflection of Tinkham Peak and its jagged flanks—a popular scramble for those with experience and no fear of heights.

From the unsigned trailhead, take off through a couple open patches of vegetation and enjoy the smatterings of wildflowers. The trail climbs gently for most of its length. The trailside sights remain interesting, and in a little over 0.75 mile you reach Cottonwood Lake, a glassy pool cradled by tall ridges. Less than 0.5 mile later, you reach a junction with the Pacific Crest Trail (PCT) right before reaching Mirror Lake. Turn left at the junction and continue toward the east bank of the lake.

Both Mirror Lake and Twilight Lake, which is 1.0 mile farther south on the PCT, are popular for fishing. Cottonwood Lake, on the way to Mirror Lake, is too shallow to support many fish.

Miles and Directions

- **0.0** Start from the lower parking spots on FR 5480.
- **0.3** Pass the upper parking lot and continue on the trail on the left (west) side of the road.
- **0.8** Reach Cottonwood Lake and continue to the left (south) of it.
- **1.2** Turn left (south) onto the Pacific Crest Trail toward Stampede Pass.
- **1.3** Arrive at Mirror Lake.
- **1.5** Reach the first campsite at the lake. Return the way you came.
- **3.0** Arrive back at the lower parking lot.

Options

From the lake there are several options for hiking farther. If you continue on the PCT past the lake, you'll reach Twilight Lake and Yakima Pass in about 1.0 mile. Yakima Pass is a low notch in the Cascades that was once a main route through this section of the range. In the other direction, the PCT goes toward Snoqualmie Pass, with plenty of lakes, peaks, and views along the way. Hiking 1.5 miles from the lake in this direction brings you to the base of Silver Peak, one of the tallest mountains in the immediate area. An adventurous trail leads to the top of Silver Peak, where you can find grand views of Tinkham and Abiel Peaks, as well as Humpback Mountain and Annette Lake.

Hike Information

Local Information

Kittitas County Chamber of Commerce, 609 N. Main St., Ellensburg 98926; (509) 925-2002; kittitascountychamber.com

Lodging

Iron Horse Inn Bed & Breakfast, 526 Marie Ave., South Cle Elum; (509) 674-5939; ironhorseinnbb.com

Restaurants

El Caporal Mexican Restaurant, 105 W. First St., Cle Elum; (509) 674-4284
Village Pizza, 105 W. Pennsylvania Ave., Roslyn; (509) 649-2992

16 Rachel Lake and Rampart Lakes

The Alpine Lakes Wilderness area includes more than 700 lakes, ranging from deep tarns to shallow ponds. Rachel Lake and Rampart Lakes are fine examples and easily accessible. Rampart Lakes, above Rachel Lake, is a collection of about a dozen blue pools with an incredible variety in sizes. The calm blue waters reflect snow and the numerous cliffs on the ridge they are named after—Rampart Ridge.

Start: Parking lot and trailhead at the end of FR 4930

Distance: 10.6 miles out and back

Hiking time: About 5 hours

Difficulty: Difficult due to length and steep sections

Trail surface: Dirt and rock trail

Elevation gain: 2,300 feet

Land status: Federal wilderness

Nearest town: Cle Elum

Best season: Mid-July to Oct

Other trail users: None

Canine compatibility: Leashed dogs allowed

Fees and permits: Northwest Forest Pass required to park at trailhead

Maps: USGS Chikamin Peak; Green Trails no. 207, Snoqualmie Pass, and no. 208, Kachess Lake

Trail contacts: Okanogan/Wenatchee National Forest, Cle Elum Ranger District; (509) 852-1100; www.fs.usda.gov/okawen

Finding the trailhead: From Seattle drive 61 miles east on I-90 to exit 62. Turn left onto Kachess Lake Road (FR 49) and continue for 5.2 miles. Turn left onto FR 4930. In 4.1 miles park in the large parking lot on the left side of the road. GPS: N47 24 03' / W121 17 03'

The Hike

Rachel Lake and Rampart Lakes are some of the most tightly concentrated lakes in the Alpine Lakes Wilderness. The beautiful lakes and meadows are best seen in a day trip—they're an extremely popular overnight destination because of the tranquil campsites surrounding the lakes. The area is just too pleasant. Mountain hemlocks shade the shores of the rugged lakes, and views of neighboring peaks add to the atmosphere.

The hike begins in a deep forest with patches of meadow alongside Box Canyon Creek. The trail is relatively flat for most of the first 3.0 miles as it ambles alongside the creek. The creek's clear water is surrounded by polished rock and there are some cool miniature waterfalls along the way. Several huge logs lie across the trail. spread out over the first few miles. None of them are impassible, but stepping over them when you're carrying a heavy pack gets tiring.

Dense vegetation and wildflowers in an incredible variety of colors grow in a couple openings in the forest. Delicate white flowers of bunchberry—a dwarf member of the dogwood family—cover the ground. Monkshood, lupine, goatsbeard,

Queen Anne's lace, tiger lily, and red columbine grow among a short understory of thimbleberries, salmonberries, lady ferns, and devil's club.

After gradually gaining 600 feet of elevation in nearly 3.0 miles, the route begins to climb straight up toward Rachel Lake. A notorious staircase of roots, logs, and rock rises 1,200 feet in the next 0.8 mile to the lake. This section resembles a dry creekbed in some short sections, and you may need free hands to pull yourself up several rocky ledges. Luckily, even the steepest sections of trail aren't loose, and occasional flat spots in the trail let your legs rest in between climbs.

At 3.5 miles the trail emerges from the trees at a spectacular waterfall. Box Canyon Creek fans out as it plummets down a wide rock face and into a shallow pool next to the trail. Even more wildflowers reach for the sun in this open spot. Red columbines, with their bright red-and-yellow lanterns, are most numerous. These falls are reason enough to make the hike. But Rachel Lake awaits.

Rachel Lake is a huge alpine lake—one of the biggest in the Alpine Lakes Wilderness. It's surrounded by the cliffs of Rampart Ridge on its western shore, and several well-established campgrounds line the near (east) side of the lake. If you camp here or at Rampart Lakes, make sure to camp only in an established campsite. The fragile meadows around the lakes have already been trampled by too many boots.

The landscape changes dramatically in the next 1.0 mile of trail to Rampart Lakes. The trail takes a fairly direct route up Rampart Ridge with a couple short switchbacks. From this trail, views down to Rachel Lake are breathtaking. You can see how the steep walls of the lake yield on its east side, creating an outlet for the headwaters of Box Canyon Creek to plunge down a steep slope. It's also a good perspective of the long, glacier-carved valley curving back toward Kachess Lake.

Above Rachel Lake, pink heather and purple lupines take over as the main wildflowers. The show of colors continues into the fall, long after the wildflowers wilt, when huckleberries and mountain ash turn a fiery red.

At 5.2 miles from the trailhead, you reach Rampart Lakes at last. About ten lakes of all shapes and sizes are nestled into this flat spot beneath Rampart Ridge. A web of trails leads between them, probing into every nook and cranny of the basin. Creeks splash between the lakes and across the trails. Most of the lakes are small, but a couple large ones loom underneath Rampart Ridge at the south end of the basin. Some lakes are broad and shallow. Others are small and deep. There's amazing variety in these glacier-carved bodies of water.

Miles and Directions

- **0.0** Start from the trailhead at the end of FR 4930.
- **0.4** Cross a creek.
- **0.7** Cross a section of bridges and elevated trail.
- **1.1** Pass a section of Box Canyon Creek where the water cascades over polished rock. The creek is easy to access from the trail here.
- **3.1** Pass a small waterfall. After a long flat section, the trail begins climbing steeply here.

Rachel Lake and Rampart Lakes

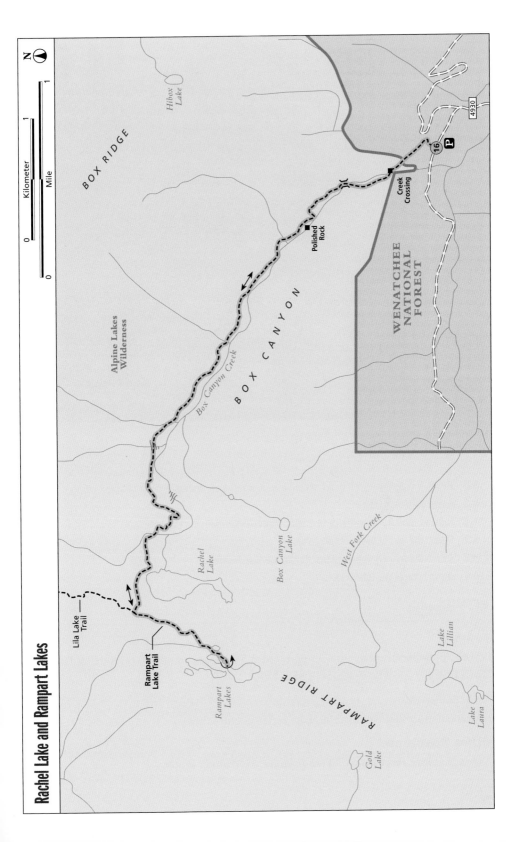

Fall color at Rampart Lakes. RON JOHNSON

3.6 Reach a bigger waterfall that fans out over a broad rock, ending in a pool at the bottom.

4.2 Arrive at Rachel Lake.

4.6 Turn left atop Rampart Ridge at a signed intersection with the Lila Lake Trail.

5.2 Reach the first of the Rampart Lakes.

5.3 Reach the main Rampart Lakes. Return the way you came.

10.6 Arrive back at the trailhead.

Hike Information

Lodging

USDA Forest Service Kachess Campground, 5.5 miles north of I-90 on Kachess Lake Road (FR 49) and FR 4930; (509) 852-1100

Restaurants

Easton Saloon, 1860 Railroad St., Easton; (509) 656-2309

Other Resources

Snoqualmie Pass: From Indian Trail to Interstate, by Yvonne Prater

17 Lake Ingalls

Lake Ingalls is probably the most scenic spot in the Teanaway valley on the east slope of the Cascades. Slick red rock surrounds the deep blue water of Lake Ingalls. Beyond the deep tarn, Mount Stuart scrapes the sky. With its rugged looks and incredible height, Mount Stuart is perhaps the most dramatic peak in the Cascades. The wide-open terrain, exceptional weather, and an alpine forest full of larches are the icing on the cake at Lake Ingalls.

Start: Esmerelda Basin Trailhead at the end of FR 9737
Distance: 9.0 miles out and back
Hiking time: About 5 hours
Difficulty: Difficult due to elevation gain and a rocky scramble near the lake
Trail surface: Dirt trail, rock scramble
Elevation gain: 2,400 feet
Land status: Federal wilderness
Nearest town: Cle Elum

Best season: Mid-July through Oct
Other trail users: None
Canine compatibility: No dogs allowed
Fees and permits: Northwest Forest Pass required to park at trailhead
Maps: USGS Mount Stuart; Green Trails no. 209, Mount Stuart
Trail contacts: Okanogan/Wenatchee National Forest, Cle Elum Ranger District; (509) 852-1100; www.fs.usda.gov/okawen

Finding the trailhead: From Cle Elum go east on WA 970 for about 8 miles. A mile after crossing a bridge over the Teanaway River, turn left onto Teanaway Road and continue north. In 7.3 miles bear right onto North Fork Teanaway Road. In 6 miles (13.3 from WA 970) the pavement ends at FR 9737, signed for Beverly Campground. Follow this dirt road to its end at the trailhead, 23.1 miles from the highway. GPS: N47 26.40' / W120 55.34'

The Hike

The Teanaway Valley has a unique blend of the Cascades' sharp peaks and glacier-polished terrain with the beautiful weather and pine forests of the dry side of the state. It's a peak bagger's paradise—you can hike across open ridges and scramble up to many rocky high points in one day.

Lake Ingalls, at the far north end of the Teanaway, is the epicenter for larches and views in the area. Mount Stuart, often called the crown jewel of the Central Cascades, looms high above the dark blue water of Lake Ingalls. The stark granite peak is the tallest mountain between Mount Rainier and Glacier Peak. From the larch-dotted vantage of Lake Ingalls, you get a close-up view of the couloirs on the south side of the big guy. The lake sits in a basin of glacier-polished brown rock below Ingalls Peaks. Both climbers and mountain goats like to scale the solid rock on the tallest of the three Ingalls Peaks, and you're likely to see a party of either.

The trail begins along the upper reaches of the North Fork Teanaway River. It starts out by climbing through forests of lodgepole and white pine below Longs

Mountain goats on the shore of Lake Ingalls

Pass, a notch in the ridge with a trail leading to Ingalls Creek. The Ingalls Way Trail is one of those rare trails that seem to climb at a perfect grade—not too steep, but steep enough that you get to where you're going at a decent rate. The first of the wildflowers start below Longs Pass. Lupines, monkshood, paintbrush, and scarlet gilia grow among the pines.

In 1.5 miles the Longs Pass Trail peels off to the right. Go straight to continue up to Ingalls Pass. Stretches of this trail are narrow and cling to smooth, steep slopes that can be challenging if you meet another hiker, so cross your fingers. As you crest Ingalls Pass, Mount Stuart appears and you leave views of Mount Rainier and the North Fork Teanaway valley behind. The white granite of the Stuart Range provides an interesting contrast to the amber rocks of the Lake Ingalls basin. The Teanaway valley contains a complex and diverse collection of rock, making it a popular spot for rock lovers. Look for several interesting striped intrusions in the rock surrounding the lake.

▶ **Mountain goats crave salt. They can't get much of it in the mountains, so they look for deposits of human urine. When you're high in the mountains, pee on bare rocks; otherwise goats will damage the vegetation while digging for their favorite treat.**

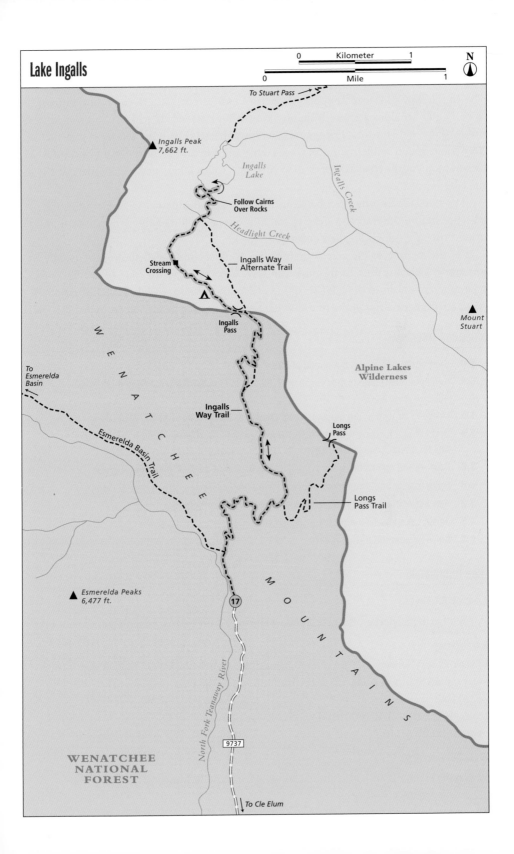

Lake Ingalls

0   Kilometer   1

0   Mile   1

N

To Stuart Pass

▲ Ingalls Peak
7,662 ft.

*Ingalls
Lake*

Ingalls Creek

Follow Cairns
Over Rocks

Headlight Creek

Stream
Crossing

Ingalls Way
Alternate Trail

Ingalls
Pass

▲ Mount
Stuart

**Alpine Lakes
Wilderness**

To
Esmerelda
Basin

W
E
N
A
T
C
H
E
E

Ingalls
Way
Trail

Longs
Pass

Esmerelda Basin Trail

Longs
Pass Trail

▲ Esmerelda Peaks
6,477 ft.

M
O
U
N
T
A
I
N
S

17

North Fork Teanaway River

9737

**WENATCHEE
NATIONAL
FOREST**

To Cle Elum

The trail splits just beyond Ingalls Pass in the Headlight Creek basin. The Ingalls Way Trail stays higher, passing through stunted trees at the top of a larch-filled basin. The Ingalls Way Alternate Trail dips deeper into the larches, where you'll find bigger trees. The lower alternate trail is slightly longer but is mandatory in larch season and makes a nice return route. The scenery here is unbeatable, and the setting is parklike. You could spend endless time staring, taking photos, and wandering the beautiful terrain atop Ingalls Pass. This spot is so nice that some hikers never even make it to the lake.

The trail stays mostly level between Ingalls Pass and the final scramble up to the lake. Just before the trail gets steep again, it crosses a small meadow with a trickle of water flowing through it called Headlight Creek.

On the far side of the creek, scramble up boulders and rocky shelves to a saddle just above Lake Ingalls. Cairns guide the way. Walk down to the base of the lake or scramble across slabs to the left (west) side of the lake beneath Ingalls Peak. Either spot is a nice place for a rest and a fine vantage for viewing the beauty all around.

Miles and Directions

0.0 Start at the parking lot at the end of FR 9737.
0.3 Turn right (east) onto Ingalls Way Trail (1390) at the junction with the Esmerelda Basin Trail.
1.5 Continue straight at the junction where Longs Pass Trail peels off to the right (east).
2.9 Stay left at a junction with the Ingalls Way Alternate Trail. (**Option:** Return on the alternate trail for a nice lollipop loop, especially in larch season.)
3.6 Pass several campsites spread along the north side of the trail, and cross a creek.
3.9 Follow cairns and scramble across boulders and up ledges.
3.2 Stay left at the second junction with the Ingalls Way Alternate Trail.
4.5 Reach Lake Ingalls. Return the way you came.
9.0 Arrive back at the trailhead.

Hike Information

Local Events
Roslyn Farmers Market, Roslyn; Sundays during summer; roslynfarmersmarket.com

Lodging
USDA Forest Service Beverly Campground, on North Fork Teanaway Road; Teanaway Guard Station Cabin, 2.2 miles from the end of the pavement, on FR 9737; (509) 852-1100

Iron Horse Inn Bed & Breakfast, 526 Marie Ave., Cle Elum; (509) 674-5939; ironhorseinnbb.com

Restaurants
El Caporal Restaurant and Cantina, 105 W. First St., Cle Elum; (509) 674-4284

Honorable Mentions

A Church Mountain

You have to hike a long way up for this one—3,600 feet to be exact. The 8.5-mile out and back trail starts in the foothills west of Mount Baker and the crest of the Cascades on the Mount Baker Highway. It passes through old-growth forests above the Nooksack River on the way to spectacular meadows. Keep going through the meadows of lupines, paintbrush, and asters to views of the Nooksack Valley, Mount Baker, and Mount Shuksan.

Drive east on the Mount Baker Highway for 39 miles. Five miles past the Glacier Public Service Center, turn left onto FR 3040 (East Church Mountain Road). Continue for 2.7 miles to the trailhead at the end of the road.

B Winchester Mountain

Lookouts are well known for their 360-degree views, and Winchester Mountain near the Mount Baker Highway is no exception. The views of the Pickets, Mount Baker, Yellow Aster Butte, Tomyhoi Peak, and the American and Canadian Border Peaks are exceptional. Even more exceptional is that you'll walk just 3.5 miles round-trip to reach this perch at the top of the world. Not only is the destination beautiful, but so is the journey. The hike starts between two crystal-clear alpine lakes called Twin Lakes. The only downside is that snow lingers in a steep gulley on the trail late into summer.

From Bellingham go east for 47 miles on the Mount Baker Highway (WA 542). You'll pass the Glacier Public Service Center in 34 miles. Just past the Department of Transportation garage on the left (north) side of the highway, turn left onto FR 3065, signed TWIN LAKES ROAD. Immediately turn left at another junction to stay on FR 3065; continue for 4.7 miles. The Yellow Aster Butte Trailhead is on the left. The trailhead at Twin Lakes is 2.5 miles farther down the road, but the road gets rough. It may be best to park here if you don't have a high-clearance vehicle.

C Ira Spring Trail, Mason Lake

This stunning alpine lake is extremely popular, but if you can go during the week you may find some solitude in the deep basin surrounding the water. The hike is 6 miles round-trip. A gentle old road bed from the trailhead gives way to a final mile of steep trail. After a brief but stunning view of Mount Rainier, you cross over a ridge into the Alpine Lakes Wilderness and leave the sound of the freeway behind. From the lake, Mount Defiance is a quick side trip. On the clearest of days, you can see Seattle's Space Needle from the mountain's flowery summit.

Drive east from Seattle on I-90 to exit 45. At the bottom of the exit ramp, go left and cross under I-90. Turn left onto FR 9030 and then left again onto FR 9031 in about 1 mile. Follow this road for 3 miles to the parking lot and trailhead,

D Cutthroat Pass

This is a classic North Cascades day hike, with the option to make it an overnighter or a multi-night backpacking trip and venture on to Golden Horn, a stunning peak of colorful, glacier-scraped rock. The hike to Cutthroat Pass follows the Pacific Crest Trail on one of its most scenic stretches. Five miles of trail lead to forests of larches and views of incredible crags.

Drive east 51 miles from Marblemount on the North Cascades Highway to Rainy Pass. At Rainy Pass, turn left when you see a sign for the Cutthroat Lake Trailhead. Follow this road for 1 mile to the trailhead.

E Mount Dickerman

Expansive views and wildly productive blueberry bushes make the grind up Mount Dickerman worthwhile. You'll gain nearly 4,000 feet in 4.3 miles to get to the top of this popular hike on the Mountain Loop Highway. Views of Del Campo Peak, Big Four Mountain, and Glacier Peak dominate the skyline from the cliffy summit. The switchbacks in the beginning are relentless, but this hike is worth every drop of sweat.

Drive east from Granite Falls on the Mountain Loop Highway. Park at the signed lot at the trailhead, 27 miles east of Granite Falls. The trailhead is 1.8 miles east of the Big Four Picnic Area and 3 miles west of Barlow Pass.

F Boulder River

This year-round hike meanders alongside a roaring river in the old-growth forest of the Boulder River Wilderness for 8.5 miles round-trip. The river flows over waterfalls and through rapids, providing several viewpoints. Four miles in, you come to a camp with views up the river canyon to jagged mountains.

From Arlington follow WA 530 to milepost 41, 19.8 miles east of Arlington. Turn right (south) onto FR 2010. This junction can be hard to spot, so look for the milepost. Follow this dirt road for 3.8 miles, passing French Creek Campground, to the trailhead and parking area.

G Raptor Ridge

This is another lowland gem in the Chuckanut Mountains south of Bellingham. The 3.8-mile one-way trip to Raptor Ridge leads through dense forests to a high ridge in the heart of the Chuckanuts. You can see the water from a rocky viewpoint, but even more impressive is the expanse of forest so close to the cities of Bellingham and Burlington.

From Bellingham go south on Chuckanut Drive (WA 11) for 1.5 miles to the Chuckanut Mountain Trailhead and parking area on the left. A map of the trail system is available at www.co.whatcom.wa.us/parks/chuckanut/.

⊢ Meander Meadow

This gorgeous hanging valley in the Henry M. Jackson Wilderness is a good base camp for countless hikes along the Pacific Crest Trail, as well as an excellent destination on its own. The 12.5-mile round-trip hike to the meadow, which is north and east of Stevens Pass, passes through thick jungles of false hellebore, thimbleberry, and slide alder. Forests, grasses, and heather make a mosaic of colorful greens all around the trail at higher elevations. At the meadow you'll find a good-size stream of fresh snowmelt meandering in long loopy curves through the colorful valley.

From Monroe go 70 miles east on US 2 or 15 miles west from Leavenworth to Cole's Corner (a junction with WA 207). Go north on WA 207, toward Lake Wenatchee, for 4.3 miles and bear left onto North Shore Road. Continue 14 miles to the trailhead at the road's end.

South Cascades

A triangle of white volcanoes climb into the thin air of the South Cascades, dwarfing the surrounding mountains. You're never far from a spectacular view of at least one of these icy giants in the region between Snoqualmie Pass and the Columbia River. The state's two tallest mountains—Mounts Rainier and Adams—are both in this region, as are the blown-out but still towering remains of Mount St. Helens. As a bonus, Mount Hood lies just beyond the Columbia River in Oregon.

With some exceptions, such as the Goat Rocks Wilderness and the Tatoosh Range, the rest of the mountains south of I-90 aren't quite as tall or jagged as those in the North Cascades. Much of the rest of the mountains are a full mile or two shorter than the volcanoes, with dense forests covering their tops. This makes the massive volcanoes incredibly dramatic as they loom above their surroundings. Compared with the North Cascades, not as much of the Cascade crest south of I-90 is protected. Outside of the wilderness areas and Mount Rainier National Park, the hills are heavily logged.

Some of the best hikes in the state are in the parklike meadows surrounding the volcanoes. It must be the perfect climate for wildflowers, because it's rare to find wildflowers denser than the gardens around Mount Rainier or in the Goat Rocks. The trails in Mount Rainier National Park—being iconic and relatively easy to get to—draw huge crowds. It's well worth hiking with the crowds just to be in the presence of 14,410-foot-tall Mount Rainier. Twenty-five separate glaciers cover 35 miles of the mountain's slopes. Those glaciers occupy the skyline from all over the state—and also decorate beer cans and license plates. Mount Adams is a little more remote, so fewer people roam its high country. The trails surrounding Mount Adams have a wilder feel than those around Mount Rainier, and many experienced hikers prefer Mount Adams. Mount St. Helens isn't as tall or aesthetic as it once was, but it reminds Washingtonians of the violent eruption in 1980 and the potential power of the region's other volcanoes. It also serves as an interesting study in ecology. The Norway Pass Trail shows off a landscape slowly rebuilding in the active volcano's shadow.

It's not just the active volcanoes that are shaped by eruptions and lava flows. High-volcanic plateaus spread out between the trio of giants, such as the high country in the Indian Heaven Wilderness, and the lake-filled meadows surrounding Tumac Mountain.

Adventures and hikes at lower elevations are also abundant in the South Cascades. Spring wildflowers, epic views, and a long hiking season attract many to the Columbia River Gorge. A smattering of state parks in the area preserve the hills, waterfalls, and flowery meadows along the mighty river. The Lewis River and many other lowland river valleys offer trails through big woods, along streams, and to beautiful waterfalls that are accessible nearly year-round.

Mount Rainier from Tumac Mountain (hike 24)

18 Summerland and Panhandle Gap

Possibly the best day hike in Mount Rainier National Park, this section of the Wonderland Trail from Fryingpan Creek to Summerland and Panhandle Gap traverses a huge variety of terrain and ecosystems. It starts deep in an old-growth forest next to a roaring creek but soon leaves the dense forest behind in exchange for meadows and wildflowers. Panhandle Gap, the highest point on the Wonderland Trail around Mount Rainier, is in a world of rock and ice.

Start: Fryingpan Creek Trailhead on Sunrise Road
Distance: 10.6 miles out and back
Hiking Time: 5.5 hours
Difficulty: Difficult due to length and elevation gain
Trail surface: Dirt trail
Elevation gain: 3,000 feet
Land status: National park
Nearest town: Packwood
Best season: Mid-July through Oct

Other trail users: None
Canine compatibility: No dogs allowed
Fees and permits: Fee required to enter Mount Rainier National Park. A free permit is required for wilderness camping; permits are available at any ranger station in the park.
Maps: USGS Sunrise/White River Park; Green Trails no. 270, Mt. Rainier East
Trail contacts: Mount Rainier National Park; (360) 569-2211; nps.gov/mora

Finding the trailhead: From Enumclaw: Drive east on WA 410 for 37 miles. Enter Mount Rainier National Park White River entrance and turn right onto Sunrise Road. Continue on Sunrise Road for 7.8 miles from WA 410. Park in the lot on the right side of the road just past the bridge over Fryingpan Creek.

From Yakima: Drive west on US 12 for 12 miles and then continue onto WA 410. Go east on WA 410 for 54 miles, and then turn left onto Sunrise Road and enter the Mount Rainier National Park White River entrance.Continue on Sunrise Road for 7.8 miles from WA 410. Park in the lot on the right side of the road just past the bridge over Fryingpan Creek.

GPS: N46 53.31' / W121 36.65'

The Hike

Glaciers slowly creep down Mount Rainier, snow-fed streams dance through wildflower meadows, and goats roam the knoll between Summerland and Panhandle Gap. This section of the Wonderland Trail—a 93-mile trail encircling Mount Rainier—makes one of the best day hikes in Mount Rainier National Park. It passes through old-growth forests and meadows bursting with color before the final climb to Panhandle Gap (6,750 feet)—the highest point on the Wonderland Trail.

At Summerland and Panhandle Gap you can bask in the presence of colossal Mount Rainier. Its sheer size is hard to comprehend until you see it up close. Even from Summerland, the top of the icy behemoth looms 8,000 feet above the trail. It

The view from Panhandle Gap—white slopes above the Ohanapecosh Valley

protrudes so far into the sky that its complicated faces, ridges, and icefalls glow pink in the sunset for hours after the evening shadows have crept up and over every other ridge and peak in the park.

The trail starts out as a flat path through big trees next to Fryingpan Creek. The whitewater of the creek roars down several waterfalls. At the end of the first flat 1.0 mile you begin climbing a series of long switchbacks, with each right-hand turn opening up a view down into the drops, pools, and cliffs of the creek.

In 2.9 miles the woods open up and the trail crosses Fryingpan Creek for the last time. Here the creek is wide and steep. Little flowers grow between the gravel and big boulders of the ever-changing creek. Downstream the creek disappears into the forest; upstream it tears a gash in the raw landscape above the tree line.

Lupines, scarlet columbine, yarrow, and many other flowers crowd the opening in the trees. As the trail passes through this brilliant garden, Mount Rainier and Little Tahoma are dead ahead. The trail continues climbing toward the crevassed dome of

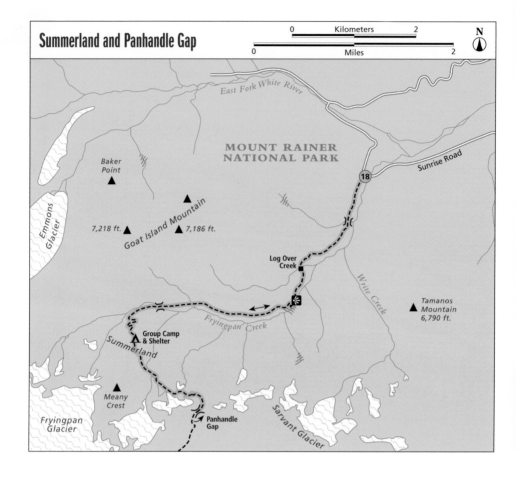

East Fork White River

MOUNT RAINER
NATIONAL PARK

Sunrise Road

Baker
Point

Emmons
Glacier

18

7,218 ft.   Goat Island Mountain   7,186 ft.

Log Over
Creek

White Creek

Tamanos
Mountain
6,790 ft.

Fryingpan Creek

Group Camp
& Shelter

Summerland

Meany
Crest

Fryingpan
Glacier

Sarvant Glacier

Panhandle
Gap

Mount Rainier, beginning a series of tight switchbacks through heather and ava-lanche lilies. Across the valley, lupine grows so thick that it seems as though a dusting of purple Dr. Seuss snow fell on the meadows of Goat Island Mountain.

At the top of this climb is Summerland—a series of wide-open meadows filled with heather, phlox, lupines, and a variety of other wildflowers. The trail winds through the patches of purple, white, pink, and yellow. Stick to the trail—the sur-rounding meadow is fragile.

Turn around at Summerland and you have done a reasonable-length day hike through some of the best terrain in the park. But it only gets better in the next 1.3 miles to Panhandle Gap. The trail continues through mostly bare ground and snow up to Panhandle Gap—a notch in a rocky ridgeline. From the gap you can peer into the glacier-covered Ohanapecosh Valley. Look for mountain goats between Panhandle Gap and the meadows of Summerland.

Miles and Directions

0.0 Start on the Wonderland Trail at the Fryingpan Creek Trailhead on Sunrise Road.

0.5 Cross a tributary of Fryingpan Creek on a wooden footbridge.

1.2 Cross Fryingpan Creek on a sturdy log bridge.

1.6 At a switchback in the trail, reach a viewpoint of Fryingpan Creek tumbling over a waterfall.

2.9 Cross another footbridge over Fryingpan Creek and enter a meadow.

4.0 Arrive above the tree line at Summerland. A sheltered group camp is to the left (east) of the trail.

5.3 Staying on the Wonderland Trail, continue climbing to Panhandle Gap, a notch in a rocky ridge dividing Summerland and the Ohanapecosh Valley. Return the way you came.

10.6 Arrive back at the trailhead.

Hike Information

Lodging

Mount Rainier National Park White River Campground, 2.5 miles south of Sunrise on Sunrise Road; (360) 569-2211

Copper Creek Inn at Mount Rainier, 35707 SR 706 E, Ashford; (360) 569-2799; coppercreekinn.com

Paradise Inn, 55106 Kernahan Rd. E, Ashford; (360) 569-2275

Other Resources

Mac's Field Guide to Mount Rainier National Park: Mammals and Birds, by Craig MacGowan

Vanilla leaf in bloom

19 Burroughs Mountain: Second Burroughs Loop

Starting from the highest paved parking lot in Washington State, the Burroughs Mountain loop wastes no time in getting to a mountain realm of alpine tundra, bare rock, and snow. Spectacular views of Mount Rainier start immediately and only get better. The top is a table set for two, with just you and the mountain staring each other in the face. On the return path you'll see deep moraines and acres of lupines.

Start: Trailhead at Sunrise, behind the visitor center

Distance: 6.3-mile lollipop

Hiking time: About 3 hours

Difficulty: Moderate due to steep sections

Trail surface: Rock and dirt trail

Elevation gain: 1,100 feet

Land status: National park

Nearest town: Packwood

Best season: Mid-July to Oct

Other trail users: None

Canine compatibility: No dogs allowed

Fees and permits: Fee required to enter Mount Rainier National Park. A free permit is required for wilderness camping; permits are available at any ranger station in the park.

Maps: USGS Sunrise; Green Trails no. 270, Mount Rainier East

Trail contacts: Mount Rainier National Park; (360) 569-2211; nps.gov/mora

Finding the trailhead: From Enumclaw: Drive east on WA 410 for 37 miles. Enter Mount Rainier National Park and turn right onto Sunrise Road. Follow Sunrise Road for 15.5 steep and windy miles to the visitor center and parking lot at the road's end.

From Yakima: Drive west on US 12 for 12 miles and then continue onto WA 410. Go east on WA 410 for 54 miles, and then turn left onto Sunrise Road and enter the Mount Rainier National Park White River entrance. Follow Sunrise Road for 15.5 steep and windy miles to the visitor center and parking lot at the road's end.

GPS: N46 54.86' / W121 38.52'

The Hike

The Burroughs Mountain loop brings you to close-up views of Mount Rainier and through meadows packed with wildflowers. While the hordes of roped climbers queue up to ascend Mount Rainier with crampons and ice axes, hikers on Burroughs Mountain can enjoy Mount Rainier without all the hassle.

Burroughs is a high-elevation experience. This is as close as many hikers will get to Mount Rainier. At 6,400 feet, even the trailhead is higher than many peaks in the Cascades. The meadows of wildflowers near the beginning of the hike quickly give way to alpine tundra—a rugged, treeless landscape of broken rock and stunted vegetation. Plants in the tundra zone have just a couple months to eke out an existence on sunlight and thawed soil and look much different from their relatives 1,000 or 2,000 feet below. Snow clings to the north-facing slopes of the trail into August. If you're not comfortable traversing patches of steep snow, wait until late summer to hike up Burroughs Mountain.

Asters, lupines, and Mount Rainier

From the north side of the Sunrise parking lot, take the wide gravel trail that goes up the hill behind the restrooms. From here, trails wind in all directions. Fortunately the paths are well signed, and finding the way to Burroughs Mountain isn't challenging. The wide, graveled trail begins by climbing a series of wooden steps toward an intersection below Sourdough Ridge. At the intersection, go left and follow the trail as it climbs steeply up the ridge. Occasional viewpoints face north toward Mount Fremont, McNeeley Peak, Antler Peak, and sometimes Glacier Peak far in the distance.

The meadows on the side of Sourdough Ridge are absolutely covered in lupines, with occasional miniature white phlox flowers and red-orange Indian paintbrush mixed in.

After passing Frozen Lake, the trail climbs steeply up a barren ridge with only the occasional dwarf version of lupine, heather, or paintbrush holding the scree and mineral dirt in place; tread lightly. The trail soon plateaus at First Burroughs. This wide, flat spot doesn't feel much like a peak, but it sports nice views, and there's a chance you'll see mountain goats grazing on top. The park's mountain goats are often together in big herds, and you may see as many as twenty goats grazing near this trail. This is also prime terrain for marmots, so keep your eyes peeled and listen for their whistling.

A short, steep climb leads to Second Burroughs, where you'll find a circular rock bench. Scramble up and you can sit across from Mount Rainier. Second Burroughs

Burroughs Mountain: Second Burroughs Loop

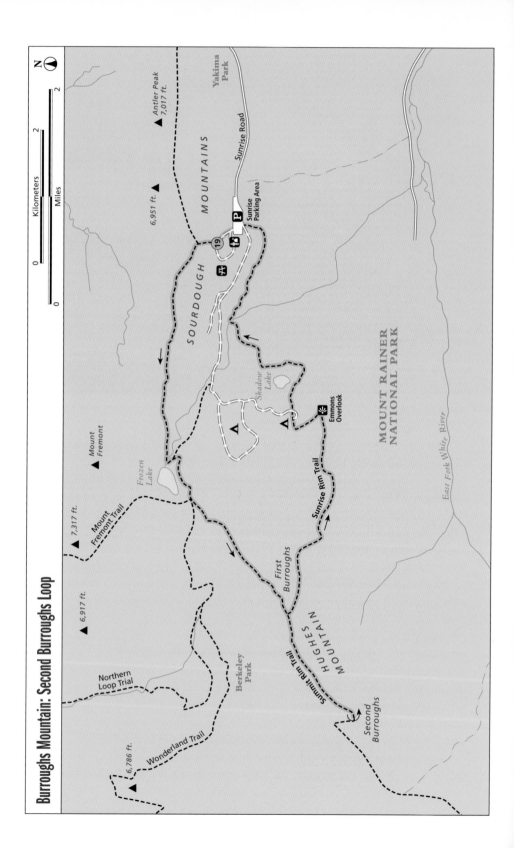

N

Kilometers
0 · 2 · 2

Miles
0 · 2

Antler Peak
7,017 ft. ▲

Yakima Park

Sunrise Road

6,951 ft. ▲

SOURDOUGH

MOUNTAINS

19

Sunrise Parking Area

P

MOUNT RAINER
NATIONAL PARK

Shadow Lake

Emmons Overlook

East Fork White River

Mount Fremont ▲

Frozen Lake

7,317 ft. ▲

Mount Fremont Trail

6,917 ft. ▲

Sunrise Rim Trail

First Burroughs

HUGHES MOUNTAIN

Summit Rim Trail

Second Burroughs

Northern Loop Trial

Berkeley Park

6,786 ft. ▲

Wonderland Trail

has views in all directions, but chances are you won't be able to take your eyes off Mount Rainier and the Emmons and Winthrop Glaciers.

Experienced scramblers can continue on through more scree and snow to Third Burroughs. This is a strenuous summit, with a high point of 7,828 feet and a round-trip distance of nearly 10 miles. This unmaintained trail traverses fragile plant environments. Stay on the trail!

On the way down from Second Burroughs, turn right at the junction near First Burroughs to make a loop back to the Sunrise parking lot. This trail descends toward Shadow Lake, affording views of the White River flowing through the Emmons Moraine. The lower slopes near Shadow Lake make the loop worthwhile. The variety and density of wildflowers is second to none. This route is similar in length to the way you came up, on Sourdough Ridge. When you begin to see crowds and families with lots of small children, the parking lot is near.

Miles and Directions

0.0 Start at the trailhead behind the visitor center on the north side of the Sunrise parking lot. Follow the wide gravel trail with wooden steps up the hill, and turn left at an intersection in 200 yards.

1.5 Come to an intersection with the Mount Fremont and Wonderland Trails. Continue up the ridge, following the sign for Burroughs Mountain.

2.2 Just past First Burroughs—a broad high point—reach an intersection with the Sunrise Rim Trail and continue upward.

2.9 Arrive at Second Burroughs. Turn around to retrace your steps.

3.5 Reach the intersection with the Sunrise Rim Trail and go right to make a loop back to the parking lot.

4.6 Continue past a viewpoint of Mount Rainier, Little Tahoma, and the White River flowing through the Emmons Moraine.

4.8 Continue straight at an intersection with an outhouse on the left. In 100 yards continue straight at an intersection that goes to Shadow Lake, to the left (north) of the trail.

6.3 Arrive back at the parking lot.

Hike Information

Lodging
Mount Rainier National Park White River Campground, 2.5 miles south of Sunrise on Sunrise Road; and Ohanapecosh Campgrounds, 3 miles north of the National Park Boundary on SR 123; (360) 569-2211

Other Resources
Mac's Field Guide to Mount Rainier National Park: Mammals and Birds, by Craig MacGowan

20 Naches Peak Loop

The meadows surrounding this high loop around Naches Peak burst with flowers. After an initial climb, the trail stays flat as it contours around the mountain, making for an easy hike. You'll cross over snow-fed streams that trickle through peaceful wildflower gardens. The scenery seems too good to be true, until it gets better. The views of Mount Rainier from the last third of the trail are breathtaking. This is a great hike to do with kids or anyone who wants to experience exquisite alpine beauty without working too hard for it.

Start: Tipsoo Lake Picnic Area at the top of Chinook Pass
Distance: 3.5-mile loop
Hiking time: About 2 hours
Difficulty: Easy
Trail surface: Dirt trail
Elevation gain: 550 feet
Land status: National park, federal wilderness area
Nearest town: Enumclaw
Best season: July to Oct
Other trail users: Equestrians and pack animals on the Pacific Crest Trail portion of the hike; hikers only in the national park
Canine compatibility: No dogs allowed
Fees and permits: Fee required to enter Mount Rainier National Park. A free permit is required for wilderness camping; permits are available at any ranger station in the park.
Maps: USGS Chinook Pass; Green Trails no. 270, Mount Rainier East, and no. 271, Bumping Lake
Trail contacts: Mount Rainier National Park; (360) 569-2211; nps.gov/mora

Finding the trailhead: From Enumclaw drive east on WA 410 for 44 miles. At the top of Chinook Pass on WA 410, park at the Tipsoo Lake Picnic Area on the left side of the highway. GPS: N46 52.19' / W121 31.18'

The Hike

Mount Rainier National Park and the surrounding area have some of the highest paved roads in the state. You can drive to the kind of rugged terrain and subalpine meadows that usually require a long uphill march to experience. The Naches Peak Loop uses the topography to its advantage by circling through exquisite meadows without gaining much elevation. The trail climbs about 500 feet in the first 1.0 mile and stays relatively flat after that as it contours through the meadows below the steep peak.

As the trail winds around Naches Peak, it passes through the William O. Douglas Wilderness, Mount Rainier National Park, and some of the most vibrant wildflower gardens on the planet. The peak is dotted with clumps of old, gnarled alpine firs, purple carpets of lupines, and patches of snow melting into clear streams that zigzag through the gardens.

Lupine is the most prevalent wildflower here, and sometimes it seems as though the meadows and hillsides are more purple than green. You'll also find plenty of

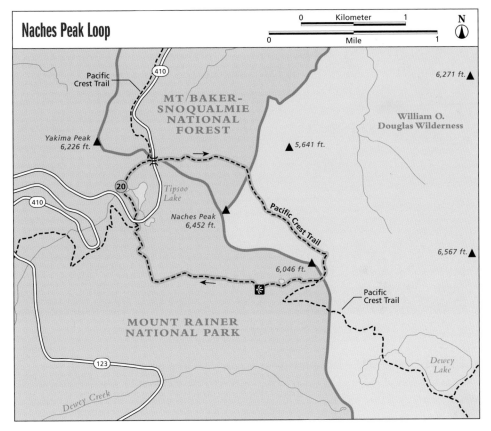

Naches Peak Loop

Pacific Crest Trail

410

MT BAKER-
SNOQUALMIE
NATIONAL
FOREST

Yakima Peak
6,226 ft.

6,271 ft. ▲

William O.
Douglas Wilderness

▲ 5,641 ft.

20

Tipsoo
Lake

410

Naches Peak
6,452 ft.
▲

Pacific Crest Trail

6,567 ft. ▲

6,046 ft.
▲

Pacific
Crest Trail

MOUNT RAINER
NATIONAL PARK

123

Dewey
Lake

Dewey Creek

0   Kilometer   1
0   Mile   1

N

Indian paintbrush, scarlet columbine, asters, Queen Anne's lace, heather, bear grass, glacier lilies, arnica, hellebore, and more. The sparse forest of subalpine firs and the occasional cedar allows plenty of sunlight to reach the flowers. Bring sunscreen, though; shade is scarce on the trail.

The loop is beautiful in both directions, but going clockwise offers better views of Mount Rainier. This way you get to stare at the massive volcano while you are walking toward it on the last half of the hike, where the views are best. Of course the wildflowers are equally good no matter which direction you walk.

For the clockwise loop, hike up the north side of Tipsoo Lake toward Chinook Pass, cross a bridge over the highway, and continue climbing up the side of Naches Peak on the trail. Soon you'll be skirting underneath the peak's cliffy north face. Make sure to savor the view of Yakima Peak, the cone-shaped mountain across WA 410, before Naches Peak hides it from view. The best wildflowers start on the northeast side of Naches Peak. Above the colorful meadows, cliff bands at the top of Naches Peak shade little snowfields, which feed creeks that dance downhill between the flowers. Several little trickles of water splash over cliffs directly above the trail.

Two miles from the parking lot, the trail rounds the south side of Naches Peak and Mount Rainier appears. On this side of the mountain, huckleberries and mountain ash dot the trail with red foliage and fall color late in the hiking season, making the

Flowers surround a shallow pond on Naches Peak.

Naches Peak Loop trail a fantastic hike even after the summer flower show is over. On the left side of the trail you can look down into the valley at Dewey Creek and WA 123, nearly 2,000 feet below. On a clear day you can even see the Goat Rocks and Mount Adams to the south, far beyond the deep valley.

Miles and Directions

0.0 Start from the trailhead at the Tipsoo Lake parking lot and picnic area at the top of Chinook Pass. Go north on the trail next to Tipsoo Lake.

0.3 Cross WA 410 on the Chinook Pass footbridge.

1.9 Pass a trail leading to Dewey Lake.

2.1 Pass a small lake in the middle of a flowery meadow.

2.2 Mount Rainier comes into view from behind Naches Peak.

3.5 Arrive back at the parking lot and picnic area.

Hike Information

Lodging

USDA Forest Service Silver Springs Campground, 1 mile west of Mount Rainier National Park on WA 410; (541) 338-7869

Other Resources

Mac's Field Guide to Mount Rainier National Park: Mammals and Birds, by Craig MacGowan

21 High Rock Lookout

The top of High Rock, in the Gifford Pinchot National Forest, is the perfect place to gaze at Mount Rainier. You're far enough from the massive mountain to get a sense of its incredible height and bulk, but close enough to pick out such details as icefalls and crevasses on its glaciers. The trip to the old fire lookout atop High Rock is short and sweet.

Start: High Rock Trailhead at Towhead Gap on FR 8440
Distance: 3.6 miles out and back
Hiking time: About 2 hours
Difficulty: Easy
Trail surface: Dirt trail with steep rock at the top
Elevation gain: 1,400 feet
Land status: National forest
Nearest town: Ashford

Best season: Late June to Oct
Other trail users: Horses and bicycles allowed but not recommended by the forest service
Canine compatibility: Leashed dogs allowed
Fees and permits: Northwest Forest Pass required to park at trailhead
Map: Green Trails no. 301, Randle
Trail contacts: Gifford Pinchot National Forest, Cowlitz Valley Ranger District; (360) 497-1100

Finding the trailhead: From Elbe, where WA 7 becomes WA 706, drive east on WA 706. In 7.9 miles, at Ashford, continue east for 2.9 miles and turn right at Kernahan Road. From here turn right in 1.5 miles onto Osborn Road after crossing the Nisqually River. Immediately turn left from Osborn Road onto FR 85. Continue 6.5 miles on a narrow, paved, badly potholed road, and then turn left onto FR 8440. Continue 5 miles to the parking area at Towhead Gap. The signed trailhead is on the left (west) side of the road.

For a longer but smoother road to the trailhead, go left onto Skate Creek Road (FR 52) from Kernahan Road, 1.5 miles from the junction with WA 706. Turn right onto FR 8440 in 3.3 miles and continue 9.5 miles to the parking area and trailhead at Towhead Gap. GPS: N 46 39.96' / W121 53.48'

The Hike

If it's views of the one and only Mount Rainier that you desire, forgo the crowds at the national park and go to High Rock instead. The short jaunt ends at a fire lookout on a perch high above the rolling forested hills south of the Nisqually River and Mount Rainier.

The trail is gradual and enjoyable, and the view at the top is almost perfect. The fire lookout is close enough to Rainier to see crevasses and the creeping, fragmented ice at the noses of the Tahoma, Kautz, Wilson, Nisqually, and Cowlitz Glaciers. It's just far enough to see the entire cone and the absurd difference in height between the mountain and the surrounding landscape. From inside the lookout, Rainier's glaciers and rock ridges fill the entire row of windows on the lookout's north side.

Sawtooth Ridge from High Rock

The view from High Rock spans the entire horizon, and the other directions also require much gawking. Also from the tower you can see the Tattoosh Range in the foreground just to the right of the mountain and the snowcapped Goat Rocks farther east. Turn around for views of Mounts Adams and St. Helens far beyond lush green hills.

High Rock is a high point of Sawtooth Ridge in the Gifford Pinchot National Forest. The ridge is made up of sharp peaks of uplifted rock. The northern slopes of the ridge shelter several forested lakes. Cora Lake, a beautiful dish of water, is 2,000 feet almost straight down from High Rock.

The hike to the tower is a direct trip up a ridge covered in second-growth forest with a few wildflowers. The trail is straightforward for most of the way. Just before the lookout is a lone switchback. The trail ends at mostly bare rock just below the summit. You must make your way up this steep rock to get to the tower. This part isn't dangerous, but be careful of the cliffs on three sides of the rock summit.

The view isn't quite perfect—if you can take your eyes off Rainier, you'll find plenty of evidence of clear-cutting on the nearby ridges. But the perspective of the mountain rising from rolling hills can't be beat. It's a short hike, so you can spend half the time walking and the other half staring wide-eyed.

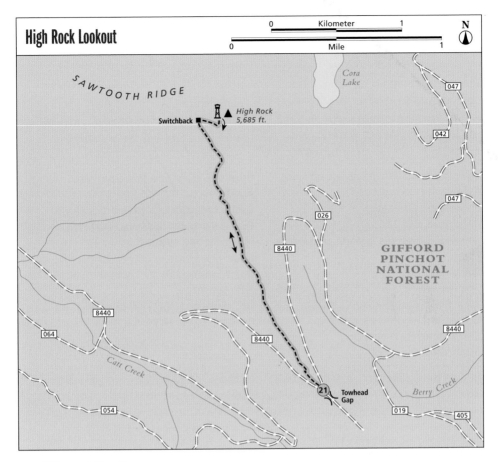

Miles and Directions

0.0 Start from the signed High Rock Trailhead at Towhead Gap.

1.7 Follow the trail as it switchbacks just below the rocky summit.

1.8 Reach the lookout tower and summit of High Rock. Return the way you came.

3.6 Arrive back at the trailhead.

Hike Information

Lodging

Big Creek Campground, Skate Creek Road, Gifford Pinchot National Forest; (360) 497-1100

Outfitters

Whittaker Mountaineering (maps and hiking gear), 30027 SR 706 E, Ashford; whittakermountaineering.com

Other Resources

Lookouts: Firewatchers of the Cascades and the Olympics, by Ira Spring and Byron Fish

22 Snowgrass Flat and Goat Ridge Loop

The gardens beneath the Goat Rocks—which are the core of an ancient volcano—rival any on Earth. This popular loop hike passes through miles of these magical gardens. Vibrant lupines and Indian paintbrush hug the sides of icy streams, and dark mountains with patchy snow hang overhead. Warning: There will be crowds.

Start: Snowgrass Flat Trailhead on loop road 96A
Distance: 14.7-mile loop
Hiking time: 7 to 9 hours
Difficulty: Difficult due to length and elevation gain
Trail surface: Dirt trail
Elevation gain: 1,200 feet to Snowgrass Flat; 2,000 feet to Goat Lake and Goat Ridge
Land status: Federal wilderness area
Nearest town: Packwood
Best season: Aug to Oct

Other trail users: Equestrians and pack animals
Canine compatibility: Leashed dogs allowed
Fees and permits: Northwest Forest Pass required to park at trailhead
Maps: Green Trails no. 302, Packwood; no. 303, White Pass; no. 304, Blue Lake; and no. 335, Walupt Lake
Trail contacts: Gifford Pinchot National Forest, Cowlitz Valley Ranger District; (360) 497-1100

Finding the trailhead: From Morton drive 30 miles east on US 12 and turn right onto Johnson Creek Road (FR 21), 1.7 miles west of Packwood. In 15.5 miles turn left onto FR 2150, signed CHAMBERS LAKE CAMPGROUND. In 3 miles turn right onto FR 2150-040 and right again onto Spur 2150-405 (signed SNOWGRASS FLAT). Continue to the trailhead and parking loop at the end of the road. GPS: N46 27.84' / W 121 31.17'

The Hike

A blanket of brilliant purple and red wildflowers cover the slopes and hang over the creeks underneath the Goat Rocks. The wildflowers are unbeatable, and aside from the volcanoes, the snowy mountains are the tallest and most rugged peaks between the Central Cascades and the Columbia River.

The flowery meadows can be seen in a day, and the nearby trails and peaks can fill multiple days of exploring. Strong hikers can make a 14.7-mile loop trip by returning on the Goat Ridge Trail and taking day hikes to Old Snowy Mountain and Hawkeye Point—one is a gentle but giant pile of loose rock with spectacular views; the other is a steep peak that makes a fine vantage for spotting mountain goats grazing around Goat Lake.

While the exploring is bountiful, so are the crowds. This makes day tripping to Snowgrass Flat a much simpler outing than having to hope and pray for a camping spot. Think twice about trying to camp at Snowgrass Flat on a weekend.

Wildflowers beneath the Goat Rocks

The trail gets dusty in summer as hooved animals beat down on it. It's dustiest near the parking lot. At 1.8 miles cross Goat Creek on a sturdy bridge and enter the Goat Rocks Wilderness. The path climbs higher from here, and before you know it you're surrounded by wildflowers. As soon as the subalpine fir thins out, the dense lupines fill the high meadows. Lupines crowd one another, grasping for sunlight. They are most numerous and the star of the flower show. But between the dense clumps of lupines, you'll see bear grass, asters, paintbrush, avalanche lilies, arnica, tiger lilies, Hooker's fairy bells, and much more.

The flowery climax is near Trail 96's junction with the Pacific Crest Trail (PCT). It's one of the state's best gardens, and it's in an idyllic setting. Snow melting from beneath the ridge of loose rock between Old Snowy Mountain and Ives Peak splashes between the clumps of flowers. Up above, hanging gardens of flowers drape themselves

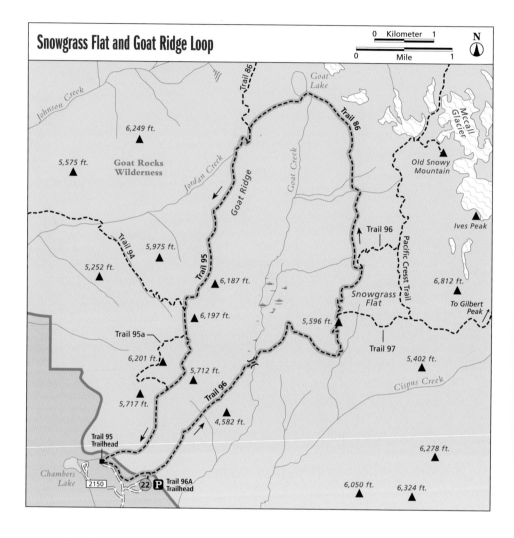

Snowgrass Flat and Goat Ridge Loop

0   Kilometer   1

0   Mile   1

N

Johnson Creek

Trail 86

Goat Lake

Mccall Glacier

6,249 ft.

5,575 ft.

Goat Rocks Wilderness

Jordan Creek

Goat Ridge

Goat Creek

Trail 86

Old Snowy Mountain

Ives Peak

Trail 96

Pacific Crest Trail

5,975 ft.

Trail 95

6,812 ft.

To Gilbert Peak

5,252 ft.

Trail 94

6,187 ft.

Snowgrass Flat

6,197 ft.

5,596 ft.

Trail 95a

Trail 97

5,402 ft.

6,201 ft.

5,712 ft.

Trail 96

Cispus Creek

5,717 ft.

4,582 ft.

Trail 95 Trailhead

6,278 ft.

Chambers Lake

2150

22 P Trail 96A Trailhead

6,050 ft.

6,324 ft.

over rocky shelves of andesite. The rock here is all volcanic. The Goat Rocks are the withered ruins of an ancient volcano the size of Mount Adams.

For a journey into the alpine world of rock and ice, where the growing season is too short for all but the hardiest of wildflowers, ramble up Old Snowy. To do this, follow the PCT north to a saddle, the highest point on the PCT in Washington, and continue up the ridge to the mountaintop on a way trail. The summit climb isn't technical, but watch for loose rock. From the summit, you can see Mount Curtis Gilbert to the east, the only point in the Goat Rocks that's higher than Old Snowy. Snowfields and glaciers cover the northern slopes of the ridge of Goat Rocks.

From the big junction at Snowgrass Flat, take the Lily Basin Trail through more colorful meadows to make the loop trip to Goat Lake and Goat Ridge. You'll soon come to a tall waterfall. Goat Lake barely thaws, and Hawkeye Point, above the lake, is a good spot to look for mountain goats around the icy lake. The white alpine ungulates hang out in the lake basin but seem to disappear when dogs come walking down the trail.

The trail continues climbing past the lake, traversing steep slopes of endless wild-flowers. The ever-prominent paintbrush, lupine, and bear grass are now joined by thick clumps of western pasque flower, which look like Dr. Seuss's truffula trees. They flower early, and then their delicate white flower petals shrivel and a shock of fuzzy hair envelops the flower.

The return trail on Goat Ridge is less busy than the trail through Snowgrass Flat, and several campsites on the ridge offer alternatives to the more-crowded camps near Snowgrass Flat.

Miles and Directions

0.0 Start at the trailhead for Trail 96A on Spur 2150-405.

0.2 Turn right onto Trail 96 to walk the route in a counterclockwise direction.

1.8 Cross Goat Creek on a wooden bridge and pass a campsite.

3.9 Reach the bypass trail, which bypasses the junction with the Lily Basin Trail and connects to the Pacific Crest Trail.

4.6 Arrive at Snowgrass Flat and the junction with the Lily Basin Trail. (**Option:** Turn around here for a 9.2-mile round-trip.) The Snowgrass Flat Trail continues to the PCT in 0.7 mile.

6.5 Pass a sign that reads No Campfires Beyond This Point.

7.0 Arrive at Goat Lake.

8.5 Turn left at a junction and continue on the Goat Ridge Trail.

11.8 Bear left at a junction with Trail 95A, which leads to a 6,201-foot high point on Goat Ridge.

12.5 Pass the lower junction with Trail 95A; bear left.

14.0 Reach the horse/alternate parking lot and trailhead. Go left for the 96A trailhead.

14.7 Arrive at the trailhead for Trail 96A.

Hike Information

Local Information
Destination Packwood, 103 Main St., Packwood; destinationpackwood.com

Lodging
USDA Forest Service Walupt Lake Campground, Gifford Pinchot National Forest, Cowlitz Valley Ranger District; (360) 497-1100

Restaurants
Cruiser's Pizza, 13028 US 12, Packwood; (360) 494-5400

23 Juniper Ridge

Unfortunately for hikers, motorcycles are allowed on many of the trails in Gifford Pinchot National Forest. Some of these mixed-use trails lead to beautiful destinations like Juniper Ridge. If motorcycles don't deter you, try this seldom-used hike to a grassy ridge with Mounts Adams, Rainier, and St. Helens all on the horizon. Smart hikers know they can find crowd-free roaming where motorcycles are allowed.

Start: Trailhead near the end of FR 2904
Distance: 6.0 miles out and back
Hiking time: About 3 hours
Difficulty: Moderate due to elevation gain
Trail surface: Dirt trail
Elevation gain: 2,000 feet
Land status: National forest
Nearest town: Randle

Best season: Summer, fall
Other trail users: Motorcycles, bicycles, horses
Canine compatibility: Dogs allowed
Fees and permits: Northwest Forest Pass required to park at trailhead
Map: *Green Trails no. 333, McCoy Peak*
Trail contacts: Gifford Pinchot National Forest, Cowlitz Valley Ranger District; (360) 497-1100

Finding the trailhead: From Randle go south on FR 25. Cross the Cowlitz River and turn left onto FR 23 in 1 mile. Stay on this road for 8 miles, and then turn right on FR 28. Continue 1 mile and turn left onto FR 29. Four miles down FR 29, turn left onto FR 2904, which is a relatively good gravel road but has countless speed bumps. Park on the left side of FR 2904, 4 miles from FR 29. The signed trailheads for Juniper Ridge and Tongue Mountain are on either side of the road. GPS: N46 23.80' / W 121 45.92'

The Hike

The lush forest below Juniper Peak is alive with leafy green, and the views from the ridge take in all three South Cascades volcanoes. It's a beautiful spot, but there's a good chance you'll have it to yourself. That's because this trail, like many of the trails in the Gifford Pinchot National Forest, is open to motorcycles. Its being open to motorcycles means most hikers leave it alone, but you're unlikely to actually encounter any motorcyclists—the trail isn't long enough to appeal to them.

There is ample evidence of motorcycles use though, and because of this Juniper Ridge is not the most serene wilderness experience. But it is beautiful, and a prime example of the lesser-traveled paths in the Gifford Pinchot National Forest. While your hike might be marred by the smell of motorcycle exhaust, which lingers among the stately trees long after the noisy bikes are out of sight, there's a good chance it won't be. By taking this risk you'll be rewarded with solitude, lush forest, a spacious ridge, and prime views in all directions.

The trail to these lonely views climbs the base of a low knoll covered in second-growth forest. The gentle slopes are covered in lush vegetation, including huge false hellebore, ferns, trilliums, bunchberry, and vanilla leaf. In 0.5 mile the path begins to

The long crest of Juniper Ridge

get gradually steeper. In a couple of the steepest spots, motorcycles have gouged small U-shaped ditches into the path. This is awkward and annoying, but there really isn't too much motorcycle damage.

After a couple short switchbacks, the trail gains a higher ridge 1.6 miles from the trailhead. From here you can get a brief view into the Cispus River basin and much of the Dark Divide roadless area. The roadless area, which includes Juniper Ridge, is one of the largest Roadless Areas in Western Washington. The US Senate eliminated the Dark Divide from the Wilderness Act of 1984. If it ever is designated as a wilderness, it will surely become popular for the hiking masses.

Indian paintbrush, asters, and red columbine peak out through openings in the trees along the ridge. After a final steep grunt up a sandy slope, you reach the top of a broad ridge below Juniper Peak. A grassy meadow on top of this long ridge is filled with wildflowers. A trail leads 5.0 miles along the top of the ridge until the ridge ends and the trail descends to Dark Meadow. A faint path leads to the top of Juniper Peak, where you can see snowy volcanoes and rolling hills in all directions. Juniper Peak and much of the top of Juniper Ridge is rocky and well draining. Several species

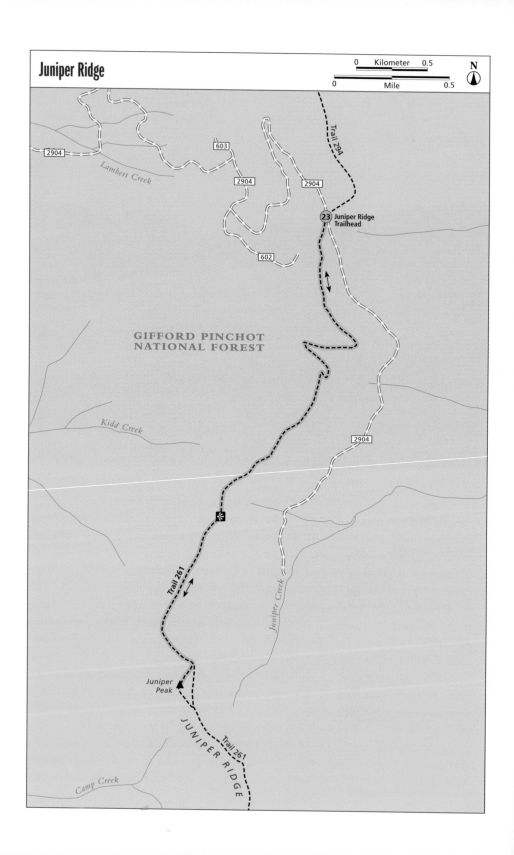

Juniper Ridge

0 Kilometer 0.5
0 Mile 0.5

N

2904

603

Lambert Creek

2904

2904

602

Trail 294

23 Juniper Ridge
Trailhead

GIFFORD PINCHOT
NATIONAL FOREST

Kidd Creek

2904

Trail 261

Juniper Creek

Juniper
Peak

Trail 261

J U N I P E R   R I D G E

Camp Creek

of stonecrop, a plant with water-storing succulent leaves and small yellow flowers, grow atop the ridge. The ridge would make a fantastic backpacking trip, but there's no water along the way.

Miles and Directions

0.0 Start at the Juniper Ridge Trailhead on the south side of FR 2904.

0.6 Hike through a long switchback.

2.1 Pass through an opening in the trees with views toward the Cispus River valley.

3.0 Reach Juniper Peak. The final 500 feet to the peak is on a scramble trail from the main trail on Juniper Ridge. Return the way you came.

6.0 Arrive back at the trailhead and parking lot.

Hike Information

Restaurants

Mount Adams Cafe, 9794 US 12, Randle; (360) 497-5556

Sunlight filtered through a Douglas fir

24 Twin Sisters Lakes and Tumac Mountain

For a short hike, Twin Sisters Lakes is a great destination. Berries, meadows, flat high country, and subalpine forests surround the big lakes. Hikers looking for a more serious leg-stretch can continue up Tumac Mountain to breathe alpine air and survey the lake-dotted plateau that surrounds the cindery mountain.

Start: Trailhead at the end of FR 1800 (Bumping River Road), at Deep Creek Campground
Distance: 9.6 miles out and back
Hiking time: About 5 hours out and back
Difficulty: Moderate due to length and relatively gentle terrain and elevation gain
Trail surface: Dirt trail
Elevation gain: 1,950 feet to Tumac Mountain
Land status: Federal wilderness area
Nearest town: Yakima
Best season: Mid-July through Oct

Other trail users: Equestrians
Canine compatibility: Leashed dogs permitted
Fees and permits: Northwest Forest Pass required to park at trailhead
Maps: *USDA Forest Service William O. Douglas Wilderness map; Green Trails no. 271, Bumping Lake,* and *no. 303, White Pass*
Trail contacts: Wenatchee National Forest, Naches Ranger District; (509) 653-1400

Finding the trailhead: From Yakima drive east on US 12 for 17.5 miles to the junction with WA 410 to Chinook Pass. Continue on WA 410 for 30 miles and turn left onto Bumping River Road. (Or reach Bumping River Road from the west by driving on WA 410 62 miles east from Enumclaw.) The pavement ends in 11.5 miles and the road becomes FR 1800. Continue 7.5 more miles to Deep Creek Campground, a very primitive campground at the road's end. The trailhead is on the right at the beginning of the campground loop. GPS: N46 45.16' / W121 21.68'

The Hike

On the east side of the South Cascades, just south of Mount Rainier, a pair of lakes below Tumac Mountain make a great destination for kids and hikers looking for a wilderness destination just 2.0 miles from the car. The open forests and meadows on this plateau above Deep Creek bristle with heather, lowbush huckleberries, and wildflowers. The two lakes, one slightly larger than the other, fill deep basins in this east-slope subalpine forest.

Several sandy nooks surround each lakeshore, and the smaller lake has a complicated shoreline with miniature bays, fingers, and inlets confining the blue water. Camp 100 feet from the lakes to protect the fragile lakeside vegetation (and to give other campers privacy).

Deep Creek Road was closed from 2006 to 2013 after a washout. During those years, few hikers ventured to these once-popular lakes. In 2013 the trail showed the lack of use, and some sections of trail above the lake were overgrown.

Little Twin Sisters Lake

The trail enters the William O. Douglas Wilderness as you cross a bridge over Deep Creek 0.1 mile from the trailhead. The trail climbs alongside Deep Creek through wildflowers and mature groves of trees. It passes a small rocky canyon at about 1.5 miles, with deeper water pooling beneath short cliffs. Several species of penstemon grow near the trail. Their tubular flowers come in a variety of blues and lavenders. Keep an eye out for bear grass and subalpine spirea, which thrive in these east-slope forests and meadows.

In 2.0 miles the trail meets the shore of the smaller of the Twin Sisters, and a path to the right leads to the slightly larger Sister. Twin Sisters Lakes mark the northern end of a wide plateau with a couple dozen lakes (and a couple dozen places for mosquitoes to breed). Several different trails loop through the area.

The lakes are glorious, and there's no need to go farther. However, a jaunt up Tumac Mountain completes the trip like a scoop of ice cream completes warm apple pie. Tumac Mountain, a young but extinct volcanic cone, rises from the middle of the plateau it helped create with its volcanic activity.

WILLIAM O. DOUGLAS

US Associate Supreme Court Justice William O. Douglas loved the natural world and the wild places of his home state. The wilderness that now bears his name was among his favorite areas. Douglas, who grew up in Yakima, wrote in his book *Of Men and Mountains* that the meadows around Blankenship Lakes, just east of Tumac Mountain, were his favorite place in the Cascades.

Douglas defended wild places, and in 1958 he led a 20-mile beach march from Cape Alava to Rialto Beach to draw attention to a proposed road on the wild stretch of coastline. Reporters and photographers tagged along to document the journey, and the road never intruded into the wild beach.

Apparently Douglas hiked fast. The late Ira Spring—a celebrated Washington wilderness photographer, guidebook author, and strong hiker and climber—said he had a hard time keeping up with Douglas while also photographing him on the beach walk.

To get to Tumac, go left (southeast) at the smaller Twin Sister and bear right in 0.6 mile onto Trail 44 at a junction with the Sand Creek Trail. By some trick of the eye, Tumac looks far away. It's surprising how quickly you begin climbing slopes covered in huckleberries and white and pink heather on the mountain. Most of the way is a gradual uphill, but the trail gets steep as it makes a few switchbacks up the cinder slopes to Tumac Mountain's summit. On top of Tumac you'll find the footing of an old fire lookout, stunted subalpine firs, and 360-degree views.

The region's star volcanoes—Adams, St. Helens, and Rainier—are all visible. Rainier commands much of the northern skyline, but trees are crowding the view toward Rainier from the summit. The glaciered north side of the Goat Rocks, another ancient volcano, is directly between Tumac and Mount Adams. The group of high yellow mountains behind Blankenship Lakes is Nelson Ridge; Mount Aix is the 7,766-foot-tall high point. Even Mount Stuart protrudes into the skyline beyond Nelson Ridge. In the foreground in nearly every direction, sparkling lakes reflect the sky above the high plateau surrounding the mountain.

Miles and Directions

0.0 Start from the trailhead at Deep Creek Campground.

0.1 Cross Deep Creek on a sturdy wooden bridge and begin hiking up several long switchbacks.

2.0 Arrive at a junction at the smaller of the Twin Sisters Lakes. (*Option:* Turn around here for a shorter out and back hike. The 4.0-mile round-trip will take about 2 hours. Elevation gain: 800 feet.) The trail to the right leads to the bigger lake. Go left to continue to Tumac Mountain.

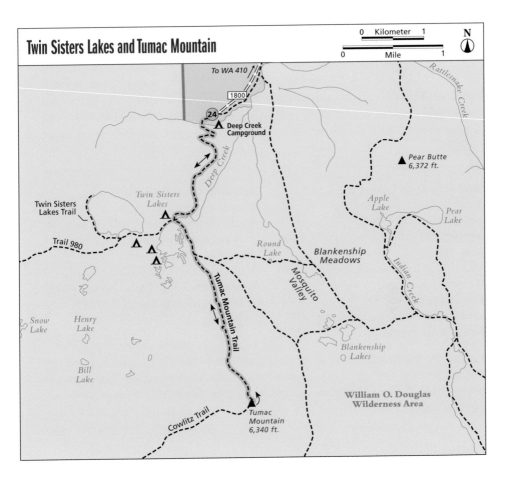

Twin Sisters Lakes and Tumac Mountain

0 Kilometer 1

0 Mile 1

N

To WA 410

1800

24

▲ Deep Creek
Campground

Deep Creek

Rattlesnake Creek

▲ Pear Butte
6,372 ft.

Twin Sisters
Lakes

Twin Sisters
Lakes Trail

Trail 980

Apple
Lake

Pear
Lake

Round
Lake

Blankenship
Meadows

Mosquito
Valley

Indian Creek

Snow
Lake

Henry
Lake

Tumac Mountain Trail

Bill
Lake

Blankenship
Lakes

William O. Douglas
Wilderness Area

Cowlitz Trail

Tumac
Mountain
6,340 ft.

2.6 On the trail to Tumac Mountain, bear right at a junction with the Sand Ridge Trail, which leads to Blankenship Lakes.

4.8 Reach the summit of Tumac Mountain. Return the way you came.

9.6 Arrive back at the trailhead.

Hike Information

Lodging
USDA Forest Service Bumping Lake Campground, Bumping River Road, Goose Prairie; USDA Forest Service Deep Creek Campground at the trailhead at the end of FR 1800 (Bumping River Road), Naches Ranger District, 10237 US 12, Naches; (509) 653-1400

Other Resources
Of Men and Mountains: The Classic Memoir of Wilderness Adventure, by William O. Douglas

25 Killen Creek Meadows

The hike to Killen Creek Meadows samples the best scenery and open meadows on Mount Adams's west side. You can fill days of wandering in this high country, but this shorter hike leads to several sights you can't miss—lava flows; a plateau of rock and stunted trees beneath the steep, broken Adams Glacier; and waterfalls in an alpine meadow.

Start: Killen Creek Trailhead on FR 2329
Distance: 8.2 miles out and back
Hiking time: About 4 hours
Difficulty: Difficult due to length and elevation gain
Trail surface: Dusty dirt trail; rock and ash on the way to High Camp
Elevation gain: 1,500 feet
Land status: Federal wilderness area
Nearest town: Randle

Best season: Mid-July through Oct
Other trail users: Equestrians
Canine compatibility: Leashed dogs permitted
Fees and permits: Northwest Forest Pass required to park at trailhead
Map: Green Trails no. 367S, Mount Adams
Trail contacts: Gifford Pinchot National Forest, Mount Adams Ranger District; (509) 395-3400

Finding the trailhead: From I-5, 15 miles south of Centralia, take exit 68 for US 12 toward Morton and Yakima. Turn right in Randle onto FR 25. In 1 mile, after crossing the Cowlitz River, bear left onto FR 23. Continue 31 miles to a junction, and turn left onto FR 2329. Continue 6 miles to the Killen Creek Trailhead on the right. GPS: N46 17.31' / W121 33.12'

The Hike

The meadows around Mount Adams offer miles of alpine roaming to massive glaciers, otherworldly lava flaws, pine forests, and flowery meadows with flowing creeks. The second-tallest volcano in Washington isn't quite as iconic as Mount Rainier—you won't find it on a beer can or license plate. In spite of this (or maybe because of it), hiking near Mount Adams is a much different and in some ways better experience than hiking in Mount Rainier National Park.

The more remote trailheads than those in Mount Rainier National Park result in smaller crowds. FR 23 runs much of the way around the west side of the mountain. From it, access roads branch off uphill, ending at trails that continue up the mountain. Many of these trails eventually link up with Pacific Crest Trail (PCT) and the Around the Mountain Trail, two separate paths that run nearly the whole way around Mount Adams. The path on these high trails is mostly at elevations between 5,700 and 6,900 feet, where views are plentiful. These trails end on the mountain's northeast slopes, and completely encircling Mount Adams requires bushwhacking and possibly glacier travel. Thanks to this circular network of trails, there's many ways to get high on Mount Adams.

Amanita muscaria *is generally considered to be toxic.*

The Killen Creek Trail to Killen Creek Meadows shows off much of Mount Adams's variety and beauty. A mixed forest of pines and firs covers the first section of the trail. It can be hot and dusty and much drier than other Washington volcanoes. In fact, ponderosa pines, which are drought and fire resistant, grow on the south and east slopes of Mount Adams.

The Killen Creek Trail isn't brutally steep, but it is direct as it climbs toward the massive mountain. The Killen Creek Trail starts near Killen Creek but only gets farther and farther from its namesake creek as it veers toward Adams Creek. In 2.5 miles you reach East Fork and meadows thick with lupines and huckleberries. This creek offers the first water on the route and the location of several campsites.

In 3.1 miles the trail reaches a junction with the PCT. A 1.0-mile-long spur trail continues up the mountain to popular High Camp beneath the Adams Glacier. If you have the time and the energy, don't miss this side trip—see option below. Just above the camp the Adams Glacier tumbles down the mountain between the Pinnacle and the North Cleaver, grinding ever deeper into the massive mountain. These huge wedges and blocks of ice creep toward the high camp down one of the mountain's steepest faces. Ragged pine trees grow in the volcanic soil, but they don't grow very tall. The windswept trees spread out into rows, and they're always facing downwind. To the north, the view of Mount Rainier and the Goat Rocks is eye-popping. Notice how the land south of Mount Adams is a high plateau extending all the way to the Goat Rocks.

To continue, it's 1.0 short mile east to Killen Creek Meadows. Killen Creek flows year-round. On its course down the mountain, it tumbles over several low-angled

Mount Adams from a lake beneath Killen Creek Meadows

waterfalls and meanders neatly through the meadow. These meadows have it all—waterfalls, flowers, breathtaking views, and even a hidden lake.

Reverse your path to get back to the trailhead, or go south on the PCT 1.5 miles past the junction with Killen Creek Trail (113) to Trail 112. Trail 112 descends for 1.8 miles through more meadows. These meadows aren't as scenic as the Killen Creek Meadows, but they are bigger and more open. From the trailhead for Trail 112, walk about 3.0 miles on FR 2329 to get back to the Killen Creek Trailhead.

Miles and Directions

- **0.0** Start at the Killen Creek Trailhead.
- **2.5** The trail reaches East Fork and several campsites.
- **3.1** Trail 113 reaches an intersection with the Pacific Crest Trail. (See option below.) Turn left for Killen Creek Meadows.
- **4.1** Reach a waterfall in the meadows of Killen Creek. Return the way you came.
- **8.2** Arrive back at the trailhead.

Option

At the intersection with the Pacific Crest Trail at mile 3.1, continue straight for a side trip to High Camp. This option adds 2 miles to your route—1 mile to High Camp, then turn around and return to the PCT junction. Turn right at the junction to continue to the meadows of Killen Creek.

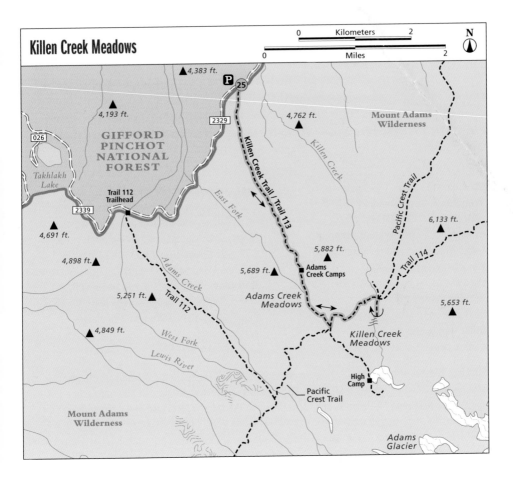

Killen Creek Meadows

Hike Information

Lodging

USDA Forest Service Takhlakh Lake and Horseshoe Lake Campgrounds, Gifford Pinchot National Forest, Mount Adams Ranger District, 2455 Washington 141, Trout Lake; (509) 395-3400

Restaurants

Cruiser's Pizza, 13028 US 12, Packwood; (360) 494-5400

Other Resources

The Wildflowers of Mount Adams, Washington, by Susan McDougall

26 Norway Pass

This hike through the blast zone of Mount St. Helens leads towards some of the most unusual and spectacular views in the Cascades. The way up through a slowly regenerating forest is punctuated by views of Mounts Rainier and Adams. From Norway Pass, Mount St. Helens's gaping crater is less than 10 air-miles away across log-choked Spirit Lake.

Start: Boundary Trail 1 trailhead
Distance: 4.4 miles out and back
Hiking time: About 2 hours
Difficulty: Easy due to short distance
Trail surface: Dirt and pumice trail
Elevation gain: 908 feet
Land status: National monument
Nearest town: Randle
Best season: July through Oct
Other trail users: None
Canine compatibility: No dogs allowed

Fees and permits: Northwest Forest Pass required to park at trailhead; Mount Margaret backcountry permit required for camping
Maps: USGS Spirit Lake SE; Green Trails no. 332, Spirit Lake; Mount St. Helens National Volcanic Monument visitor map
Trail contacts: Gifford Pinchot National Forest, Mount Saint Helens National Volcanic Monument; (360) 891-5000; www.fs.usda.gov/giffordpinchot

Finding the trailhead: From Randle go south 22 miles on FR 25. Turn right onto FR 99, going west toward Mount St. Helens for 9 miles. FR 99 is paved, but it's washing out and narrow in a few places. Turn right onto FR 26 and continue 0.9 mile to the Norway Pass Trailhead parking area. GPS: W46 18.30' / W 122 04.96'

The Hike

Mount St. Helens used to be a tidy snowcapped pyramid, symmetrical and aesthetic. The eruptions and forces that built the mountain were recent enough that the mountain wasn't gouged and shaped much by glaciers. When it erupted on May 18, 1980, with the power of a hydrogen bomb, immense landslides broke free, trees toppled like dominoes, and ash blew around the world and piled up nearly 3 inches deep in Yakima, more than 100 air miles away.

▶ After the eruption on May 18, 1980, then-President Jimmy Carter said, "Mount St. Helens' devastation makes the moon look like a golf course." He is also rumored to have been horrified by clear-cut logging on the way to the blast zone, which he mistook for damage from the eruption.

The hike to Norway Pass takes you to a view of the vast crater left by the eruption. The sheer amount of missing material is startling. A new glacier, the Crater Glacier, is forming in the bottom of the crater. Snow accumulates as it sloughs off the crater walls, which shade the collected snow at the bottom. It's a postcard view from Norway Pass, with log-choked Spirit Lake directly between the trail and the mountain.

Mount St. Helens and Spirit Lake

The trail climbs and traverses through blast flattened trees and incinerated slopes east of Norway Pass. Soon after the blast, mycelium, the underground roots of fungi, began recolonizing the lifeless dirt. Fireweed, a quick-growing annual plant, appeared in the landscape the next spring. After its pink flowers bloomed and spread seed, the plant mass added organic matter to the soil. Gophers helped by tilling the soil and transporting seeds from nearby areas. Fireweed still lingers on the trail, but it's now just one member of an orchestra of plants that include huckleberries, monkey flowers, Indian paintbrush, salmonberry, thimbleberry, and even young trees. Tangled alders choke the moist spots and creekbeds, while young subalpine firs grow on the hillsides.

Among all the new growth are the bare bones of the former forest. Everywhere, white logs lie on the ground. They're nearly always pointing away from the volcano, the origin of the explosion that laid them flat.

The trail gets to the pass quickly and directly. As you climb the trail of pumice and ash, Mount Rainier comes into view to the north, and then Mount Adams appears to the east about 1.25 miles in. At about 1.5 miles the trail contours through a steep, north-facing drainage that may by covered in snow into July. In 2.2 miles the trail reaches Norway Pass, a notch in a ridge with a fantastic view. For even better views,

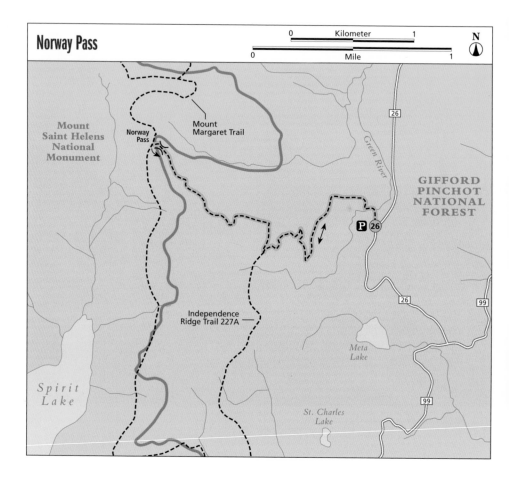

you can follow the Mount Margaret Trail up the ridge a short way to the north of Norway Pass or continue all the way to Mount Margaret, an 11.4-mile round-trip from the parking lot.

On the drive out through the national forest, look for stands of trees that were replanted after the eruption. These forests have grown in much quicker than in the terrain you hiked through on the way to Norway Pass, where no trees were replanted. But these forests are less diverse and have a more sterile, uniform appearance than those inside the national monument.

Miles and Directions

0.0   Start on the Boundary 1 Trail at the Norway Pass Trailhead parking area. Stay left at a junction with the Independence Pass Trail in 50 yards.

1.2   Arrive at a junction with Independence Ridge Trail (227A), which connects to Independence Pass Trail (227) in 1.3 yards. Turn right toward Norway Pass.

2.2 Reach Norway Pass, a notch in the ridge at a junction with the trail to Mount Margaret. Return the way you came.

4.4 Arrive back at the trailhead.

Hike Information

Local Information

Mount St. Helens Visitor Center at Seaquest/Silver Lake, 3029 Spirit Lake Hwy., Castle Rock 98611; (360) 274-0962; mountsthelens.com/visitorcenters.html

Restaurants

Mount Adams Cafe, 9794 US 12, Randle; (360) 497-5556

Other Resources

Mount St. Helens: The Eruption and Recovery of a Volcano, by Rob Carson

A lone Indian paintbrush and Mount St. Helens

27 Indian Heaven Loop

Lake after lake is sprinkled throughout the high plateau that makes up the Indian Heaven Wilderness. Trails lead around the lakes through meadows and tall open forests. In season, the scent of sweet, juicy berries wafts through it all. Hike to as many lakes as you can stand, and snack on berries in between—it's hiker heaven.

Start: Indian Heaven Trail 33 Trailhead, Cultus Creek Campground
Distance: 6.9-mile loop
Hiking time: About 4 hours
Difficulty: Moderate
Trail surface: Dirt trail
Elevation gain: 1,450 feet
Land status: Federal wilderness area
Nearest town: Trout Lake

Best season: Mid-July through Oct
Other trail users: Equestrians
Canine compatibility: Leashed dogs allowed
Fees and permits: Northwest Forest Pass required to park at trailhead
Maps: *Green Trail no. 365S, Indian Heaven*
Trail contacts: Gifford Pinchot National Forest, Mount Adams Ranger District; (509) 395-3400

Finding the trailhead: From I-5 at Woodland go east on WA 503/Lewis River Road for 32 miles. At Cougar, continue east on FR 90 for 19 miles. About 50 miles from the interstate, turn right onto Curly Creek Road. In 5 miles turn left onto Meadow Creek Road; 2.8 miles later, make a slight right onto FR 30. In 7.9 miles turn right onto FR 24 and continue 4.1 rough miles to the trailhead at Cultus Creek Campground.

If you're coming from south of Woodland, drive WA 14 through the Columbia River Gorge to Carson. From Carson go north on Wind River Road for 13.4 miles and turn right onto FR 30. In 7.9 miles turn right onto FR 24 and continue 4.1 rough miles to the trailhead at Cultus Creek Campground. GPS: N 46 02.79' / W 121 45.39'

The Hike

This is a lake lover's paradise. Lakes, meadows, and mature forests perfumed with the sweet smell of blueberries and huckleberries in season cover this high plateau between Mounts St. Helens and Adams. A web of trails weaves through the land of lakes. Some trails pass through forests heavy in silver, noble, and subalpine fir. Others meander through open meadows. Wherever you roam in this approximately 10 x 4-mile strip of wilderness, huckleberries are close by.

The web of trails lends itself to sustained wandering. There are lakes to discover in every direction—more than twenty big named lakes in the Indian Heaven Wilderness and countless smaller ponds dotting the meadows.

There's not much in the way of views on this loop, although Mount Adams is visible in several spots at the beginning and end of the loop. For more views, take the spur trail toward Lemei Rock, just past Cultus Lake. The trail climbs a high shoulder

One of dozens of lakes in the Indian Heaven Wilderness

of the rocky peak, where you can look down toward Lake Wapiki and northeast toward Mount Adams.

The Pacific Crest Trail (PCT) runs the long way through Indian Heaven. Several trails connect with the PCT in different places, making two good-size loops through the wilderness. The hike described here is a loop past Deep, Cultus, and Clear Lakes and around Bird Mountain. The loop can be extended by continuing on Trail 179 past Lemei and Junction Lakes and returning on the PCT. The PCT passes through deep stands of mature trees, while Trail 179 goes through open meadows.

From the trailhead for Indian Heaven Trail 33, at the south end of Cultus Creek Campground, begin climbing up the steep and direct path to the Indian Heaven Wilderness. Compared with the surrounding mountains, the Indian Heaven area is a high plateau. The trails are nearly all at an elevation between 4,000 and 5,000 feet. But that doesn't mean the walking is flat. It seems you're constantly climbing little hills, bulges,

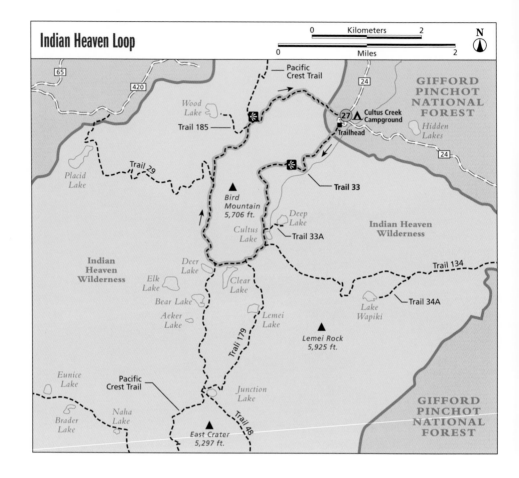

and dips in Indian Heaven. This first section of trail is the steepest climb of the trip. In 1.1 mile you come to a viewpoint facing Mount Adams. After another 1.0 mile of climbing, you reach a junction to Deep Lake, which has several campsites and a view of the top of Mount Adams beyond the trees. Cultus Lake is just beyond the junction.

From Cultus Lake you'll contour around the southern flank of Bird Mountain, passing junctions that lead toward Junction Lake and more meadows deeper in wilderness. Blocky talus crumbles off the south side of Bird Mountain toward Clear Lake and Deer Lake. This area has the highest concentration of lakes in Indian Heaven. Elk and Bear Lakes are just south. At Deer Lake, turn right onto the PCT and head south, back toward the trailhead at Cultus Creek Campground. You'll pass several more junctions leading to solitary lakes and then peekaboo views of Mount Adams on the descent to the campground and trailhead.

Miles and Directions

0.0 Start at the Indian Heaven 33 Trailhead at the south side of the Cultus Creek Campground.

1.1 After climbing forested slopes, reach a view of Mount Adams.

2.4 Bear right at a junction with a trail to Deep Lake.

2.5 Bear right at a junction with a trail to Lemei Rock and Lake Wapiki.

2.8 Turn right at a junction with Trail 179, which leads to Lemei Lake.

3.4 Reach a junction with the Pacific Crest Trail. Turn right to continue the loop.

4.4 Bear right at a junction with the Placid Lake Trail.

5.4 Turn right and go uphill (Trail 108) at a four-way intersection. The other trails lead to Wood Lake and Sawtooth Mountain.

6.9 Arrive back at the Cultus Creek Campground. Walk across the campground to the Trail 33 parking lot.

Hike Information

Lodging
USDA Forest Service Cultus Creek Campground (at the trailhead), Gifford Pinchot National Forest, Mount Adams Ranger District, 2455 Washington 141, Trout Lake; (509) 395-3400

Restaurants
KJ's Bear Creek Cafe, 2376 SR 141, Trout Lake; (509) 395-2525

28 Lewis River

The Lewis River cascades down several grand falls on its way to the Columbia River. This section of trail features a high concentration of spectacular pools and waterfalls, as well as great views of the emerald water flowing through a deep valley of old-growth forest. The falls are not only large and plentiful but also close together, and the trail between them could hardly be easier.

Start: Lower Falls Recreation Area, Gifford Pinchot National Forest
Distance: 6.4 miles out and back
Hiking time: About 3 hours
Difficulty: Easy due to gentle terrain
Trail surface: Dirt trail
Elevation gain: 400 feet
Land status: National forest
Nearest towns: Carson, Cougar
Best season: Apr to Nov

Other trail users: Mountain bikes, equestrians on first section of trail
Canine compatibility: Leashed dogs permitted
Fees and permits: Northwest Forest Pass required to park at trailhead
Map: Green Trails no. 365, Lone Butte
Trail contacts: Gifford Pinchot National Forest; (360) 891-5000; www.fs.usda.gov/gifford pinchot

Finding the Trailhead: Leave I-5 in Woodland at exit 22. Turn left onto Lewis River Road (WA 503) and continue east for 23 miles to the town of Cougar. Continue straight through Cougar for 25 miles, past Lake Merwin, Yale Lake, and Swift Reservoir, to the Skamania County line, where the road becomes FR 90. Continue east for 13.7 miles and turn into the Lower Falls Recreation Area. Park near the restrooms and take one of several paths directly behind the restrooms toward the lower falls viewpoint. GPS: N 46 09.33' / W 121 52.88'

The Hike

Before the US Army Corps of Engineers installed dam after dam on the Columbia River, the lower falls on the Lewis River was a prime fishing spot for Native Americans. The 40-foot wall of whitewater presented an impassable barrier to salmon. What was once the end of the line for spawning salmon marks the beginning of an adventure to awe-inspiring waterfalls and lowland old-growth trees for hikers.

Trees grow quickly in southern Washington. Nearly all the ancient forests have been cut over and replaced with uniform second-growth stands. Around the Lewis River you'll find ancient trees and trees of varying height. The ground is littered with rotting logs, giving life to young hemlocks and cedars.

▶ The Lewis River was not named for Meriwether Lewis but for A. Lee Lewis, an early settler who homesteaded near the mouth of the river.

Upstream, the river is a raging torrent, flowing through the volcanic terrain below Mount Adams's Adams Glacier. Downstream, it's blocked by hydroelectric dams. In these

Upper Falls on the Lewis River

woods, it flows gently and calmly, occasionally plunging over cliffs and cascades into deep pools.

The Lower Falls, a wide drop-off where the cool water splashes from platform to rocky platform, is just a couple hundred feet from the parking lot. To continue the hike from here, stay right along the river—following it upstream—through the tangle of trails to avoid getting lost in the maze of tents, RVs, barbecues, and kids on bicycles in the campground. For most of the hike you'll walk high above the river. On the trail you'll catch a glance of the shallow water only occasionally, but the tranquil sound of the stream is ever present. The trail winds through giant trees and beneath towering cliffs and caves colored neon from lichen. Look for maidenhair ferns growing on the cliffs above the river. These delicate ferns with black stems like growing on vertical cliffs near waterfalls. Here their roots find soil that drains quickly, but they can suck up constant moisture from the mist in the wake of the waterfalls.

The trail descends toward the river at each waterfall, where broad walls of whitewater roar off cliffs and into deep pools. The waterfalls are the main attraction, and the area around each falls seems to be made just for human enjoyment and relaxation,

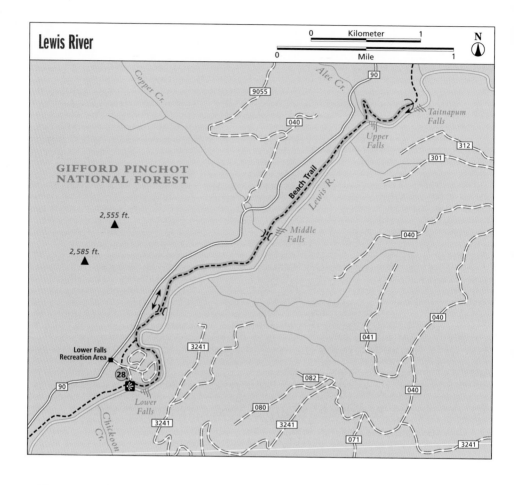

GIFFORD PINCHOT
NATIONAL FOREST

with warm rocks to rest on. Water flows, pools, and constricts in channels of solid rock before being released back into shallow stretches of river. The second falls is a stout and turbulent set of rapids. The upper waterfall is perhaps the most scenic. It's about 60-feet tall, and the pool at the bottom is huge, making a wide opening in the forest canopy. To get the most waterfalls per mileage, continue another 0.7 mile to Taitnapum Falls, which you can see from the trail through an opening in the trees.

Miles and Directions

0.0 Start from the Lower Lewis River Falls Trailhead, just behind the restrooms at the Lower Falls Recreation Area. Begin hiking upstream, and stay right along the river as you pass through the maze of trails in the campground.

0.2 Pass a boardwalk and stairs leading to a beach on the right.

1.6 Arrive at the middle waterfall.

2.5 Reach Upper Lewis River Falls. Past the falls, the trail climbs on a switchback.

3.2 Reach Taitnapum Falls, a good spot to turn around. Return the way you came.

6.4 Arrive back at the trailhead.

Hike information

Lodging

USDA Forest Service Lewis River Campground (at the trailhead), Gifford Pinchot National Forest, Mount St. Helens National Volcanic Monument; (360) 891-5000; www.fs.usda.gov/giffordpinchot

Old-growth Douglas fir

29 Hamilton Mountain Loop

[handwritten: 18 min from Skamania]

This hike in the Columbia Gorge has a little bit of everything the gorge offers—enchanting waterfalls and pools, wildflowers, views of volcanoes, and an incredible vantage of the Columbia River's deep channel. A ribbon of water dropping into a deep pothole of a pool at 1.1 miles is a highlight of the hike. It's rare to find such a long, scenic hike that you can do before the high country snow melts out.

Start: Day-use area near the campground at Beacon Rock State Park, north of WA 14
Distance: 8.3-mile lollipop
Hiking time: About 4.5 hours
Difficulty: Moderate due to length and elevation gain
Trail surface: Dirt trail
Elevation gain: 2,100 feet
Land status: State park
Nearest town: Stevenson

Best season: Year-round
Other trail users: Mountain bikers and equestrians in some sections
Canine compatibility: Leashed dogs allowed
Fees and permits: Discover Pass required to park at trailhead
Maps: USGS Beacon Rock; Green Trails no. 429, Bonneville Dam
Trail contacts: Beacon Rock State Park; (509) 427-8265

Finding the trailhead: Take exit 1A from I-5 in Vancouver and merge onto WA 14 East toward Camas. In 34.5 miles turn left (north) into the camping and day-use area at Beacon Rock State Park. GPS: N 45 37.95' / W 122 01.17'

[handwritten: Sun or mon ?]

The Hike

The Columbia River cuts right through the heart of the Cascades at the gorge. Thousand-foot-high cliffs and tall mountains on either side of the gap make for excellent early- and late-season hiking. The Oregon side of the gorge is known for its waterfalls, which cascade down the south side of the deep gorge toward the river. The Washington side is south-facing and sunnier, so it has an abundance of wildflowers. These flowers bloom in April and May, while the mountains are still snowy.

Hamilton Mountain has both spectacular waterfalls and pockets of colorful wildflowers, as well as views of Mount Hood, Mount Adams, Beacon Rock, and the big river. The trailhead is easy to get to, since it's less than an hour away from Portland, Oregon, and Vancouver, Washington, on paved roads. However, the hike is long and steep.

The trail begins climbing up the north flank of Hamilton Mountain from the day-use area at Beacon Rock State Park. It passes beneath power lines in a clear-cut thick with thimbleberries, salmonberries, and Oregon grape. Soon you're back in the forest, contouring gently up the mountain toward Hardy and Rodney Falls, which are a little more than 1.0 mile from the trailhead.

Pool of the winds on Hamilton Mountain ▶

Don't miss the path up to the Pool of the Winds, where Hardy Creek drops 30-feet into a hot tub–size pool of swirling water. The misty pool is surrounded by vertical rock on all sides, except for a narrow gap in the downhill side, where water spills out and continues its tumultuous course down rocky steps. Peer in the narrow opening and watch the spray and mist swirl around in the deep pool.

Soon after the falls, the trail passes an opening in the trees with views of the river and Beacon Rock. One-tenth mile later, go right at a junction toward the "most difficult" route up Hamilton Mountain. The route is shorter and steeper then the other trail at the fork, which the sign calls "difficult." The longer, "difficult" trail will be your return path. Now you'll begin climbing a steep ridge on the south side of Hamilton Mountain.

▶ Cascade Rapids—the riffle of water running through the Columbia Gorge—is actually the namesake for the entire Cascade Range. It's easy to forget when you're hiking in the Columbia Gorge, but the mountains on either side of the Columbia River are actually the crest of the Cascades, which the river cuts right through.

This is where the wildflowers start. There're Columbia lily, columbines, paintbrush, grass widow, gentians, Menzies' larkspur, and Indian pipe, which is a plant that doesn't use photosynthesis. Instead the waxy white plants get their energy through a parasitic relationship with certain fungi.

Continue up past wildflowers and views of broad basalt cliffs on the southeast side of Hamilton Mountain. In 3.2 miles the trail crosses the top of Hamilton Mountain. From the summit you can see Mounts Adams and Hood. Far below is Cascade Locks and Cascade Rapids on the Columbia River. The rapids were once the site of a giant landslide that made a land bridge across the river. Native Americans called the land bridge the "bridge of the gods," which is now the name of the man-made bridge across the Columbia.

From the top you can return the way you came or continue along the ridge at the top for a more gradual downhill. The trail goes north along a high open ridge until it comes to an open roadbed. Here it switches direction and continues down into the forest of Douglas firs, vine maples, and Oregon grape.

The trail traverses the west side of Hamilton Mountain above Hardy Creek until it meets up with the beginning of the loop near Hardy Falls.

Miles and Directions

0.0 Start at the trailhead at the north end of the day-use parking lot. The trailhead is signed TRAIL, and there's a map at a kiosk next to the trailhead.

0.4 Pass under power lines.

1.0 Pass a viewpoint of Hardy Falls. A downhill trail leads to a wooden platform above the falls.

1.1 Cross a wooden bridge over Hardy Creek just above Rodney Falls. A short uphill spur leads a couple hundred feet to the Pool of the Winds.

1.3 Pass a viewpoint of the Columbia River.

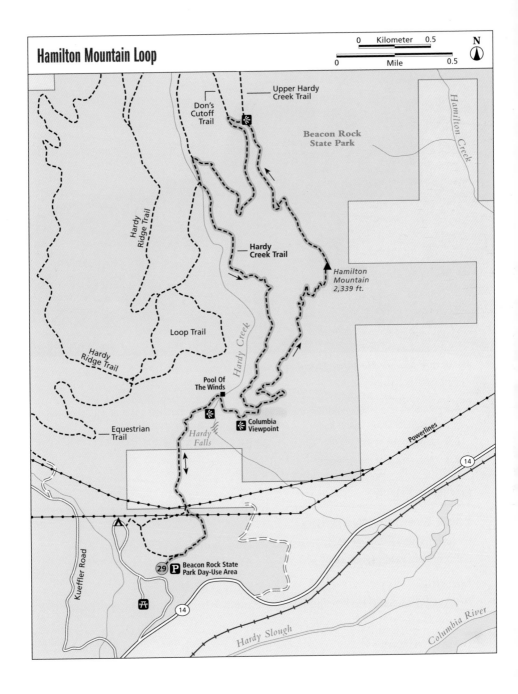

Hamilton Mountain Loop

0   Kilometer   0.5

0   Mile   0.5

N

Upper Hardy
Creek Trail

Don's
Cutoff
Trail

Beacon Rock
State Park

Hardy Ridge Trail

Hardy
Creek Trail

Hamilton
Mountain
2,339 ft.

Loop Trail

Hardy
Ridge Trail

Hardy Creek

Pool Of
The Winds

Equestrian
Trail

Hardy
Falls

Columbia
Viewpoint

Powerlines

14

Kueffler Road

29 P   Beacon Rock State
Park Day-Use Area

14

Hardy Slough

Hamilton Creek

Columbia River

1.4   Arrive at a fork in the road; go right up the "most difficult" route up Hamilton Mountain. The left path will be the return trail.

3.2   Reach the summit of Hamilton Mountain, a broad ridge.

Basalt cliffs beneath Hamilton Mountain's summit

4.2 Turn left at a junction with an equestrian trail. In 500 feet turn left again at a junction with a sign for Don's Cutoff Trail.

6.9 Arrive back at the junction with the "most difficult" trail.

8.3 Arrive back at the trailhead.

Hike Information

Local Events/Attractions

Columbia River Gorge Bluegrass Festival, Stevenson; last week in July; columbiagorgebluegrass.net

Lodging

Beacon Rock State Park (camping at the trailhead), 34841 SR 14, Stevenson; (509) 427-8625

Organizations

Friends of the Columbia Gorge; gorgefriends.org

Other Resources

Northwest Passage: The Great Columbia River, by William Dietrich

Honorable Mentions

| Dog Mountain

Dog Mountain is the go-to spot for spring wildflowers in the Columbia Gorge. It's a steep climb, and you'll gain nearly 3,000 vertical feet in the 8.0 mile round-trip. Fir trees cover the slopes on the first two-thirds of the hike, but the top third of the mountain is a bald, wide-open flowery paradise. It's covered in the sunflower-like blossoms of arrow leaf balsamroot, but an astonishing variety of flowers grow on the windy mountaintop. To really experience Dog Mountain in all its glory, you must go in spring. Most years, May is the month. If you miss the wildflower peak, relax; the views of the gorge aren't too bad either.

Take exit 1A from I-5 in Vancouver and merge onto WA 14 East toward Camas. Continue on WA 14 for 58 miles to the dirt parking lot at milepost 53 (14 miles east of Stevenson). The parking lot is signed DOG MOUNTAIN TRAILHEAD.

J Mount Beljica

Mount Beljica is similar to High Rock. It's a near-perfect vantage of Mount Rainier that's just 2.0 short miles from the trailhead. The trail is rough and steep at the beginning, but it soon levels out on a high ridge. At the halfway point you'll pass forested Lake Christine. It's a pretty little lake and a good place to pause before the final climb to the summit. The last 0.5 mile of trail is once again steep and rough to the summit, the site of an old lookout. Members of two families summited the peak in 1897 and named it with their first initials. The seven climbers were named Burgon, Elizabeth, Lucy, Jessie, Isabel, Clara, and Alex.

From Ashford drive east on WA 706 for 3.8 miles; turn left (north) onto FR 59, Copper Creek Road. Drive 3.4 miles to a junction and go left again onto FR 5920. You'll reach the Lake Christine Trailhead at the end of the road in 2.4 miles.

K Spray Park

If it were possible to rank the numerous parklike alpine meadows in Mount Rainier National Park, Spray Park would be near the top of the list. Meadow after flowery meadow spreads out between the subalpine firs, snow patches, and bare-rock moraines beneath Liberty Cap, the northwest peak of Mount Rainier. The trail to the park begins at Mowich Lake. It climbs on the wonderland trail past a short spur trail to Spray Falls and then switchbacks through forests and clearings. The out-and-back trip is 7.5 miles.

From Puyallup drive 13 miles east on WA 410 to Buckley. Turn right onto WA 165 and continue for 27 miles to Mowich Lake, passing Carbonado in 7.5 miles. The trailhead is at the south end of the Mowich Lake Campground.

L Grove of the Patriarchs

The 1.5-mile trail to Grove of the Patriarchs isn't much of a hike, but don't miss seeing the massive trees if you're on the east side of the park for other hikes. A short stroll through old-growth forest along the Ohanapecosh River leads to the main event: a grove of ancient Douglas firs, western red cedars, and western hemlocks. The behemoths have been growing for about 1,000 years on a small island in the river. Their thousands of needles grasp at the sun as their roots send water hundreds of feet upwards.

Drive 41 miles east from Enumclaw on WA 410 to a junction with WA 123. Go south on WA 123 and follow it for 11 miles to Mount Rainier National Park's Stevens Canyon entrance. Pay the entrance fee and park at the trailhead, just beyond the entrance.

M Lily Basin

Without a doubt, Snowgrass Flat is the classic hike in the Goat Rocks Wilderness. While the crowds are tromping up the dusty trail to Snowgrass Flat, you can walk a ridge 2,000 feet above Packwood Lake with Mount Rainier in the distance. It's a little more than 8.0 miles round-trip to a high point in a cirque below Johnson Peak, a 7,487-foot-tall multi-summited mass of Earth. This is a good place to turn around for a day hike, but the trail continues all the way to Goat Lake and Snowgrass Flat.

From Morton drive 30 miles east on US 12 and turn right onto FR 48 (2 miles west of Packwood). Follow this road 10 miles to the trailhead on the right.

Northeast Washington

Northeast Washington—between WA 97 and Idaho—has the state's sparsest population. Consequently, it's easy to find solitude on the hikes in this section. The region is also incredibly varied. The Okanogan Highlands and some of the western region of this section are covered in shrub-steppe desert, with sagebrush and rabbitbrush. The ice-age floods that carved deep canyons and potholes in some of Southeast Washington also altered the landscape in the northeast corner of the state. The Grand Coulee, at one end of the Northrup Canyon hike, is perhaps the state's best example of the monumental landscape changes caused by the ice-age floods.

Most of this part of the state is mountainous. The land near the Okanogan River, this section's western boundary, is a high plateau covered in sagebrush, ponderosa pines, and rolling hills. Farther east, the Kettle River Range between Republic and Kettle Falls parallels Roosevelt Lake and the Columbia River, which are east of the range. These mountains are high, remote, and beautiful, yet often overlooked by hikers. The crest of the Kettles is gentle and open, with incredible views and miles of trail.

In the far northeast corner of the state, a branch of the Selkirk Mountains extend into Washington. This area is a little wetter than the Kettle River Range, with vegetation similar to the Cascades. The Selkirks connect with vast wildlife habitat in northern Idaho and British Columbia. Grizzly bears, gray wolves, and the lower 48's last herd of woodland caribou roam the Selkirk Mountains. The Kettle Crest and the Selkirks are both covered in a mixed forest of pines and fir trees. Larches grow in both areas as well but are more prolific in the Kettles. To see the larches turn a golden yellow and lose their leaves, go in mid-fall.

This section doesn't have glaciers or volcanoes. But nearly anywhere you hike in this corner of the state you'll find solitude, peaceful forests, and big views into wild country.

Open forests on the side of Grassy Top (hike 34)
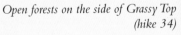

30 Northrup Canyon

The only natural forest in Grant County grows between the vertical walls of Northrup Canyon in Steamboat Rock State Park. The hike through the canyon is as rich in human history as it is in natural history. Remains of the Northrup family's homestead and other human artifacts are hidden in nooks between the 200-foot-tall walls. As the canyon narrows and begins to climb toward Northrup Lake, the trail is characterized by views of rugged granite and towering basalt.

Start: Northrup Canyon parking area on Northrup Road (The sign says NORTHRUP CANYON NATURAL AREA.)
Distance: 6.6 miles out and back
Hiking time: About 4 hours
Difficulty: Moderate due to steep sections
Trail surface: Gravel road through a flat valley, turning to dirt and rock trail over granite outcrops
Seasons: Best Oct to June, when temperatures are cooler
Other trail users: Equestrians and mountain bikers

Canine compatibility: Leashed dogs allowed
Land status: State park
Nearest town: Electric City
Fees and permits: Discover Pass required
Schedule: Year-round, dawn until dusk
Map: USGS Steamboat Rock SE
Trail contacts: Steamboat Rock State Park, PO Box 730, Electric City 99123; (509) 633-1304; stateparks.com/steamboat_rock.html
Other: No overnight camping allowed

Finding the trailhead: From Coulee City drive north on WA 155 along Grand Coulee and Banks Lake for 22 miles to Northrup Road/Northrup Canyon Natural Area. Take a right onto the gravel road marked NORTHRUP CANYON NATURAL AREA and continue 0.7 mile to the parking lot. GPS: N47 51.94' / W119 04.98'

The Hike

Northrup Canyon has everything: Grant County's only forest, with lodgepole and ponderosa pines, fir, and quaking aspen; meadows, cliffs, chunks of bedrock granite protruding in areas where ice-age floods scoured away the much more recent basalt; an old homestead with vacant buildings succumbing to gravity; and a trout-filled lake.

The lush valley, bare rock, and sharp granite ridges between the towering walls of Northrup Canyon once bustled with human activity. Four generations of the Northrup family lived between the canyon walls, where they grew fruit and vegetables and raised animals. People from neighboring counties rode into the canyon on horses and wagons on an old stagecoach road on the south wall of the canyon to sample the Northrups' produce.

Despite the many human artifacts hidden in its forgotten corners, Northrup Canyon is now a nature sanctuary and a great place to get away from the humans at nearby Banks Lake. Cougars and bears spend time in the canyon, and it's a winter

Basalt cliffs in Northrup Canyon

home for as many as one hundred bald eagles. In fact, the stagecoach road near the beginning of the trail is closed in the winter to protect roosting eagles.

As the trail enters the canyon near Banks Lake, the desert fades away and becomes a forest (or at least what passes for a forest in Grant County). Big pines and firs cast shade over the old dirt road in the first section of the hike. Later on, a creekbed provides moisture for quaking aspens, serviceberry, and squaw currant.

The trail to the right about 200 yards from the trailhead is an old stagecoach road that used to be the main road between Almira and Brewster. It leads to a plateau atop the south wall of the canyon, with views back toward Steamboat Rock. Stay left and continue on the road. This can be confusing, because the Northrup Canyon Trail is a road and the old stagecoach road is a trail.

On the left side of the trail in the first 0.25 mile of the hike is one of several large can dumps. The piles of rusted cans were left behind by Grand Coulee Dam construction workers. Apparently garbage becomes artifact at some point, because the cans are considered a historical site and should not be moved.

After the initial forested sections, you'll pass through an open meadow with views of the canyon walls. On your left, several giant ovular chunks of basalt seem to be leaning against one another on the canyon wall. Views of basalt formations surround you in all directions. Stinging nettle and even some poison oak line portions of the road in the meadow, but the road is plenty wide, and they are easy to avoid.

The views continue along the pleasant road until you reach the remains of the homestead. Several long-abandoned buildings are succumbing to the pull of gravity, while white and lavender lilacs and a peach tree live on nearby. The newer white building was used seasonally by park rangers until recently. Bearing right along the south wall of the canyon will lead you to even more forgotten fruit trees.

The hike to the homestead is gentle, scenic, and easy. Turning around here makes for a good short hike, but the gem of this hike is the next 1.5 miles of trail that climbs up the canyon toward Northrup Lake.

From the homestead the trail climbs steeply from the valley floor. Look for a sign with a hiker on it near an old henhouse. The trail goes north from the homestead. In this section, a bare spine of granite bedrock runs down the center of the canyon. Granite is rare in the Columbia Basin. Actually, any rock other than basalt is rare here. The granite ridge was covered by basalt until ice-age floods eroded the basalt from the canyon floor, exposing the ancient granite. The granite gives this steep, hilly section of the hike a high alpine feel. If you forget where you are, you may expect to see mountain goats. All the while, basalt cliffs still loom high on either side of the ridge.

After a steep climb, the trail levels out and you pass through a maze of granite and crumbling basalt boulders shaded by pine trees. This upper section of trail is also packed with wildflowers, including alumroot, balsamroot, lupines, and blue bells.

The spring-fed Northrup Lake is small, full of trout, and a haven for birds. Cliff swallows, western kingbirds, tanagers, meadowlarks, and hummingbirds play near the blue water, and you may see falcons, ravens, hawks, eagles, or turkey vultures flying high above.

The canyon has several other sights to explore that are not on the trail. You can discover several seasonal lakes, or more can dumps and other human artifacts. The bare granite face of Gibraltar Rock, near the equestrian parking lot, is a hot spot for rock climbers.

If you make it back to your car and you're hungry for more, head for Steamboat Rock, which is a couple miles west. The hike up Steamboat Rock is a short, steep grind up to a plateau with 360-degree views of Grand Coulee and 600 acres of sagebrush-filled wandering.

Miles and Directions

0.0 Start at the trailhead at the end of Northrup Road / Northrup Canyon Natural Area.

0.1 Bear left to stay on the trail. The old stagecoach road takes off to the right.

0.2 Pass a portion of a historical can dump on the left side of the trail.

1.5 Cross Northrup Creek on a wooden bridge.

1.9 Arrive at the site of old homestead with several buildings. The trail continues to the north behind the henhouse. Look for a sign with a hiker near the buildings.

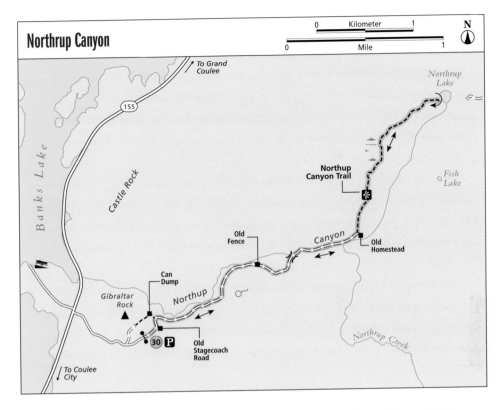

Northrup Canyon

2.2 Climb a granite ridge to a view back down into the canyon and toward the homestead.

3.3 Reach Northrup Lake. Return the way you came.

6.6 Arrive back at the trailhead.

Hike Information

Local Information

Grand Coulee Dam Area Chamber of Commerce, PO Box 760, Grand Coulee 99133; (509) 633-3074; grandcouleedam.org

Local Events/Attractions

Grand Coulee Dam; (509) 633-9265; usbr.gov/pn/grandcoulee

Lodging

Steamboat Rock State Park Campground, Jones Bay Campground, at Banks Lake on WA 155; (509) 633-1304

Restaurants

Teepee Drive-in, 211 Midway Ave., Grand Coulee; (509) 633-2111

Other Resources

Northrup Canyon: A Living History, by Norman Northrup (normannorthrup.com)

IN ADDITION: LIFE IN NORTHRUP CANYON

John Warden Northrup arrived in the canyon that now bears his name in 1829 after several failed marriages, career changes, and years of wandering in the Northwest. The fertile soil, steady supply of water, and good fishing attracted Northrup. When he moved to the canyon, it was the wettest, most fertile spot in the county, as Grand Coulee Dam and its reservoirs did not yet exist.

Northrup quickly got to work creating an irrigation system from the spring-fed stream and planting the first orchard in Grant County. He grew twenty-nine varieties of trees, along with vegetables, grains, and animals. He also successfully raised cotton, tobacco, peanuts, and a family in the canyon. By the time the last Northrup moved away from the canyon in the late 1920s, four generations had lived between the basalt walls.

The Northrups weren't just subsistence farmers. The road up the south side of the canyon was the main route between Brewster and Almira, and people came from all over Grand, Lincoln, and Douglas Counties to buy fruit and vegetables from the Northrups' farm. By the turn of the twentieth century, food from the canyon was even going to the fancier restaurants of Spokane.

The Northrups owned the majority of the canyon, but several other families also called the canyon home. The Schiebner brothers, who were hired by the government to build the section of stagecoach road through the canyon, owned a sawmill 1 mile from the entrance to the canyon. The Dillman family, who farmed goats, lived at the canyon entrance.

According to Norman Northrup, John Warden Northrup's great-grandson, the canyon was also home to a cougar with a weird sense of humor (she seemed to enjoy scaring visitors), and it was the scene of a murder.

When John Warden Northrup's health began to fail in 1894, his third wife, Caty, leased part of the farm to Israel Sanford. Shortly after, in a dispute over the ownership of fruit trees, Israel killed Caty in the sagging log house just south of the white house just before the present-day trail starts climbing toward Northrup Lake. Sanford was later acquitted by a jury for being of unsound mental health.

When John Warden Northrup died in 1901, his son George took over the farm with his wife, Joella. George had worked as a sheriff, banker, real estate agent, journalist, lawyer, preacher, and miner, and he never liked farming. When he split up with Joella over financial problems a few years later, Joella took over the farm.

Joella, with the help of a hired man and her children, worked hard to make the farm pay. She clawed her way out of the debt that George had accumulated and later became known as the "Canyon Lady." In his book *Northrup Canyon: A Living History*, Norman Northrup describes Joella as "a tough, no nonsense, feisty lady, who was not afraid to spit in the eye of the devil himself."

During the next twenty-five years, the canyon became known as a great place to picnic or visit when passing through on the stagecoach road. The road got a lot of traffic at the beginning of the twentieth century. It not only connected Almira and Brewster but also military forts in Spokane, Chelan, and Okanogan. According to Norman Northrup's book, when the Northrups spotted people coming through the canyon, they always put another chicken in the pot.

In 1926 or 1927, depending on the source, Joella and her son Charlie—the last Northrups on the farm—packed up and left. Water had become scarce in the canyon. Also, the rise of trucking had made their produce less profitable.

To learn more, check out *Northrup Canyon: A Living History*. The first half of the forty-eight-page self-published book is a historical account of the canyon; the second half is full of wild stories and tall tales about a tornado dropping thousands of fish into the canyon, the cougar with a weird sense of humor, and the Northrup boys killing snakes from horseback with whips.

31 Whistler Canyon

Sun, cliffs, and sagebrush fill this little canyon just off US 97. A herd of bighorn sheep roam the canyon and graze among the rock walls and yellow balsamroot flowers. The route snakes up between the granite cliffs to an overlook toward the meandering Okanogan River.

Start: Signed trailhead on the east side of US 97, just north of milepost 329
Distance: 4.8 miles out and back
Hiking time: About 2.5 hours
Difficulty: Easy
Trail surface: Dirt trail.
Elevation gain: 1,000 feet
Land status: Bureau of Land Management, national forest

Nearest town: Oroville
Best season: Mar through Nov
Other trail users: Equestrians, pack animals, mountain bikers
Canine compatibility: Leashed dogs allowed
Fees and permits: None
Maps: USGS Oroville
Trail contacts: Okanogan National Forest, Tonasket Ranger District; (509) 486-2186

Finding the trailhead: From Tonasket drive north on US 97 for 15.3 miles. Turn right onto the white gravel road, just after a sign for the Whistler Canyon Trailhead. Or drive 2 miles south from Oroville. The trailhead is signed from either direction. Follow the access road for 0.2 mile to the trailhead parking lot. GPS: N 48 54.19' / W119 25.37'

The Hike

This cliffy, sagebrush-filled canyon is right off US 97 and hikeable nearly year-round. The canyon is in the western edge of a 36,000-acre patch of Okanogan National Forest just east of Oroville and Tonasket. The canyon was plagued by access issues for years. In 2009 the Okanogan Valley Chapter of the Backcountry Horsemen of Washington, in partnership with the Okanogan-Wenatchee National Forest, secured a new trailhead into this scenic nook of wilderness. In December 2013 Okanogan County commissioners sold some land around the new trailhead at auction, including some of the cliffs. Kinross Gold Corp. purchased the land and a spokesperson said they plan to "preserve it as a reserve for the public."

A herd of bighorn sheep roam the canyon, browsing the grasses and shrubs amid the sagebrush, rabbitbrush, and bitterbrush. The hike described here climbs through the granite and gneiss cliffs to the western edge of a higher, mountainous area in the center of this block of forest. Here you're at more than 2,000 feet in a dense forest of pines and firs. It's much different than the shrub-steppe desert at the lower elevations of the canyon. You can explore several lakes and hidden viewpoints peeking out of the forest in the area's higher elevations, but the first few miles of trail up to the

Shrubby mountain ash trees alive with color on a gray day above Whistler Canyon

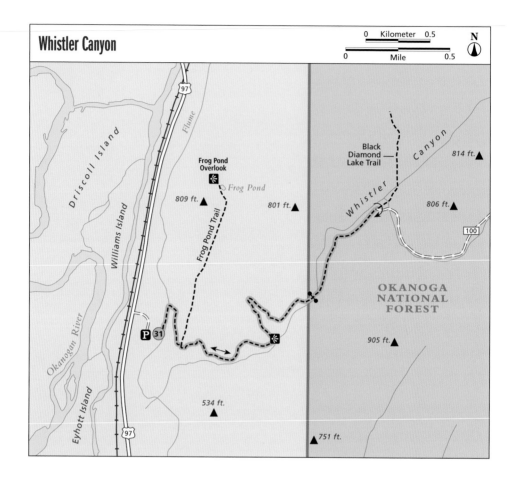

0   Kilometer   0.5

0   Mile   0.5

N

97

Flume

Driscoll Island

Frog Pond Overlook

Frog Pond

Black Diamond Lake Trail

Canyon

814 ft.

809 ft.

801 ft.

Whistler

806 ft.

100

Williams Island

Frog Pond Trail

OKANOGA NATIONAL FOREST

Okanogan River

P 31

905 ft.

534 ft.

Eyhott Island

97

751 ft.

canyon are the most exciting. They provide sweeping views of the valley and a chance to see a variety of wildlife.

The trail goes gradually uphill immediately, weaving expertly through rocky ledges, cliff bands, and giant boulders. The view improves instantly. Only an occasional ponderosa pine obscures the sight of the Okanogan River meandering through its wide floodplain. Wild roses and desert flowers bloom in spring, and fuzzy yellow flowers burst forth from the abundant rabbitbrush in fall, accompanying reddening mountain ash leaves.

At 0.4 mile from the trailhead, the Frog Pond Trail veers left from the main trail. This 0.8-mile path is a great side trip. It travels through a narrow valley below a cliff band to a tiny wet spot next to an overlook of Oroville and the river valley.

In just over 1.0 mile you'll reach a short, nearly vertical cliff band, which the trail passes under. This is the top of the steep section of climbing and the climax of the views. For the best of Whistler Canyon, turn around here and explore the Frog Pond Trail on the way out. Or continue farther into the forest. A map at the trailhead kiosk shows a maze of trails leading deeper into the trees.

Miles and Directions

0.0 Start at the parking lot and follow the gravel trail past the kiosk to the trailhead beneath the cliffs.

0.4 Continue straight at the junction with the signed Frog Pond Trail, which goes left (north). (*Option:* This trail makes a great 1.6-mile out-and-back side trip.)

1.1 Reach the beginning of the canyon and the best views down toward the Okanogan River.

1.8 Cross a gate onto national forest land.

2.4 Arrive at a junction with a trail to Black Diamond Lake. This is a good place to turn around. Return the way you came.

4.8 Arrive back at the trailhead.

Hike Information

Organizations

Okanogan Highlands Alliance; okanoganhighlands.org

Friends of the Whistler Canyon Facebook page (updated information about the status of the trailhead)

Local Events/Attractions

Tonasket Farmers Market, Tonasket; Thursdays from mid-May through October; tonasketfarmersmarket.com/

Oroville Salmon Festival, Oroville; last weekend in September; salmonfestoroville.org

32 Iller Creek Conservation Area

This low-elevation loop right outside Spokane leads through a pleasant forest to tall granite cliffs and views over the rolling green Palouse country. The granite cliffs will surprise you by appearing as you round a bend on the trail. From the top of a rocky ridge, you'll descend among grass and flowers back toward the Spokane Valley.

Start: Parking lot on the north side of the Iller Creek Conservation Area at a switchback on Holman Road
Distance: 5.0-mile loop
Hiking time: About 2.5 hours
Difficulty: Easy due to distance and gentle terrain
Trail surface: Dirt trail
Elevation gain: 1,125 feet
Land status: County-managed conservation area

Nearest town: Spokane
Best season: Spring and fall; also a popular winter snowshoe route
Other trail users: Mountain bikers
Canine compatibility: Leashed dogs allowed
Fees and permits: None required
Maps: USGS Spokane SE; Iller Creek map, available at inlandnorthwesttrails.org
Trail contacts: Spokane County Parks and Recreation Department; (509) 477-4730

Finding the trailhead: From I-90 take exit 287 for Argonne Road. Go south on Argonne Road for 1.5 miles, at which point you pass Sprague Street and Argonne Road becomes S Dishman-Mica Road. In about 2 miles turn right onto Schafer Road at a stoplight. At a stop sign in 0.9 mile, turn right (east) onto 44th Avenue. In 0.2 mile turn left onto Farr Road and continue 0.3 mile to a stop sign. Turn right (east) onto Holman Road and continue 0.7 mile to a hairpin turn. Park on the shoulder outside the gate to the Iller Creek Conservation Area. GPS: N 47 36.10' / W 117 16.90'

The Hike

This loop hike through a conservation area outside Spokane is convenient and varied. The trailhead is barely outside the urban area but quickly leads deep into the forest to a ridge full of towering granite crags. These crags, called the Rocks of Sharon, jut straight up and lean out toward the Palouse country to the south, a lowland plain of rolling green hills. It's the perfect forest for a quick wilderness escape.

This trail loops through most of the 876-acre Iller Creek Conservation Area. The area is part of the larger Dishman Hills Conservation Area, which is managed by Spokane County Parks, the state Department of Natural Resources, and the Dishman Hills Conservancy.

These naked rocks and their huge prominence are amplified by the gentle terrain of the rolling Palouse wheat fields far below. From the trail by Rocks of Sharon, you can see south out over the plain to Steptoe and Kamiak Buttes, the two tallest humps on the horizon. These hills are about 50 miles away. It's a perfect vantage for enjoying

Big Rock and the Palouse Region

the big sky of Eastern Washington. Along the trail you can also see the wide Spokane Valley and the Selkirk Mountains in Idaho to the east.

Enter the gate at the trailhead and bear right at the junction, staying on the west side of the creek. A mixed forest of pines and firs lines the trail. Thimbleberries and currants make up much of the understory. This path is wide and easy to follow, even in winter. The trip to Rocks of Sharon is a popular snowshoe. At 1.7 miles from the trailhead, bear right at a junction. The trail to the left makes a shorter loop, but it doesn't go all the way to the hilltop views.

Two miles from the trailhead you'll be walking through a lush forest that resembles Western Washington, when suddenly the Rocks of Sharon appear. Stroll beneath the monoliths along a high ridge littered with granite rock. The bigger rock faces are to the right of the trail. The biggest of the crags, simply named Big Rock, is more than 200-feet-tall.

The views don't end at Big Rock. From the hike's high point at 2.3 miles, the trail winds to the north and begins descending on an open ridge covered in phlox, balsamroot, lupines, and other wildflowers. Take in views of the Spokane Valley and the forest that surrounds you as you make your way slowly down the trail. The views

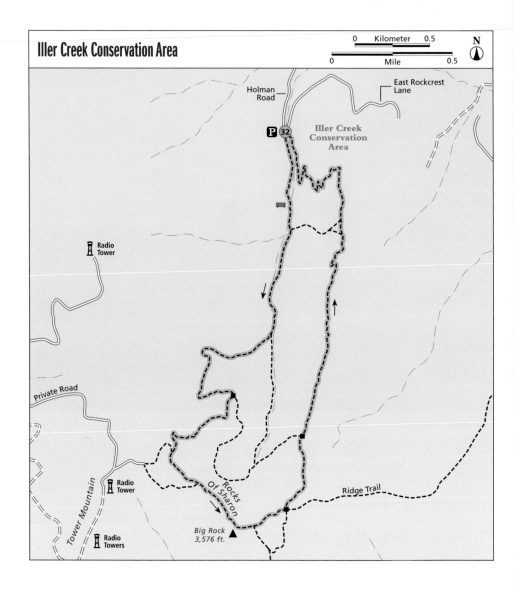

0   Kilometer   0.5

0   Mile   0.5

N

Holman
Road

East Rockcrest
Lane

P 32

Iller Creek
Conservation
Area

Radio
Tower

Private Road

Radio
Tower

Tower Mountain

Radio
Towers

Rocks
Of Sharon

Big Rock
3,576 ft.

Ridge Trail

don't cease until you begin switchbacking downhill toward the creek, 0.5 mile from the parking lot.

Miles and Directions

0.0   Start at the trailhead on Holman Road; stay right at the fork.

0.3   Pass a bench on the side of the trail.

1.7   Stay right at a junction with a cutoff trail for the shorter loop.

2.3   Pass the Rocks of Sharon to the right (south) of the trail; 0.2 mile later you'll pass the remains of a red pickup truck.

2.9 Bear left at a junction with a small trail.

3.2 Bear right at a junction with the shorter loop trail.

5.0 Arrive back at the trailhead.

Hike Information

Local Information

www.visitspokane.com

Organizations

Spokane Mountaineers; spokanemountaineers.org

Inland Northwest Trails Coalition; inlandnorthwesttrails.org

Nootka rose flower

33 Sherman Peak Loop

Sunshine, high lumpy mountains, larches, and views spanning Washington's east side from the Cascades to the Selkirk Mountains are the highlights of the loop hike around Sherman Peak. From a high, paved trailhead, it doesn't take long to get to some of the best views in the Kettle River Range.

Start: Trailhead at Sherman Pass on US 20
Distance: 6.1-mile lollipop
Hiking time: About 3.5 hours
Difficulty: Moderate due to elevation gain and distance
Trail surface: Dirt trail
Elevation gain: 1,100 feet
Land status: National forest
Nearest town: Republic

Best season: July through Oct
Other trail users: Equestrians, mountain bikers
Canine compatibility: Leashed dogs allowed
Fees and permits: None required
Map: USGS Sherman Peak and Copper Butte
Trail contacts: Colville National Forest, Republic Ranger District; (509) 775-7400

Finding the trailhead: From Tonasket drive east on US 20 for 40 miles. Turn right onto Clark Avenue in downtown Republic to stay on US 20. Continue 16.6 miles to the top of Sherman Pass to an access road going north, with a sign for recreational opportunities. Continue 0.1 mile to a parking lot. Alternately, reach Sherman Pass from Kettle Falls by driving 26.3 miles west on US 20. GPS: N 48 36.48' / W 118 28.63'

The Hike

Between the North Cascades and the Selkirks, a high, lonely mountain range called the Kettle River Range stretches into Canada. The range runs north to south between the towns of Republic and Kettle Falls and is intersected by US 20 at Sherman Pass, the highest paved mountain pass in the state. The Kettles are tall, remote, and supremely quiet. Even the Sherman Peak Loop, the easiest trailhead in the range to reach, is lonely.

▶ **The Kettle Range is sacred to the Colville Nation. Young people entering adulthood went on vision quests in the mountain range.**

Sherman Peak, a lofty mountain just south of Sherman Pass, is one of the taller peaks in the southern end of the Kettle Crest Range. A relatively easy trail loops around the peak, affording incredible views of the Kettles. At the southern end of the loop, the trail joins the Kettle Crest Trail, which roams north–south along the spine of the Kettles for about 45 miles. Some hikers climb Sherman Peak off-trail from the south end of the loop. The trail around the mountain offers views in all directions because much of the forest burned during the 1988 White Mountain Fire. Vegetation along the Sherman Peak Loop alternates between forest and charred areas quickly growing up with young larches and lodgepole pines.

Snow Peak Cabin, 1.4 miles from Sherman Peak

From the parking lot, the trail dips into a narrow drainage before climbing back toward US 20. When you get to the road, look for the other end of the trail just uphill. It's hidden from sight behind a boulder. Next you'll switchback uphill for 0.7 mile to the junction with the loop trail. Turn right (west) and come out of the forest into an open, burned area called Gleason's Gallop. Just downhill, the larches are tall and abundant. They seem to turn gold a little later than larches in the Cascades. In season, this is a fantastic spot to watch the delicate needles change colors before falling off.

Brittle, sun-bleached snags stand throughout this area and litter the ground. They frequently blow down, so expect to climb over and under some logs on this hike. The Sherman Loop Trail joins the Kettle Crest Trail 3.1 miles from the trailhead. Bear left to continue the loop, or go right to hike beneath Snow Peak and explore the Kettle Crest Trail toward the Snow Peak Cabin. The forest service and several clubs completed the cozy log cabin in 1995 after several years of work. You can reserve the cabin for a reasonable nightly fee.

On the south side of Sherman Peak, the mountain hides any evidence of the highway, giving the area a wild and remote feeling. The trail remains fairly level, swelling between 6,100 feet and 6,400 feet as it continues to contour around the mountain. The east side of the mountain yields a long, unobstructed view toward the South

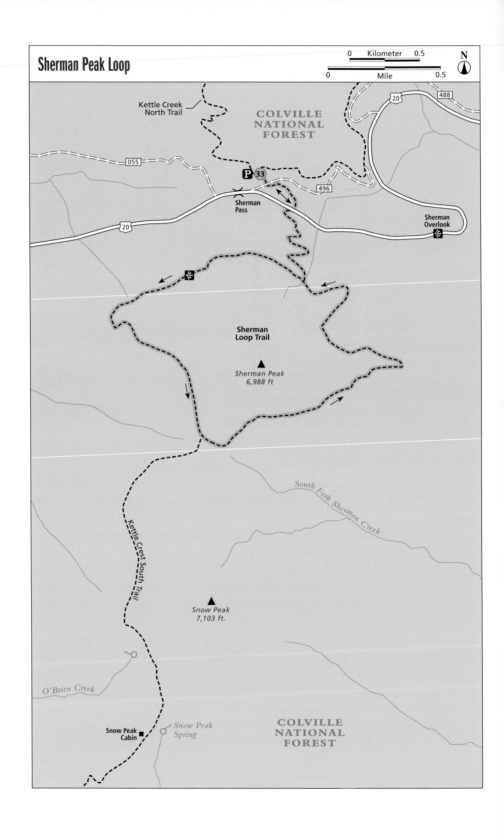

Sherman Peak Loop

Kettle Creek
North Trail

COLVILLE
NATIONAL
FOREST

055

20

P 33

Sherman
Pass

496

20

Sherman
Overlook

Sherman
Loop Trail

▲
Sherman Peak
6,988 ft

South Fork Shermon Creek

Kettle Crest South Trail

▲
Snow Peak
7,103 ft.

O'Brien Creek

Snow Peak
Cabin

Snow Peak
Spring

COLVILLE
NATIONAL
FOREST

0   Kilometer   0.5

0   Mile   0.5

N

Fork Sherman Creek valley. To the south you can see Snow Peak, Barnaby Buttes, and White Mountain, which the Kettle Crest South Trail weaves through.

After crossing a pass between Sherman Peak and a minor high point to the east, you'll switchback into a wide bowl on the mountain's east side. This is one of the most heavily burned sections of the hike. Next the trail crosses a ridge onto the north side of the peak below a cliff band high on the mountain. Talus extends almost to the trail in the final section before the path links up with the trail back to the parking lot.

Rather than climbing off-trail to Sherman Peak's summit, a better way to extend the trip is to walk an extra 1.4 miles south on the Kettle Crest South Trail to the Snow Peak Cabin, which sits in a beautiful and remote saddle between Snow Peak and Bald Mountain.

Miles and Directions

0.0 Start on the Kettle Crest South Trail 13. The trail dips into a drainage and back up toward US 20.

0.4 Cross US 20. Look for the trail just out of sight uphill, behind a boulder.

1.1 Turn right at a junction with Sherman Loop Trail 72. This is the beginning of the loop.

1.8 Pass through a burned area called Gleason's Gallop. Here there are many larches and views to the north.

3.0 Reach a junction with the Kettle Crest South Trail. Roam along this trail, or bear left to continue the loop.

5.0 Turn right onto the Kettle Crest South Trail and head back toward the parking lot, the end of the Sherman Loop Trail.

6.1 Arrive back at the trailhead.

Option

From the junction with the Kettle Crest South Trail on the south side of Sherman Peak, continue 1.4 miles south to Snow Peak Cabin.

Hike Information

Local Events/Attractions

Stonerose Interpretive Center and Eocene Fossil Site, Republic; (509) 775-2295; stonerosefossil.org

Lodging

USDA Forest Service Sherman Pass Overlook Campground, Colville National Forest, Republic Ranger District, just east of Sherman Pass on US 20; (509) 775-7400

Restaurants

Republic Brewing Company, Old Fire Hall, 26 Clark Ave., Republic; (509) 775-2700; republicbrew.com

34 Grassy Top

This 7.6-mile hike quickly climbs a tall ridge and then traverses across its top to a broad high point. From Grassy Top, the view into Idaho is supreme—ridge after ridge rolls into the distance. Grizzly bears, moose, elk, gray wolves, and woodland caribou dwell in this wild corner of the state.

Start: Trailhead just west of Pass Creek Pass

Distance: 7.6 miles out and back

Hiking time: About 4 hours

Difficulty: Moderate

Trail surface: Dirt trail

Elevation gain: 925 feet

Land status: National forest

Nearest town: Metaline Falls

Best season: July through Oct

Other trail users: Equestrians, mountain bikers

Canine compatibility: Leashed dogs allowed

Fees and permits: None required

Maps: USGS Pass Creek; Colville National Forest map

Trail contacts: Colville National Forest, Sullivan Lake Ranger District; (509) 446-7500; www.fs.fed.us/r6/colville

Finding the trailhead: From Metaline Falls drive north on WA 31 for 2.1 miles and turn right onto Sullivan Lake Road. In 4.7 miles (0.5 mile before reaching Sullivan Lake) turn left onto FR 22 (Sullivan Creek Road). At 5.3 miles from Sullivan Lake Road, go right at a junction to remain on FR 22. Continue for 7 miles to Pass Creek Pass and park on the shoulder. The trailhead is 0.1 mile west of the pass, on the south side of the road. GPS: N48 47.90' / W117 08.03'

The Hike

The part of the Selkirk Mountains in Northeast Washington is really the middle of nowhere. You're unlikely to see another hiker on these trails, and the views stretch forever into wilderness in Idaho and British Columbia.

The majority of the trail to Grassy Top's broad, forested summit runs along a high ridge north of the peak. This is the southern end of the Shedroof Divide, a prominent ridge that runs north until it meets the South Salmo River, just a couple miles from the Canadian Border. The summit isn't steep. You can walk around the area to find views in every direction, but there's always an interesting view on the ridge walk between the high trailhead and the summit.

From the trailhead west of Pass Creek Pass, the trail drops 50 feet or so until it comes to a trail register. From here you'll contour around a ridge and begin switchbacking uphill, climbing about 500 feet to the grassy open country atop the ridge. Engelmann spruce, lodgepole pines, and larches grow amid patches of grass and huckleberries. Chances are grouse will come flapping and fluttering out of the trees and brush as you walk the divide.

The trail slowly weaves from the west side to the east side of the ridge and then back and forth again. Each time, it passes beneath stubby summits on the way to

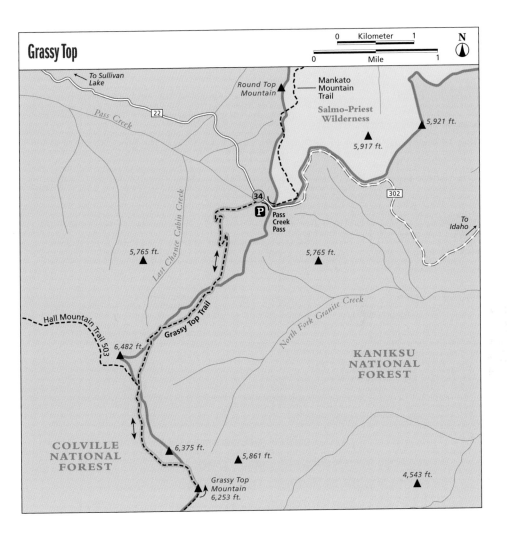

0   Kilometer   1

0   Mile   1

N

To Sullivan
Lake

Round Top
Mountain

Mankato
Mountain
Trail

Pass Creek

22

Salmo-Priest
Wilderness

5,921 ft.

5,917 ft.

34

P

302

Pass
Creek
Pass

To
Idaho

Last Chance Cabin Creek

5,765 ft.

5,765 ft.

Hall Mountain Trail 503

Grassy Top Trail

North Fork Granite Creek

6,482 ft.

KANIKSU
NATIONAL
FOREST

COLVILLE
NATIONAL
FOREST

6,375 ft.

5,861 ft.

4,543 ft.

Grassy Top
Mountain
6,253 ft.

Grassy Top. In 2.6 miles a trail goes right (west) 8.0 miles to Hall Mountain, a peak on the east edge of Sullivan Lake.

This hike is about the journey as much as the destination. Since the trailhead is so high, you don't have to climb far for the views. The summit of Grassy Top is anti-climactic. It's fairly flat, and though it is grassy, trees crowd most of the sides. It does offer a long view to the east. Hike a couple hundred more feet south from the summit to see the endless mountains, ridges, and rolling hills to the south. It's a good spot to plop down in the grass and spend some time recharging.

Miles and Directions

0.0 Start from the trailhead just west of the parking area at Pass Creek Pass.

2.6 Bear left at a junction with Trail 503, toward Hall Mountain.

3.8 Arrive at the broad summit of Grassy Top. Return the way you came.

7.6 Arrive back at the trailhead.

Hike Information

Local Events/Attractions

The International Selkirk Loop, 280-mile scenic drive through the Selkirk Mountains; selkirkloop.org

The Cutter Theatre, 302 Park St., Metaline Falls; historic theater and hotel; (509) 446-4108; cuttertheatre.com

Lodging

USDA Forest Service Sullivan Lake Campground, on the north end of Sullivan Lake, Colville National Forest, Sullivan Lake Ranger District; (509) 446-7500; www.fs.fed .us/r6/colville

Restaurants

Cathy's Cafe, 221 E. Fifth Ave., Metaline Falls; (509) 446-2447

WOLVES IN WASHINGTON

Few animals are more feared by humans than wolves. The big bad wolf is a common villain in literature and mythology throughout the world. However, the cunning pack animals are also revered in several cultures for their ability to hunt, and some mythologies credit wolves with founding civilizations and even giving birth to the first humans.

One hundred years ago, the Washington State government paid a bounty for gray wolf pelts, and the keystone species was dwindling. Now wolves are slowly returning to the Northwest. This time they're a protected endangered species in the western half of the state, and their return is celebrated by biologists and wildlife lovers.

In the mid-1990s the US Fish and Wildlife Service introduced sixty-six gray wolves from Canada into Montana, Wyoming, and Idaho. At that time, about sixty wolves were thought to already live in the northwest corner of Montana.

Lone wolves will leave the pack and roam hundreds of miles in search of a mate. In 2008 Fish and Wildlife biologists confirmed the presence of wolves near Twisp, in north-central Washington. They captured and radio-collared two adult wolves and caught six pups on video. That pack, which they named the Lookout Pack, was the first confirmed wolf pack in Washington State in more than seventy years.

By March 2013 nine confirmed packs denned in Washington, numbering at least fifty-one wolves total. The packs are concentrated in the Selkirks and other highlands in the north-

Layers upon layers of ridges rolling into Idaho

east corner of the state. But three packs—the Lookout, Teanaway, and Wenatchee Packs—live in the Cascades. The Teanaway Pack, roaming north of Cle Elum, is the farthest west.

According to Fish and Wildlife biologists, wolves are necessary for a healthy ecosystem. A study on wolves reintroduced in Yellowstone National Park found that wolves helped feed everything from bald eagles to beetles. When a pack of wolves takes down an elk or a deer, it often can't finish all the meat. Scavengers flock to finish the leftovers. In Yellowstone predatory birds benefit most from wolf leftovers because they'll travel long distances to find carrion. Ravens especially are attuned to wolf packs and will follow them for their leftovers.

While wolves in Yellowstone help control elk, moose, and deer populations, they also help maintain scavenger populations. Before wolves were reintroduced, more large ungulates starved around the same time of year, toward the end of winter. But that provided more carrion than scavengers could eat before it rotted. The presence of wolves in Yellowstone makes smaller amounts of carrion meat available more regularly throughout the year. This helps sustain scavenger species more effectively.

But not everyone likes wolves. Ranchers whose cattle graze on public lands bear most of the cost of wolf reintroduction. Wolves tend to hone their killing skills on one particular prey animal.

35 Shedroof Mountain

There's no higher point in Washington State north or east of Shedroof Mountain, in the Salmo-Priest Wilderness. Views of rugged mountains spread out to infinity. The walk to the former fire lookout passes through a landscape that's similar to the Cascades, but the terrain is more remote and has far less human presence.

Start: Trailhead at the end of FR 2220
Distance: 8.8 miles out and back
Hiking time: About 4.5 hours
Difficulty: Moderate but mentally taxing—trail frequently loses elevation on the way up
Trail surface: Dirt trail
Elevation gain: 850 feet
Land status: National forest, wilderness area
Nearest town: Metaline Falls

Best season: July through Oct
Other trail users: Equestrians
Canine compatibility: Leashed dogs allowed
Fees and permits: None required
Map: USGS *Salmo Mountain*
Trail contacts: Colville National Forest, Sullivan Lake Ranger District; (509) 446-7500; www.fs.fed.us/r6/colville

Finding the trailhead: From Metaline Falls drive north on WA 31 for 2.1 miles. Turn right onto Sullivan Lake Road and continue for 4.7 miles. Turn left onto FR 22 (Sullivan Creek Road) and bear left. In 5.3 miles bear left onto FR 2220. Drive 13 miles to the trailhead at the end of the road. GPS: N 48 57.35' / W 117 04.88'

The Hike

Shedroof Mountain rises to 6,764 feet at the very northeast corner of Washington. The views from the summit will be absolutely foreign to anyone who hasn't hiked outside Washington State before. Among the many peaks and valleys, Priest Lake in the northern end of the Idaho panhandle stands out. The 19-mile-long lake is cradled by hills beneath the tall eastern branch of the Selkirks. The Selkirk Range forks into two branches that run north–south, surrounding Priest Lake. Shedroof Mountain is on the crest of the western branch of the Selkirks.

The area blends remoteness with accessibility. Logging roads penetrate deep and high up into the mountains, but with no big cities or towns nearby, few people venture into this wilderness. There's a good chance the only mammals you'll share the trail with will be large, furry, and nonhuman. Both black bears and grizzly bears enjoy the berries in season, but grizzly bear sightings are extremely rare. Knowing of these wild inhabitants gives the remote forest a primeval feel.

The trail to Shedroof Mountain is part of a popular 19-mile loop hike that goes into Idaho and nearly grazes British Columbia. This loop turns east on Trail 512 just before the summit of Shedroof Mountain and climbs Little Snowy Top Mountain in Idaho. Then the trail descends and goes northwest until it links up with the South Salmo River Trail and goes back to the parking lot at the end of FR 22.

Priest Lake in Idaho from the summit of Shedroof Mountain

The hike to Shedroof Mountain includes the most spectacular scenery in the Washington portion of this popular loop. It's a great way to experience the northern end of the Shedroof Divide in a day hike.

The hike starts out on a flat, old road high above the South Salmo River from a nearly 6,000-foot-high trailhead. From this section of old road you can see Salmo Mountain, which is topped by a fire lookout, to the northwest. At 1.0 mile the old road ends and the trail enters the 41,335-acre Salmo-Priest Wilderness. The path climbs quickly to open meadows of bear grass in between clumps of subalpine firs. Patches of huckleberries cover the ground, and kinnikinnick is common high on the mountain. Lupines are also prolific on this portion of the Shedroof Divide.

Diehard peak baggers may get frustrated with the indirect nature of the trail. It's constantly sloughing off hard-won elevation gains. After wandering across a slope south of the summit, you finally gain a ridge high on Shedroof Mountain only to drop into a bowl on the west side of the mountain and traverse to the south ridge, which the trail finally ascends to the summit. The last 0.4 mile of trail to the top is not maintained. Experienced hikers equipped with a map, compass, and GPS unit could make a small summit loop by following the ridge north and west from the summit back to the trail on the west side of the mountain.

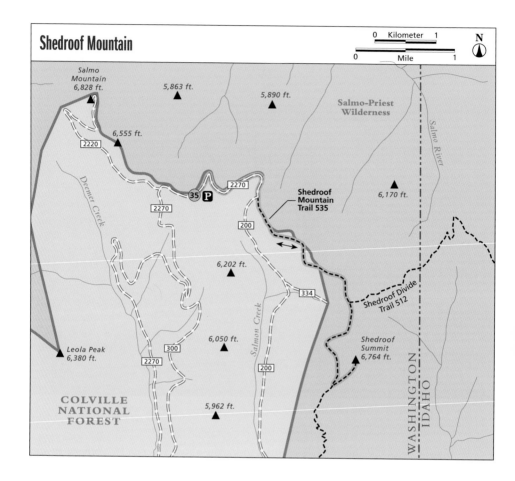

Shedroof Mountain

Miles and Directions

0.0 Start hiking at the Salmo Divide 535 Trailhead at the end of FR 2220. The trail begins as an old road.

1.0 Enter the Salmo-Priest Wilderness boundary at the end of the old road.

1.2 Pass a sign pointing left toward Shedroof Mountain.

2.0 Hike along and beside a tall ridge with views.

3.0 Go right at a junction with the Shedroof Divide Trail 512.

4.0 Go left, leaving the Divide Trail, for the final climb up Shedroof Mountain.

4.4 Reach the summit of Shedroof Mountain. Return the way you came.

8.8 Arrive back at the trailhead.

Hike Information

Local Events/Attractions

The International Selkirk Loop, 280-mile scenic drive through the Selkirk Mountains; selkirkloop.org

The Cutter Theatre, 302 Park St., Metaline Falls; historic theater and hotel; (509) 446-4108; cuttertheatre.com

Lodging

USDA Forest Service Sullivan Lake Campground, Colville National Forest, Sullivan Lake Ranger District on the north end of Sullivan Lake; (509) 446-7500; www.fs.fed .us/r6/colville

Restaurants

Cathy's Cafe, 221 E. Fifth Ave., Metaline Falls; (509) 446-2447

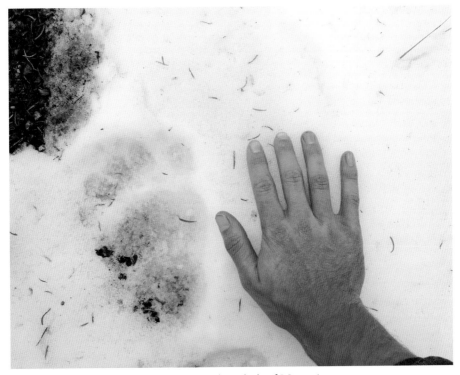

Black bear tracks in October snow on the trail to Shedroof Mountain

Honorable Mentions

N Steamboat Rock

This massive, steamboat-shaped rock in the middle of the Grand Coulee is a quick 4-mile round-trip hike, and the views are amazing. The rock is surrounded by the deep water of Bank Lake and the Coulee walls. The top of the mesa offers even more exploring on a trail that follows the perimeter of the mesa. It's also convenient—the trailhead to Steamboat Rock is a couple miles down the road from Northrup Canyon, another excellent hike.

From Ephrata go north on WA 283. In 5.5 miles, at Soap Lake, turn left onto WA 17. Continue north on WA 17 for 20 miles, and turn right onto US 2, about 4 miles past Sun Lakes State Park. In 4.3 miles, merge onto WA 155. In 15.5 miles turn left into Steamboat Rock State Park. The trailhead is on the left, 0.5 mile past the entrance station.

O Mankato Mountain

Another hike on the Shedroof Divide, the 7.0-mile hike to Mankato Mountain quickly passes Round Top Mountain and continues north along the high Shedroof Divide to Shedroof Mountain (6,590 feet). This hike is not much different from the others in this book on the Shedroof Divide, but with a high trailhead, views along a ridge, wildflowers, and abundant wildlife, what more do you need?

The trailhead is just east of the Grassy Top Trailhead, near Pass Creek Pass. From Metaline Falls drive north on WA 31 for 2.1 miles and turn right onto Sullivan Lake Road. In 4.7 miles (0.5 mile before reaching Sullivan Lake) turn left onto FR 22 (Sullivan Creek Road). In 5.3 miles come to a junction and go right to remain on FR 22. Park on the shoulder at Pass Creek Pass in 7 miles. The trailhead is just east of the pass.

P Kettle Crest North

The 30-mile section of the Kettle Crest Trail north of WA 20 is longer than the southern section, which includes Sherman Peak. The whole trail runs along a grassy ridgeline that's mostly at about 6,000 feet. Views along the lonely ridgeline stretch from the North Cascades in the west to the Selkirk's in the east. The southern end of the Kettle Crest North Trail is right off WA 20 and easy to get to. A handful of feeder trails join the Kettle Crest North Trail from logging roads north of WA 20.

For the southern access, drive east on WA 20 for 40 miles from Tonasket. Turn right onto Clark Avenue in downtown Republic to stay on WA 20. Continue 16.6 miles to the top of Sherman Pass to an access road signed with recreational opportunities.

Drive 0.1 mile to a parking lot. Alternately, reach Sherman Pass from Kettle Falls by driving 26.3 miles west on WA 20.

Q Abercrombie Mountain

Eastern Washington's second-tallest summit rises thousands of feet above its surroundings. On a clear day, the view from the top can't be beat. Nearby, Hooknose Mountain and Sherlock Peak also scrape the sky. In the distance, a roadless landscape spreads out in every direction. From the trailhead on FR 300, climb through switchbacks for 1.5 miles to a junction with the Silver Creek Trail. Hang a left and continue climbing to a ridge south of the peak and another junction below the summit. Bear left again to stay on Trail 117 and hike the final 0.2 mile to the chunky talus summit for a total of 3.2 miles.

From downtown Colville go east on WA 20 for just more than 1 mile and turn left (north) onto Aladdin Road (CR 9435). Follow it for 23 miles to a Y onto Deep Lake Road (FR 9445). Continue 7.4 miles to Leadpoint and turn right onto FR 4720. Follow it to the junction with FR 7078 in 1.9 miles and turn left. Continue 4.5 miles to a junction with FR 300. Drive on FR 300 for 3.3 miles to the trailhead at the road's end.

Southeast Washington

Southeast Washington is covered in sagebrush desert, long gentle ridges, and high-walled canyons and coulees. Hiking trails in this part of the state lead to waterfalls, towering cliffs, rolling ridges with expansive views, sandy dunes and through expanses of desert wildflowers.

Million of years of lava flows, followed by some of the biggest floods in the history of the world shaped Southeast Washington and some of Northeast Washington. Starting about 17.5 million years ago, deep lava flowed from an ancient volcano in the southeast corner of the state. Periodic lava flows covered the area for the next ten to fifteen million years, until layers of volcanic basalt more than 1 mile deep covered parts of the region.

Millions of years later—during the last ice age—a finger of ice reached down from Canada, damming ancient rivers and creating Glacial Lake Missoula. The ever-accumulating water periodically lifted the lobe of ice, unleashing cataclysmic floods. Raging water scoured the landscape, tearing away layers of basalt and creating deep canyons such as the Ancient Lakes Coulee and shaping the land into the giant ripples in the Palouse landscape near Kamiak Butte.

The periodic ice-age floods stopped more than 10,000 years ago when the ice melted, but a great quantity of water still flows through Southeast Washington, despite the arid climate. The Columbia River, which drains most of the Pacific Northwest, passes through the dry landscape from its origin in the Canadian Rockies and provides several opportunities for hiking and exploring. The river is controlled by a series of dams, but the hike along the White Bluffs overlooks the last free-flowing stretch of the West's greatest river. The Blue Mountains in the very southwest corner of the state are the tallest mountains in the region. They're an out-of-the-way range with miles of high-country trails through pine forest with beautiful, expansive views and deep canyons.

Shifting tectonic plates buckled and folded the earth in other parts of the region, creating tall ridges like Umtanum Ridge, Manastash Ridge, and the Horse Heaven Hills. These ridges are part of the Yakima Fold and Thrust Belt, which geologists are only recently beginning to understand. New research suggests that the tectonic forces causing the earth to buckle into these ridges could also produce shallow earthquakes.

Other features of hikes in Southeast Washington are flowers that rival those in the mountains, and open terrain where you can roam off-trail. It's easy to find solitude and empty trails in the desert. If nothing else, treat yourself to at least one desert walk in spring while the wildflowers are in their prime and the mountains are still covered in snow. By the middle of the hiking season, when everyone and their mother is stomping up a trail in the Cascades and Priuses choke the parking lots, even skeptics of desert hiking may find themselves yearning for a lonely desert with the aroma of sagebrush hanging in the parched air.

The Palouse region from Kamiak Butte (hike 41)

36 Manastash Ridge–Ray Westberg Trail

The Ray Westberg Trail—one of the best-loved hiking trails east of the Cascades—is a steep jaunt to a beautiful high point on Manastash Ridge. Many hikers use the trail to get in shape for longer trails and bigger mountains, but there's plenty to enjoy on the way up Manastash Ridge. The wildflowers are spectacular, as are the views of the Kittitas Valley and Stuart Range.

Start: Parking lot and trailhead at the end of Cove Road
Distance: 4.2 miles out and back
Hiking time: About 2.5 hours
Difficulty: Moderate due to elevation gain
Trail surface: Dirt trail
Elevation gain: 1,700 feet
Best season: Spring for wildflowers
Other trail users: Equestrians
Canine compatibility: Dogs allowed

Land status: State wildlife area
Nearest town: Ellensburg
Fees and permits: None required
Schedule: Year-round
Map: *USGS Badger Gap*
Trail contacts: L. T. Murray Wildlife Recreation Area, Washington Department of Fish and Wildlife; (509) 925-6746; wdfw.wa.gov/lands/wildlife_areas/lt_murray/

Finding the trailhead: From Seattle drive east on I-90 to exit 101 at Thorp. After exiting, turn right onto South Thorp Highway and follow it southeast for 2 miles. Turn right onto Cove Road and follow it south for 4.5 miles. Park on the gravel shoulder at the end of Cove Road. GPS: N46 58.06' / W120 38.73'

The Hike

In spring, Manastash Ridge can't be beat. The sky is usually clear, and the ridge is a convenient place to gain some elevation long before the snow melts in the Cascades. Several trails run from top to bottom, but the best and most popular route is the Ray Westberg Memorial Trail. The hike up Manastash Ridge is popular for its convenience—it's 5 miles from downtown Ellensburg and close enough for a day trip from Seattle on a sunny spring day—and it can be hiked almost year-round depending on the amount of snow. Locals hike the trail all year in snowshoes or boots equipped with traction devices.

Manastash Ridge is at least as beautiful as it is convenient. The ridge is covered in a variety of wildflowers, and as you climb you're treated to new species. Arrowleaf balsam root, phlox, desert buckwheat, and bitterroot are some of the most common flowers. The sagebrush and rabbitbrush could be considered old-growth—it towers overhead, perfuming the path. A variety of birds, including great-horned owls and ospreys, can be seen overhead. Deer are common, and elk and bighorn sheep live nearby.

The ridge is the northernmost of a series of undulations that make up the desert moonscape between Ellensburg and Yakima. Northward movement of the West Coast

Memorial Point on Manastash Ridge and Kittitas Valley below

is slowly buckling the ridges and pushing them ever higher. The climb is deceptive, because a series of knolls hides the top from view as you make your way up. You'll swear those tectonic plates are working extra hard and pushing the top of the ridge higher even as you climb.

From the trailhead at the end of Cove Road, walk past the gate and cross an irrigation canal. The trail begins climbing soon after and continues going almost straight up through sagebrush and ponderosa pines. After 1.0 mile of hiking, views of the Stuart Range begin, and they keep getting better the whole way up. Horned lizards scurry underfoot. There's a flat stretch after the first climb, but the trail soon continues climbing. Only a few trees provide shade on this trail, so start early if you're hiking on a hot, sunny day.

In 2.1 miles the trail arrives at Memorial Point, which has a rocky cairn and a multitude of memorials. One is for Ray Westberg, an Ellensburg High School wrestling coach and the trail's namesake.

The view from the summit is spectacular. Mount Stuart reaches into the sky to the north. To the east, Manastash Ridge winds its way toward the Yakima River. Straight ahead you can see lush green irrigated fields of timothy hay, downtown Ellensburg, and the tall plateau of Table Mountain across Kittitas Valley.

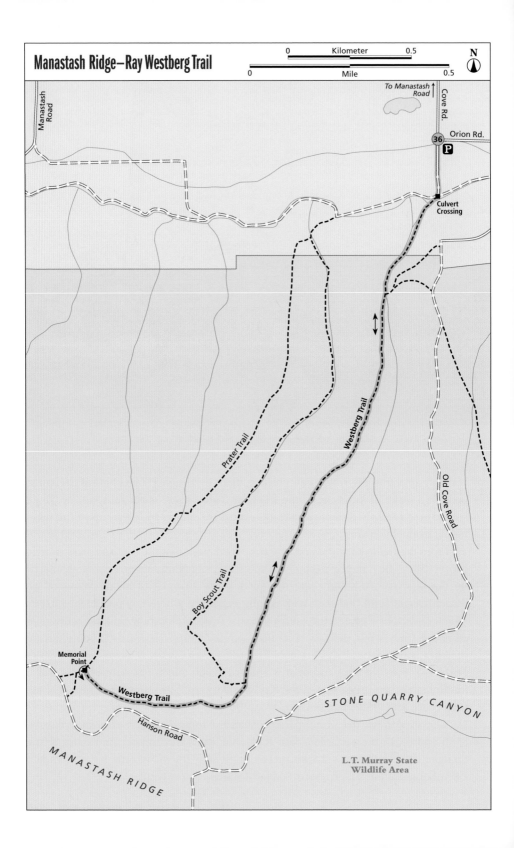

Miles and Directions

0.0 Start from the parking lot near the end of Cove Road. Cross the gate and irrigation canal at the end of the road and bear left onto the trail to begin the hike.

1.5 Continue straight up the ridge, past a trail on the right.

2.1 Reach Memorial Point on top of the ridge. Return the way you came.

4.2 Arrive back at the trailhead.

Hike Information

Local Information
Kittitas County Chamber of Commerce, 609 N. Main St., Ellensburg 98926; (509) 925-2002; kittitascountychamber.com

Local Events/Attractions
Jazz in the Valley, Ellensburg; last weekend in July; (509) 925-2002; jazzinthevalley .com

Lodging
Ellensburg KOA Campground, 32 S. Thorp Hwy., Ellensburg; (509) 925-9319

Restaurants
Ellensburg Pasta Company, 600 N. Main St., Ellensburg; (509) 933-3330
Rossow's U-Tote-Em, 807 W. University Way, Ellensburg; (509) 925-1500

Other Resources
Northwest Arid Lands: An Introduction to the Columbia Basin Shrub-Steppe, by Georganne P. O'Connor and Karen Wieda

THE LEGEND OF MEL'S HOLE

Mel's Hole, one of Washington's weirder legends, is a bottomless pit rumored to lurk somewhere on Manastash Ridge. The fabled hole with magical powers was made famous on the *Coast to Coast AM* radio show in 1997. Mel Waters, a caller on the radio show, claimed to have discovered a mysterious, rock-lined hole more than 15 miles deep. (He said he measured it with 20 pounds of fishing line and a weight.) Don't look too hard for the hole, because Waters claimed in 2008 that the hole is now elaborately camouflaged by the government. According to public records checks by local reporters at the time, no Mel Waters ever lived in Kittitas County.

37 Black Canyon

This hike follows a trickle of water up through a wildflower-filled canyon to Umtanum Ridge, where you're treated to views of Kittitas Valley, the Stuart Range, Mount Rainier, and the Wenas Valley, where the hike begins. The canyon walls aren't especially tall or steep, but they make up for it with a plethora of wildflowers, stunning views, varied terrain, and a chance to see bighorn sheep and elk.

Start: Parking lot in the L. T. Murray Wilderness, off North Wenas Road
Distance: 7.6 miles out and back
Hiking time: About 4 hours
Difficulty: Moderate due to length and elevation gain
Trail surface: Dirt/gravel road and trail through the bottom of a canyon
Best seasons: Spring for wildflowers; fall for golden quaking aspens
Other trail users: Equestrians, all-terrain vehicles (ATVs) in the last 1.5 miles of trail
Canine compatibility: Dogs allowed (watch out for ticks and rattlesnakes)
Elevation Gain: 1,500 feet
Land status: State wildlife recreation area
Nearest town: Ellensburg/Selah
Fees and permits: Discover Pass required for parking

Schedule: Closed in winter to protect wildlife. Check with Washington Department of Fish and Wildlife.
Maps: USGS Wenas Lake; Ellensburg 15-minute quad
Trail contacts: L. T. Murray Wildlife Recreation Area, Washington Department of Fish and Wildlife; (509) 925-6746; wdfw.wa.gov/lands/wildlife_areas/lt_murray/; Wenas area: (509) 697-4503
Special considerations: The road to the trailhead is rough. Although the last 1.3 miles of road between North Wenas Road and the Black Canyon Trailhead are doable in most cars, you'll be crawling in first gear and gripping the wheel. Walking this section is wise if your vehicle doesn't have high clearance.

Finding the trailhead: From Seattle drive 109 miles east on I-90 to exit 109 in Ellensburg. Take a right and drive under the freeway on Canyon Road. Turn left onto Umptanum Road in 0.7 mile. Continue on Umptanum Road for 22.5 miles; it turns to gravel in 5.2 miles and back to pavement in 18.5 miles, when it becomes North Wenas Road. Turn left onto a rough dirt road 4 miles after the road becomes pavement. The road is unmarked expect for a large Wildlife Area sign. From North Wenas Road drive (or walk) 0.5 mile to a gate at the boundary of the L. T. Murray State Wildlife Recreation Area. Close the gate behind you, and continue another 0.8 mile to a parking lot at the end of the road. GPS: N46 50.98' / W121 42.13'

The Hike

Often in this part of the state, you must choose between a hike through a canyon filled with vegetation or a hike to a high point with open views. Black Canyon has both. The trail through the canyon ends on Umtanum Ridge, where you can see Mount Rainier to the east and the jagged Stuart Range, Kittitas Valley, and the narrow

The remains of an old cabin in Black Canyon

gash carved by Umtanum Creek to the north. Even Mount Adams is visible on clear days. The walls of Black Canyon aren't as steep as nearby Umtanum Canyon, but Black Canyon is more remote and better illustrates the stark contrast of lush canyon bottoms and dry ridges found in the many canyons above the Wenas Valley.

Black Canyon is the deepest of a series of canyons that lead from the floor of the Wenas Valley up to the crest of Umtanum Ridge. Green vegetation surrounds the creek at the bottom of the canyon, but dry hills of wildflowers, steep talus, and basalt cliffs loom above on the canyon walls. The canyon is also home to abundant wildlife (including the occasional rattlesnake). If the beauty of the canyon itself doesn't impress you, surely the view from Umtanum Ridge will.

The trail starts on an old road beside a streambed. The trail is rocky and loose in a few spots, but the grade is mostly gentle. The streambed is surrounded by walls of basalt talus and rolling brown hills capped with cliffs on either side and a sparse forest of mixed lodgepole and ponderosa pines as you get higher up.

The water running through the canyon is just a trickle, but it's enough to keep the gulch lush year-round. It was also enough for homesteaders to build a cabin in the canyon, the remains of which can be seen at 1.4 miles from the trailhead. The cabin sits in a shaded flat spot with easy access to the creek. It's surrounded by tall dogwoods, birches, and quaking aspens, which give shelter to northern pygmy owls and barred owls. The presence of water in the desert means that rattlesnakes may be nearby, so watch where you step. The trail is exposed to the sun for most of the hike, so this patch of shade is an ideal lunch spot or water break on hot days. Don't forget your sunscreen.

Just past the cabin, stay right at a fork in the road. Here the canyon opens up and the trail winds though a forest of tall, mixed pines. Elk and deer abound in these woods. The trees are tall and sparse, and the ground blooms with white and pink phlox in spring. The occasional sagebrush, which is much more abundant at the beginning of the hike, still hangs around up here to perfume the air between red ponderosa pine trunks.

▶ **Road construction in the Wenas Valley in 2005 uncovered the left-front leg bone of a mammoth. Scientists from Central Washington University spent the next five years studying the site and uncovered hundreds of surprisingly well-preserved mammoth bones.**

The upper half of this trail is open to motor vehicles as part of the L. T. Murray Green Dot road system. Tire tracks can detract from the wilderness experience, but you are unlikely to see any vehicles here. This is a rough and remote set of roads.

The hike through the trees is short, and you quickly top out on Umtanum Ridge. The 4,000-foot-tall ridge features views in nearly every direction and abundant wildflowers. The L. T. Murray State Wildlife Recreation Area is more than 54,000 acres, and the road at the top is one of the main routes through it. Turn right at the road and continue about 0.2 mile to a local high point. If you went east on this road for nearly 5.0 miles, you could connect to the Old Durr Road and the Yakima Skyline Trail, which goes south most of the way to Yakima.

Horned toads will likely scurry away from your boots, and you can watch western tailed-blue and Karner blue butterflies gather nectar as you explore the desert landscape high above the Kittitas and Wenas Valleys. Pink and orange bitterroot flowers, a desert treasure, poke out of the rocky ridge in late spring. Underground is a bitter carrot-like edible root that supplies the plant with moisture and nutrients during the long stretches between rain. The flowers have many petals and range in color from almost white to salmon pink. Some tribes in the inland Northwest believed the plant could ward off attacking bears.

Other flowers along the trail include pink and white phlox, bluebells, desert parsley, sagebrush false dandelion, and common spring-gold. Hedgehog cactuses are also common atop Umtanum Ridge. Look closely from the road atop the ridge and you'll see the dome-shaped cactuses or, if you're lucky, their dark pink flowers, which

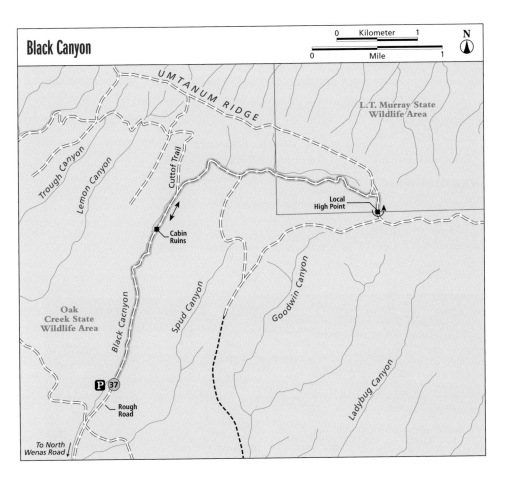

Black Canyon

0   Kilometer   1

0   Mile   1

N

UMTANUM RIDGE

L.T. Murray State
Wildlife Area

Cuttof Trail

Trough Canyon

Lemon Canyon

Cabin
Ruins

Local
High Point

Oak
Creek State
Wildlife Area

Black Cacnyon

Spud Canyon

Goodwin Canyon

Ladybug Canyon

P 37

Rough
Road

To North
Wenas Road

typically bloom in May. Like most hikes in the Washington desert, the wildflowers are best from late April to early June, but fall colors are also worth seeing in the leafy canyon. Quaking aspens put on a spectacular fall show.

Miles and Directions

0.0 Start from the trailhead on unsigned Black Canyon Road, off North Wenas Road. (**Note:** The road is rough. If your vehicle has low clearance, park at the start of Black Canyon Road and hike 1.3 miles to the trailhead.)

1.4 Pass the remains of an old cabin on the left side of the road.

1.8 Turn right at a fork in the road.

3.6 Reach the crest of Umtanum Ridge. Go right (west) and hike up to a high point on the ridge.

3.8 Reach a high point on Umtanum Ridge. Return the way you came.

7.6 Arrive back at the trailhead.

Hike Information

Local Information

Yakima Valley Visitors and Convention Bureau, 10 N. Eighth St., Yakima 98901; (509) 575-3010; visityakima.com

Restaurants

Ellensburg Pasta Company, 600 N. Main St., Ellensburg; (509) 933-3330
The Yellow Church Cafe, 111 S. Pearl St., Ellensburg; (509) 933-2233

Organizations

Wenas Audubon (local birding group); wenasaudubon.org

Other Resources

Northwest Arid Lands: An Introduction to the Columbia Basin Shrub-Steppe, by Georganne P. O'Connor and Karen Wieda

Bitterroot flowers on Umtanum Ridge

38 Ancient Lakes

This hike through a cliff-rimmed shrub–steppe desert ends at a waterfall tumbling into a spectacular set of lakes. Crumbling talus and 500-foot basalt cliffs covered in orange and green lichen surround the lush basin. The walk to the lakes is short, but there's plenty to explore in and above the basin.

Start: Ancient and Dusty Lakes Trailhead, at the end of Ancient Lake Road (Road 9 NW)

Distance: 4.8 miles out and back

Hiking time: About 2 hours

Difficulty: Easy due to flat terrain

Trail surface: Dirt/sand road and trail

Elevation gain: 175 feet

Best season: Mar through May

Other trail users: Equestrians, mountain bikers

Canine compatibility: Leashed dogs allowed

Land status: Wildlife area

Nearest town: Quincy

Fees and permits: Discover Pass required for parking

Schedule: Year-round

Map: USGS Babcock Ridge

Trail contacts: Columbia Basin Wildlife Area, Washington Department of Fish and Wildlife, 6653 Road K NE, Moses Lake; (509) 925-6746; wdfw.wa.gov

Finding the trailhead: From Ellensburg drive east 40 miles on I-90 to exit 149 for WA 281. After exiting, take a left onto WA 281 North toward Quincy. After 5.6 miles turn left onto White Trail Road. In 7.8 miles turn left onto Ancient Lake Road (Road 9 NW). The road descends to Babcock Bench, a flat plateau above the Columbia River, and becomes gravel in 2.1 miles. From here continue 3.7 miles to the gravel parking lot for Ancient and Dusty Lakes. The trail starts at the gate at the south end of the parking lot. GPS: N47 09.58' / W119 58.84'

The Hike

The trail through Potholes Coulee showcases two of the most beautiful features of the Columbia Basin: rock deposited by one of the greatest basalt flows on the Earth's surface, and deep channels carved by floods during the last ice age. The coulee also hides something seldom found in the desert—lakes and waterfalls.

Between 15,000 and 13,000 years ago, Glacial Lake Missoula released some of the biggest floods on Earth. When the lake became full enough to lift the ice sheet that blocked its way to the west, water scoured Eastern Washington. Potholes Coulee, like its neighbor to the north, Frenchmen Coulee, drained this floodwater toward the Columbia River. The water gouged a 500-foot-deep channel that is now home to a series of irrigation-fed lakes.

The abundant water is surrounded by parched rock and sagebrush. Thick vegetation clings to the edge of the lakes, and waterfowl including mallards and mergansers splash and feed. The glassy water of the three main lakes reflects the surrounding cliffs, buttes, and sky, which is usually blue in the Columbia Basin.

The Ancient Lakes Trail is beautiful from the very beginning, with views in every direction. The coulee is surrounded by orchards and vineyards, and you can see power lines from some parts of the hike. Most of the time, though, the deep walls cut off the surrounding civilization.

Start hiking on a sandy jeep trail at the south end of the parking lot. The trail is surrounded by rabbitbrush, big sagebrush, and wildflowers. Lupine, desert buckwheat, pink phlox, and arrowleaf balsamroot are the most prevalent flowers. The lavender-petaled sagebrush mariposa lily is also common along the north wall in the first 1.0 mile of the hike. Rattlesnakes sun their scaly bodies on rocks in the coulee, so keep your eyes on the trail.

From the jeep trail, the first trail to the left leads toward Ancient Lakes. It hugs the north rim of the coulee, where several waterfalls splash down the black cliffs, providing moisture for the bounty of vegetation. At 0.5 mile down the jeep trail is a second trail that also goes to Ancient Lakes, but it takes a path through the center of the coulee, away from the cliffs. The jeep trail continues south to Dusty Lake. The wall to the south of the trail isn't the south rim of Potholes Coulee but a 1,000-foot-wide finger that stretches directly down the center of the coulee. On the other side of the finger is Dusty Lake, a large lake that's popular for fishing.

The hike to the lakes and back is short, flat, and easy. But you can spend most of a day exploring around the coulee. From the lake basin, trails wander off in all directions. Trails wind around most of the lakes, and a trail with a short but steep talus scramble goes up the ridge south of the lakes. From there you can gaze 500 feet down into Dusty Lake and the south side of Potholes Coulee. A steep, scrambly trail leads past the waterfall to a network of paths that go to lakes and rock formations at the west end of the coulee.

Miles and Directions

- **0.0** Start at the Ancient and Dusty Lakes Trailhead at the south end of the parking lot at the end of Ancient Lakes Road (Road 9NW).
- **0.5** Turn left off the jeep road and onto singletrack leading east into the coulee.
- **1.8** Arrive at a view of the waterfall on your left (north wall of the coulee).
- **2.1** Reach an established campsite at the westernmost lake.
- **2.4** Reach the end of the trail on a ridge between two lakes at the eastern edge of the coulee. Return the way you came.
- **4.8** Arrive back at the trailhead.

Hike Information

Local Events/Attractions

Gorge Amphitheatre, 754 Silica Rd., Quincy; (509) 785-6262; www.livenation.com

Campers in Ancient Lakes basin. RON JOHNSON

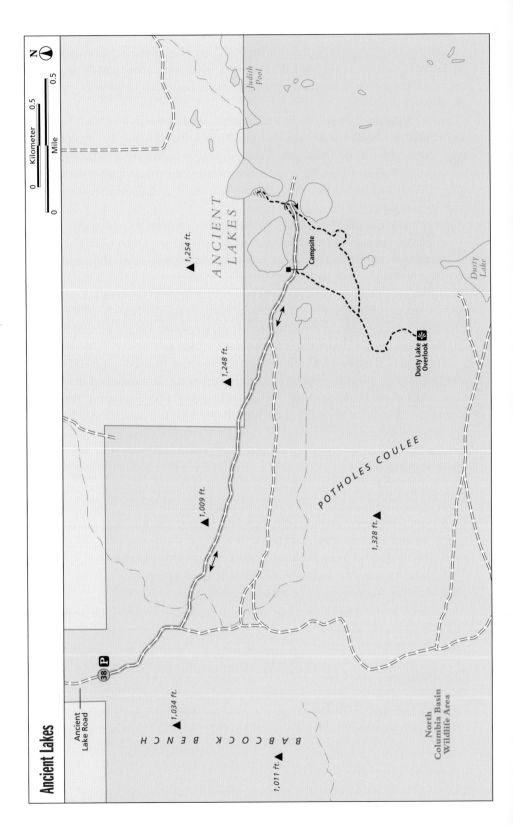

Ancient Lakes

Ancient Lake Road

38 P

BABCOCK BENCH

1,034 ft. ▲

1,011 ft. ▲

▲ 1,009 ft.

POTHOLES COULEE

1,328 ft. ▲

North
Columbia Basin
Wildlife Area

▲ 1,248 ft.

ANCIENT LAKES

▲ 1,254 ft.

Judith
Pool

■ Campsite

Dusty Lake
Overlook ☼

Dusty
Lake

N

0   0.5   Kilometer   0.5
0   Mile   0.5

Hikers above Ancient Lakes

Lodging

Wanapum Recreation Area, Vantage; (509) 856-2700 or (888) 226-7688

Cave B Inn & Spa, 334 Silica Rd., Quincy; (509) 785-2283

Other Resources

On the Trail of the Ice Age Floods: A Geological Field Guide to the Mid-Columbia Basin, by Bruce Bjornstad

39 Cowiche Canyon

One of the best rail trails in the state, Cowiche Canyon is an interesting pocket of wilderness surrounded by orchards, vineyards and other forms of civilization. Go in spring for the show of colorful wildflowers. Nearly anytime you go, a radiant blue sky will hang over the canyon's steep, rocky walls.

Start: East trailhead at the end of Cowiche Canyon Road or the west trailhead at the end of North Wiekel Road
Distance: 6.2 miles out and back
Hiking time: About 3 hours
Difficulty: Easy due to flat terrain
Trail surface: Gravel
Elevation gain: 200 feet
Land status: Bureau of Land Management, Cowiche Canyon Conservancy
Nearest town: Yakima

Best season: Spring for wildflowers; fall for colorful aspens
Other trail users: Bicyclists, equestrians
Canine compatibility: Leashed dogs allowed
Fees and permits: None required
Maps: Cowiche Canyon maps, available online at Cowichecanyon.org. (Maps are also sometimes available at a trailhead kiosk.)
Trail contacts: Cowiche Canyon Conservatory, Yakima; (509) 248-5065; cowichecanyon.org

Finding the trailhead: East trailhead: from I-90 2 miles east of Ellensburg, take exit 110 to merge onto I-82 South toward Yakima. Take exit 31A to merge onto US 12W. (If coming from downtown Yakima or points south on I-82, take exit 31 for US 12W.) In 3.8 miles turn left onto Ackley Road and then left again onto Powerhouse Road. Continue south on Powerhouse Road for 0.2 mile, and then turn right onto Cowiche Canyon Lane. In 1 mile, park at the widened end of the road. GPS: N46 37.33' / W120 36.90'
   West trailhead: From US 12W, turn left onto Ackley Road, left again onto West Powerhouse Road, and then immediately right onto Naches Heights Road. In 3.8 miles continue left onto Zimmerman Road at an intersection with Dahl Road. Turn left onto Weikel Road 1.1 mile later, following signs for Cowiche Canyon. Park at the gravel lot at the end of the road.
   Or from downtown Yakima, go west on Summitview Avenue for 9.1 miles. Turn right onto North Weikel Road and turn right in 0.5 mile at the signed trailhead. GPS: N46 37.88' / W120 39.93'

The Hike

In between acres of vineyards, rows of hops, and sprawling orchards, east of Yakima is a wild desert canyon. Cowiche Canyon is a convenient nook that's filled with sunshine, bare basalt rock, dark teal sagebrush, and dry-land flowers. Cowiche Creek meanders through this parched landscape giving life to a flush of dense growth. Tiny fish mill in the channel. Just 10 feet away from this desert oasis, only the hardiest desert plants can suck moisture from the dry crust.

   A trail leads through the canyon on an old railroad bed. Side trails leading up to the canyon rim intersect the straight path. One such path leads to a high plateau with views of Mounts Rainier and Adams and eventually to a winery and tasting room.

Andesite formations in the canyon

Many of the basalt canyons in Washington's desert are coulees carved by ice-age floods. Most of these canyons no longer have any water flowing through them. Cowiche is an exception. Cowiche Creek still flows through the walls of Columbia River basalt and Tieton andesite that it carved. Ice-age floods didn't reach this spot, but geologists still find plenty of interest in Cowiche Canyon. The Columbia River Basalt flows that blanket the area and are visible in much of the canyon may be the single largest basalt flow in the world. Andesite from the world's longest andesite flow (which started in an ancient volcano near the Goat Rocks Wilderness) tops portions of the north wall.

In spring, wildflowers push through the crust of lichen and rocky soil toward the dark blue sky and puffy clouds. Clumps of desert phlox and bright yellow balsamroot flowers grow alongside the fragrant sagebrush. Bitterroot, whose flowers range in color from salmon pink to white, is especially abundant on the canyon's sloping walls. Only the plant's flower pushes its way above the ground. Below the surface, a carrot-like root stores energy for winter.

From the east end of the canyon, you'll pass several homes as the canyon walls slowly get steeper and narrower. Soon you'll see views of the creek. Cowiche Creek meanders back and forth through the canyon. Nine different bridges cross the creek

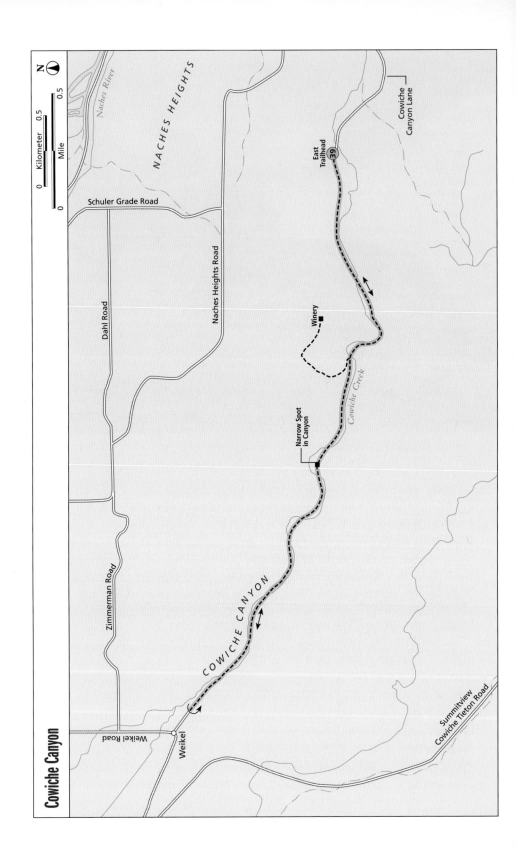

Cowiche Canyon

NACHES HEIGHTS

Naches River

Schuler Grade Road

Dahl Road

Zimmerman Road

Naches Heights Road

COWICHE CANYON

Weikel Road

Weikel

Narrow Spot in Canyon

Winery

Cowiche Creek

East Trailhead

39

Cowiche Canyon Lane

Summitview Cowiche Tieton Road

N

Kilometer   0   0.5

Mile   0   0.5

Nootka Rose in Cowiche Canyon

on the rail trail. The junction to a winery and tasting room is marked with a sign at 1.2 miles. The trail toward the winery is worth exploring, even if not for the wine. You can gaze at the canyon from above and see the Cascade Mountains in the distance. The scenery is similar throughout the canyon, but subtle changes along the way keep the walk interesting.

Miles and Directions

0.0 Start from the east trailhead, at the end of Cowiche Canyon Lane.

1.2 Reach a junction with a trail up the north side of the canyon to the Wilridge Winery.

1.7 Pass through a narrow spot in the canyon.

3.1 Reach the west trailhead. Return the way you came.

6.2 Arrive back at the east trailhead.

Hike Information

Organizations

Cowiche Canyon Conservancy; (509) 248-5065; cowichecanyon.org

Other Resources

Northwest Arid Lands: An Introduction to the Columbia Basin Shrub-Steppe, by Georganne P. O'Connor and Karen Wieda

40 White Bluffs North Slope

White bluffs and bare sand dunes—naked nature—rise above the last free-flowing stretch of the Columbia River in one of the driest parts of Washington. A desert ecosystem thrives on the sandstone formations, and birds gather en masse in the water below. You can gaze down to the river and imagine the Columbia before it was shackled by dams or roam the wide open dunes and enjoy views of the Saddle Mountains to the north.

Start: Trailhead at White Bluffs Landing in the Wahluke State Wildlife Recreation Area
Distance: 5.0 miles out and back
Hiking time: About 3 hours
Difficulty: Easy due to flat terrain
Trail surface: Sandy dirt and sections of sand dunes
Best season: Spring for wildflowers; scorching hot in summer
Other trail users: None
Canine compatibility: Leashed dogs allowed

Land status: National monument
Nearest town: Othello
Fees and permits: Discover Pass required
Schedule: Day use year-round
Map: USGS Locke Island
Trail contacts: Hanford Reach National Monument; (509) 546-8300; fws.gov/refuge/Hanford_Reach/
Other: Camping and overnight parking are prohibited in Hanford Reach National Monument.

Finding the trailhead: From Vantage cross the Columbia River on I-90 and take exit 137 to merge onto WA 26 East toward Othello/Pullman. In 1 mile turn right onto WA 243 South. Drive south for 30 miles and turn left onto WA 24 East. In 18.9 miles turn right just after milepost 63 into the Wahluke State Wildlife Recreation Area. Continue on this dirt road for 4 miles until you come to a four-way intersection. Take a right, following the sign for White Bluffs Landing. Continue 1.6 miles (5.6 from the highway) to the parking lot for White Bluffs Landing. From here the hiking trail is faint but visible on the bluff to the north. GPS: N46 40.53' / W119 27.19'

The Hike

This 15-mile ridge of white sandstone bluffs and dunes rises high above the banks of the Columbia River on the great river's last remaining free-flowing stretch in the United States. This is what the Columbia River looked like when Woody Guthrie sang about it rolling and rambling to the sea. For just 51 miles between Priest Rapids Dam, 30 miles upstream, and the McNary Dam downstream in Umatilla, Oregon, the river still rolls. This stretch has been preserved since World War II, thanks to the plutonium production facility across the river from the bluffs. Ironically, the most pristine place on the Columbia was preserved by material used in weapons that killed hundreds of thousands of people.

The continent's fourth-largest river forms in the wilds of Canada. It collects water from two Canadian provinces and the melting snowpack and glaciers of the Rockies

White Bluffs and the Columbia River

before slaloming its way south through Washington. Over the course of the river's 1,243 miles, fourteen hydroelectric dams block its flow. The river that once supported the largest salmon runs in the country is now a strictly controlled series of nearly stagnant pools and reservoirs.

However, at Hanford Reach, wild chinook still splash in free-flowing waters, as do pelicans, geese, and ducks. Flocks of fifty or more Canada geese and other waterfowl parade up and down the river nearly constantly. The Hanford Reach is a surprisingly pristine area, and the trail on the White Bluffs is the best way to see it.

From the river, the crumbling sandstone bluffs rise steeply to meet the dunes above them. The top

▶ Clumps of dark yellow flowers called White Bluffs bladderpod grow near the dunes atop the bluffs. The flower is so rare it has only been found on the bluffs and some nearby farms. When US Fish and Wildlife scientists surveyed the plant in 2007, they estimated there were about 59,000 plants in a 17-kilometer section of the bluffs.

of the bluffs and the surrounding 57,000 acres that make up Hanford Reach National Monument are home to coyotes, elk, and mule deer. A bouquet of the usual desert flowers like parsleys and buckwheats thrive on the bluffs.

From the parking lot, walk in the general direction of the bluffs to the north. The trail is faint and hard to find at the beginning, but a wide, well-established trail is visible going up the first hill. You'll be hiking on a mix of sand and sandstone covered in sagebrush, rabbitbrush, and wildflowers. Wind blows wisps of sand over the top of long dunes with their bases anchored in place by sand dock.

After a couple short sandy hills, you are treated to views of the river and Locke Island. The island and the opposite riverbank were once popular fishing spots for Native Americans. The dunes and rolling hills are scenic, but the real beauty is the wide-open land with the great river gently flowing through. This view is easy to reach and is never far away as you roam the trail north and west along the river.

One mile from the parking lot the trail becomes faint in places, but route finding is simple. Just stay on top of the bluffs and wander upstream. The trail braids, reappears, and disappears a few times in this section. The top of the bluffs is blanketed in wildflowers and sagebrush. With such pleasant wandering in this remote stretch of river, it's easy to forget how close you are to Hanford.

The sandy trail along the top of the bluffs eventually comes to a couple of tall, wind-rippled sand dunes. From here you can climb and roam the dunes, turn around, or keep hiking another 1.0 mile until you reach the second dune. The dunes are tall and bare and make a great place to contemplate the power of the untamed river. From here the rolling Saddle Mountains form a backdrop to the sandy riverside landscape.

Five miles downstream from the parking lot, another trail meanders over the southern section of the White Bluffs. This area is slightly more barren due to a recent wildfire. To find it, drive back to the four-way stop and go right. In 4 miles you'll reach a parking area at a viewpoint. Follow the old roadway and look for trails in 1 mile.

Miles and Directions

0.0 Start from the White Bluffs Landing parking lot and walk northeast toward the bluffs. The trail is faint at the beginning but soon becomes well established.

0.4 Begin ascending on a wide, sandy trail.

1.0 Reach a sandstone overlook above the river.

2.1 Reach a second sandstone overlook.

2.5 Reach the first of two bare sand dunes. Turn around here. (**Option:** Or continue 1.0 mile to a second dune.) Return the way you came.

5.0 Arrive back at the trailhead.

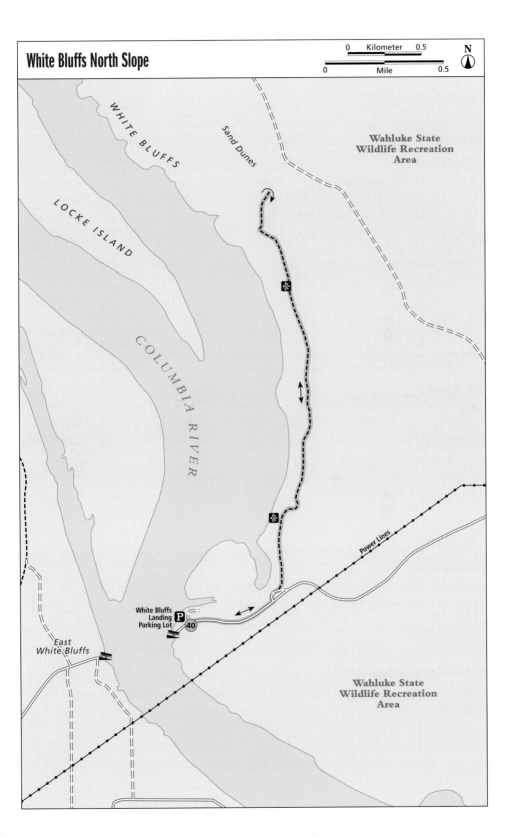

White Bluffs North Slope

0   Kilometer   0.5

0   Mile   0.5

N

WHITE BLUFFS

Sand Dunes

Wahluke State
Wildlife Recreation
Area

LOCKE ISLAND

COLUMBIA RIVER

Power Lines

White Bluffs
Landing
Parking Lot

P

40

East
White Bluffs

Wahluke State
Wildlife Recreation
Area

Sand dock and a dune on top of the White Bluffs

Hike Information

Restaurants

Atomic Ale Brewpub and Eatery, 1015 Lee Blvd., Richland; (509) 964-5465
White Bluffs Brewing, 2000 Logston Blvd. #126, Richland; (509) 554-7059

Organizations

Hiketricities.com (a collection of hikes and trip reports from trails near the Tri-Cities)

Other Resources

On the Trail of the Ice Age Floods: A Geological Field Guide to the Mid-Columbia Basin, by
Bruce Bjornstad

41 Kamiak Butte Pine Ridge Trail

The Pine Ridge Trail makes a quick loop up and down one of the Palouse region's rare mountains. The 2.5-mile trip starts in a dense forest, where the trail begins to switchback up a steep hillside to the top of a ridge. From the ridge, the wrinkles and folds and patches of wheat and lentils of the Palouse stretch in all directions. Photographers flock to the Palouse to capture its wide-open beauty, and Kamiak Butte is a unique vantage point.

Start: Day-use area at Kamiak Butte County Park
Distance: 2.5-mile loop
Hiking time: About 1.5 hours
Difficulty: Easy due to short distance and a smooth trail
Trail surface: Dirt and gravel trail
Best season: Spring through early summer
Other trail users: Equestrians
Canine compatibility: Leashed dogs allowed

Elevation gain: 700 feet
Land status: County park
Nearest town: Palouse
Fees and permits: Discover Pass required for parking
Schedule: Year-round
Map: USGS Albion
Trail contacts: Kamiak Butte County Park; (509) 397-6238

Finding the trailhead: From Pullman drive north on WA 27 for 12 miles. Turn left onto Clear Creek Road and continue onto Fugate Road, following signs for Kamiak Butte County Park. In 1 mile turn left into Kamiak Butte County Park; follow the road all the way to the wooded park and day-use parking lot. GPS: N46 52.22' / W117 09.15'

The Hike

The rolling hills that make up the Palouse region of southeastern Washington are surprisingly uniform. From above, your eyes can trace lines and ridges for miles; there is no shortage of beauty, but the ripples are all a similar size. The landscape is a giant version of a sandy beach covered in emerald-green grasses and crops. That's because it was formed by huge flows of water released by the Ancient Lake Missoula ice-age floods. North of Pullman, two islands of quartzite protrude from the gentle landscape—Steptoe Butte and the slightly taller Kamiak Butte. From Kamiak Butte, the fertile Palouse farmland looks like a wrinkled green quilt with patches of every shade. At 3,600 feet, Kamiak Butte may not be tall compared to the mountains of the Cascades, but it towers over its surroundings.

Kamiak Butte is an incredible example of microclimates. The north and south sides of the butte have very different vegetation. The butte's north face is covered in pines, firs, western larches, thick vegetation, and even some cedars. The trail is mostly on this side of the butte, and it winds through a shaded understory of thimbleberries, lady ferns, miner's lettuce, nootka rose, Oregon grape, and mallow ninebark bushes

The Palouse region from Kamiak Butte

with their thick bouquets of little white flowers. The sunnier south slope is a different world. Because the sun bakes it all day, it's mostly free of trees and the lush vegetation of the north slope. Instead it supports the kind of dry grassland ecosystem that covered the Palouse before agriculture took over.

The butte has even more to show off than views of two entirely different ecosystems. From the high point of the butte and most of the ridge along the top, you can see Pullman and Moscow to the south. On clear days, the Blue Mountains are also visible. The sea of solidified magma and silt continues rolling to the north. The region's other quartzite island, Steptoe Butte, is 15 miles northwest of Kamiak Butte and just 29 feet lower in elevation. The rolling hills, waving sea of grains, and rustic barns of the Palouse are popular with photographers, and Kamiak Butte offers a rare chance to get high above this uniform landscape.

The butte is really a long ridge. The Pine Ridge Trail switchbacks up to the low point on the ridge and then follows the ridge dividing the two microclimates. At a high point at the west end of the ridge, the trail dives back into the forest. A short spur from the ridge atop the butte leads to a viewpoint before dead-ending at private property. From the high point, the views are about the same as they are along the ridge.

On top of the ridge, the sunbaked soil is too dry for firs or larches. The occasional deep-rooted ponderosa pine manages to carve out an existence here, but mostly the ridge is covered in wildflowers that bloom from March to July. Indian paintbrush, shooting stars, and asters add bright highlights to the rolling green backdrop. The flowers on top of the butte are stunning, but the flowers in the forest are even more impressive because they are so rare in Eastern Washington. Among the shade-loving species more typical of the Cascades are trillium, foxglove, glacier lilies, and several orchids, as well as flowering dogwoods and hawthorns.

The wildflower season is long on Kamiak Butte thanks to their diversity. The best time to hike the butte is the peak of the flower season in April. Early summer is also a great time to hike Kamiak Butte because the rolling fields of wheat show their dark green hues from the middle of June until late July, when the harvest begins.

The loop can be hiked either way, but if you go left (clockwise), you reach the ridge faster. Start up the trail from the lower parking lot and continue going straight when you encounter a trail to the right in 200 feet. When you descend from the high point of the ridge, the vegetation quickly changes. Soon you are in a dense, humid forest choked with small trees and shrubs. The dense vegetation provides food and cover for deer, voles, porcupines, wrens, sparrows, warblers, and the rufous-sided towhee. A young bull moose and its grumpy mother made Kamiak Butte County Park their home in winter 2012.

A section of this trail passes through an old ski run that the park service built in the 1950s. It soon failed because of a lack of snow. Nearby trees quickly reseeded the open slope, making for a thick growth. Northern saw-whet, pygmy, and great horned owls hang out in the tops of the pines. At the base of the butte there is a quiet

WHAT IS A STEPTOE?

Kamiak Butte, named for Yakama Indian Chief Kamiakin, is a classic steptoe—an isolated mountain of bedrock that was surrounded by a lava flow. The result is a relatively flat or uniform landscape with a surprisingly tall mountain poking out of it. Several times in its life, Kamiak Butte has been an island surrounded by fiery magma.

The magma has cooled, but the steptoes in the Palouse remain ecological islands with different flora than the surrounding grasslands. Dense trees cover most of the butte, which is home to a variety of animals and wildflowers rarely seen in Eastern Washington.

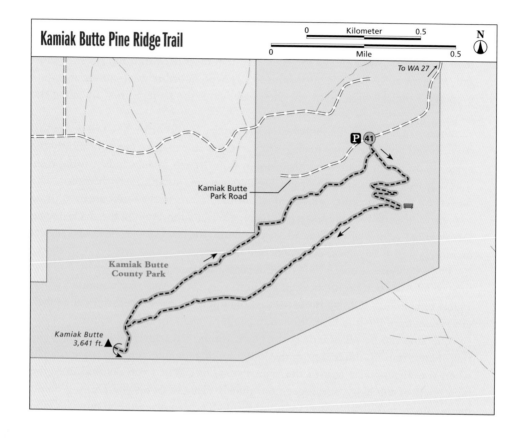

Kamiak Butte Pine Ridge Trail

campground with shaded car and walk-in campsites and a picnic area with restrooms and a playground. The 298-acre park used to be a state park, but Whitman County took it over in 1976 when the state threatened to close it. You'd be hard pressed to find a more pleasant outing in a county park.

Miles and Directions

0.0   Start from the trailhead at the lower lot in the county park's day-use area.

0.1   Go left at the fork for the more direct route up the ridge.

0.3   Begin switchbacks; you'll pass by a bench shortly.

0.5   Bear right at the top of the switchbacks, following a sign for the Pine Ridge Trail. Go right again to continue up the ridge.

1.5   Reach an intersection. Go left for the 0.1-mile spur to the summit, or turn right to complete the loop.

2.4   Arrive back at the first intersection and go left toward the parking lot.

2.5   Arrive back at the parking lot.

Hike Information

Local Events/Attractions

National Lentil Festival, Pullman; usually the third weekend in August; lentilfest.com

Lodging

Kamiak Butte County Park Campground (at the trailhead), 902 Kamiak Butte Park Rd.; (509) 397-6238

Wesson Bunkhouse Bed & Breakfast, 284 Hayward Rd., Pullman; (509) 338-5030; wessonbunkhouse.com

Restaurants

Paradise Creek Brewery, 245 SE Paradise St., Pullman; (509) 338-9463

The Green Frog Cafe, 100 E. Main St., Palouse; (509) 878-1490

Other Resources

Roadside Geology of Washington, by David D. Alt and Donald W. Hyndman

Foxglove on Kamiak Butte's shadier north slope

42 Palouse Falls

This short hike shows off the upper Palouse Falls and the deep canyon of sheer rock that the river travels through before taking the 200-foot drop into a massive punchbowl. It may not be much of a hike, but it offers solitude in a crowded state park—and you won't find views like this anywhere else in Washington.

Start: Parking lot above the falls at Palouse Falls State Park
Distance: 2.0 miles out and back
Hiking time: About 1 hour
Difficulty: Easy due to short distance
Trail surface: Gravel and dirt trail that crosses over several boulders
Land status: State park
Nearest town: Washtucna
Elevation gain: 100 feet
Best season: Spring, when the river is deepest

Other trail users: None
Canine compatibility: Leashed dogs allowed
Fees and permits: Discover Pass required for parking
Schedule: Year-round
Map: USGS Palouse Falls
Trail contacts: Washington State Parks, Palouse Falls State Park; (360) 902-8844; parks.wa.gov
Other: Don't feed the park's yellow-bellied marmots.

Finding the trailhead: From Ellensburg drive east on I-90 for 30 miles. After crossing the Columbia River, take exit 137 to merge onto WA 26E toward Othello and Pullman. Continue east on WA 26 for 83 miles, then turn right onto WA 260. In 6.4 miles turn left onto WA 261 south. After 8.7 miles on WA 261 South, turn left onto Palouse Falls Road. Enter the state park in 2.4 miles and park in the lot. GPS: N46 39.83' / W118 13.63'

The Hike

Palouse Falls is a leg-stretching stop for most area travelers. All you have to do for a view of one of the biggest waterfalls in the Northwest is drive to the parking lot. That's where most people stop. But it's one of the most scenic places in the state, and there's plenty to explore on a short walk to the canyon upstream of the falls. Just 0.5 mile upstream you'll find views of the upper falls and canyon, where you can watch the Palouse River gently flow through a deep basalt chasm.

The falls are among the most impressive anywhere, and they take most tourists by surprise. The surrounding terrain—rolling Palouse farmland known for growing grain—conceals the massive waterfall, and you can't see it until you reach the edge of the canyon. After splashing over a 200-foot drop into a perfectly round basin, the Palouse River winds through a deeply gouged basalt canyon with snaking walls as high as 700 feet.

The canyons upstream and downstream of the falls are home to a huge variety of birds and plants. Red-tailed hawks, peregrine falcons, golden eagles, ospreys, and other birds of prey use their giant wingspans to float above the falls and the canyon rim. Swallows nest in the cliffs and flit about the park in pursuit of insects.

Palouse Falls

The hike begins on the bluffs above the falls. From here the view into the falls borders on terrifying. Even the top of the waterfall is far below the trail. Below the falls, the river slows and flows between the huge canyon walls that cradle it. One riverbank is a vertical cliff; the other is an idyllic patch of green at the bottom of a steep talus slope. After 0.6 mile of hiking along the bluff, descend toward the railroad bed on a steep trail. Don't miss the chance to gawk at the deep gash carved into the basalt for the railroad tracks.

Descend the steep slope beneath the railroad tracks to a vegetated area at a scenic bend in the river. This loose, rocky slope is the only difficult section of the hike. It doesn't last long though. Rattlesnakes enjoy this sunny spot and are frequently seen here, so keep your eyes on the trail and listen for rattling. Squaw currant, sagebrush, balsamroot, lupine, buckwheat, desert parsley, and sagebrush thrive in this pleasant nook between the naked canyon walls.

From here you can walk upstream through the canyon until the trail ends around the bend or scramble downstream along the rocky bank. The downstream route is

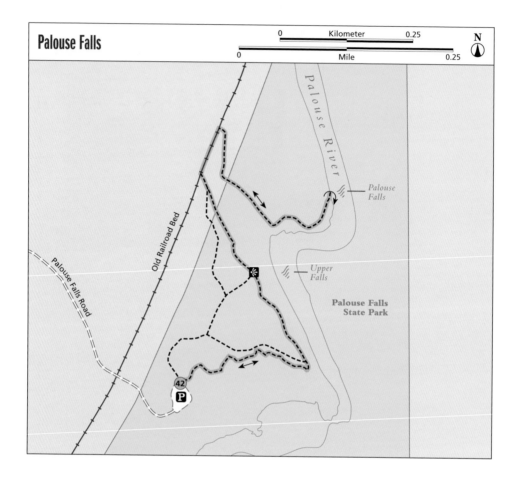

Kilometer

0   0.25

Mile

0   0.25

N

Palouse River

Palouse
Falls

Old Railroad Bed

Palouse Falls Road

Upper
Falls

**Palouse Falls
State Park**

42

P

more dangerous, as it leads to a cliff above the falls and Castle Rock—a set of spires at the head of the waterfall.

Upstream, you enter a land of color and contrast. The deep green river flows against vertical walls of black rock splotched with green and orange lichen. Above the canyon rim, clouds float by in the endless blue sky. This is a great spot to enjoy the tranquility of the river slowly cutting its way deeper into the canyon and get away from the crowds of the park.

Several families of yellow-bellied marmots live in the park. If you go at the right time (late afternoon is good), you'll hear their squeals and see them foraging. Some of the marmots are entirely unconcerned with human presence, while others will barrel toward their nests in the cliffs at the first sight of a person.

Palouse Falls is popular with photographers. They camp out all day with their cameras on tripods to catch the golden colors of sunrise and sunset. Also, the state park has en exceptionally dark sky, making it a popular spot for year-round stargazing. What better way to spend a spring evening than treating your eyes to a feast of bright stars while the heavy flow of the falls purifies your ears.

Miles and Directions

0.0 Start from the parking lot at the end of Palouse Falls Road. Follow the trail on the bluffs upstream and above the falls.

0.4 Reach a viewpoint that looks out over upper Palouse Falls.

0.6 Scramble down a steep trail toward the railroad bed; then continue descending the loose slope below the tracks.

0.8 Reach the upper falls. Continue upstream into the canyon or downstream toward the main falls.

1.0 The trail terminates in the canyon upstream of the upper falls. Return the way you came.

2.0 Arrive back at the parking lot.

Hike Information

Lodging

Camping is available in Palouse Falls State Park (10 first-come first-serve tent sites).

Other Resources

On the Trail of the Ice Age Floods, by Bruce Bjornstad and Eugene Kiver
Audubon Society "Great Washington Birding Trail"; wa.audubon.org/
great-washington-state-birding-trail

A yellow-bellied marmot above the falls

43 Oregon Butte

A gentle ramble to the highest point in Washington's Blue Mountains, this hike through the dry, forested landscape is a fine introduction to this wild corner of the state. The Blues are characterized by tall, gentle mountains divided by deep, entrenched river canyons. They hold many delights, such as cold, clear, springs high in the mountains and a plethora of wildlife.

Start: Mount Misery Trailhead at the east end of the Teepee Campground parking lot, end of FR 4608

Distance: 5.8 miles out and back

Hiking time: About 3 hours

Difficulty: Moderate due to length and modest elevation gain

Trail surface: Dirt trail

Elevation gain: 900 feet

Land status: Federal wilderness area

Nearest town: Dayton

Best season: mid-June through Oct

Other trail users: Equestrians

Canine compatibility: Leashed dogs allowed

Fees and permits: Northwest Forest Pass required to park at trailhead

Maps: *USGS Oregon Butte; USDA Forest Service Wenaha-Tucannon Wilderness* map and *Umatilla National Forest* map

Trail contacts: Umatilla National Forest, Pomeroy Ranger District, 71 West Main St., Pomeroy 99347; (509) 843-1891; www.fs.usda.gov/umatilla

Finding the trailhead: From Dayton turn south from US 12 onto Fourth Street, where a sign points toward the Bluewood ski area. Drive 4.9 miles on the paved road, which becomes Touchet Road, and go left onto gravel Hatley Gulch Road. Follow the roller coaster of Hatley Gulch Road for 5.4 miles and turn right at an intersection onto CR 1424. In 5.9 miles (16.2 miles from Dayton), turn right onto FR 46 at the Kendall Monument and continue 12 miles (26.8 miles from the intersection in Dayton). Turn left onto FR 4608 just before reaching the Godman Guard Station. Follow 4608 to its end, 6 miles from Godman Guard Station, and park at the trailhead at Teepee Campground. GPS: N46 07.07' / W117 42.86'

The Hike

The Blue Mountains and Wenaha-Tucannon Wilderness are an intriguing nook in Washington's southeast corner. Miles of trails traverse the Blue Mountains on mellow ridges and through deep canyons. The mountains comprise a high basalt plateau, deeply cut by rivers and streams into long ridges and canyons. Sun bakes the mountains more often than not, but they're high enough to collect passing moisture and form clouds to water forests of pine, larch, spruce, and subalpine fir.

From Oregon Butte, the highest point in the Wenaha-Tucannon Wilderness, the surrounding sights are exquisite and exotic. Oregon Butte has one of the few remaining staffed fire lookouts in the state, and from the top you can see forever into the distant horizon. On extra-clear days, Cascade volcanoes and the Stuart Range line

The fire lookout on Oregon Butte

the horizon to the west, far beyond the wheat fields and desert. To the east you'll see Oregon's Wallowa Mountains and the towering Seven Devils peaks, above Hells Canyon in Idaho.

The Blue Mountains have many other charms. Most of the trails are snow-free by mid-June. A variety of wild animals, from abundant elk and bear to bighorn sheep and rattlesnakes, populate the ridges and valleys. The area is uncrowded and remote. The civilization that surrounds it is very rural, and the wilderness itself has a primitive appeal. You won't see many signs here, so bring a map.

The trailhead to Oregon Butte starts at nearly 5,400 feet. It's a long steep drive to the trailhead, but it makes the hike to the top of the Blue Mountains pretty easy, with just under 1,000 feet of elevation gain. There's primitive car camping on the way to the trailhead. Teepee Campground, at the trailhead, has a privy, a few picnic tables, and places for tents (no water though). There's also a USDA Forest Service campground nearby on Tucannon Road.

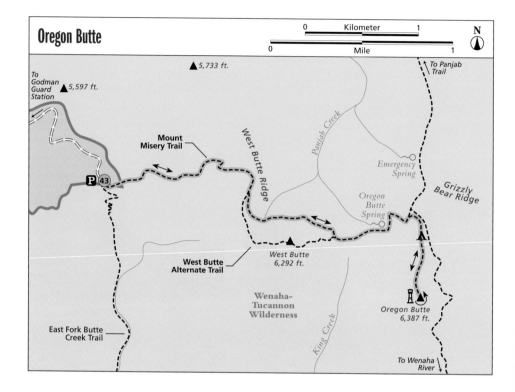

0   Kilometer   1

0   Mile   1

N

▲ 5,733 ft.

To Panjab Trail

To Godman Guard Station ▲ 5,597 ft.

Mount Misery Trail

West Butte Ridge

Panjab Creek

Emergency Spring

Grizzly Bear Ridge

Oregon Butte Spring

P 43

West Butte Alternate Trail

West Butte 6,292 ft.

Wenaha-Tucannon Wilderness

King Creek

Oregon Butte 6,387 ft.

East Fork Butte Creek Trail

To Wenaha River

The trail starts at the east end of the parking lot and is signed MOUNT MISERY TRAIL. The trail gently climbs forested, north-facing slopes. In 1.1 miles you reach a junction. The newer trail goes left, descending slightly. The trail to the right goes to the top of West Butte and then links up with the newer trail in a saddle between West and Oregon Buttes. This older trail isn't maintained, so expect downed trees in the path.

After crossing the north slope of West Butte in a forest of subalpine fir, lodgepole pine, and larch, the new trail rejoins the West Butte Trail at 1.9 miles. In 2.1 miles you'll pass a watering trough fed by Oregon Butte Spring.

Snowmelt in the Blues percolates into the porous basalt rock, creating springs throughout the wilderness. On most trails in the Blues' high country, springs trickle out of the rock every couple miles, allowing hikers to refill water bottles near the tops of mountains. It's a surreal experience in such a dry climate. The Oregon Butte Spring is one of the highest in the region. To be safe, filter the springwater before drinking. Forest service employees aren't allowed to say the springwater is drinkable, but locals drink it straight and argue about which springs produce the tastiest water.

From the spring, turn right at one last junction on the ridge just south of Oregon Butte. The airy views begin on this ridge. Deep ravines snake into the distance toward wild corners of Idaho and Oregon.

Miles and Directions

0.0 Start from the trailhead signed M<small>OUNT</small> M<small>ISERY</small> T<small>RAIL</small>, at the east end of the Teepee Campground parking lot.

1.1 Come to a junction with trail to West Butte. This trail rejoins the Mount Misery Trail in less than 1.0 mile, after climbing West Butte. Stay left for the more direct route to Oregon Butte.

1.9 Reach a junction at a saddle where the trail up West Butte rejoins the Mount Misery Trail.

2.1 Pass a hollowed-out log used as a watering trough at Oregon Butte Spring.

2.3 Bear right at the top of the ridge and head toward the lookout tower atop Oregon Butte.

2.9 Arrive at Oregon Butte and the fire lookout. Return the way you came.

5.8 Arrive back at the campground parking lot.

Hike Information

Lodging
USDA Forest Service Teepee Campground, Tucannon Campground, Umatilla National Forest, Pomeroy Ranger District, 71 West Main St., Pomeroy; (509) 843-1891; www.fs.usda.gov/umatilla
The Weinhard Hotel, 235 E. Main St., Dayton; (509) 382-4032; weinhard.com

Restaurants
Whoopemup Hollow Cafe, 120 Main St., Waitsburg; (509) 337-9000

Other Resources
Hiking Washington's Geology, by Scott Babcock and Bob Carson

A buck on the trail to Oregon Butte

Honorable Mentions

R L.T. Murray Area Hikes—Umtanum Canyon, Umtanum Falls, Yakima Skyline

Trails abound in the L. T. Murray Wildlife Recreation area between Ellensburg and Yakima. The lush Umtanum Canyon is packed with life! The basalt-walled canyon starts out wide with broad, sweeping hills and a carpet of sagebrush. The canyon narrows and fills with vegetation, especially around the bubbling creek. The canyon continues to narrow until about 3.0 miles in, when the trail begins to peter out. This is a good spot to turn around—or set up camp and explore the canyon walls off-trail. Wildflowers paint the gash in an array of colors in spring, and the aspens, alders, and cottonwoods put on a spectacular fall show. At a different trailhead, the short walk to Umtanum Falls is easy, shaded, and beautiful any time of year. The Yakima Skyline Trail is a classic, and one of the longest hikes you'll find in Eastern Washington. Motor vehicles seem to be trespassing in the area more frequently, and many of the roads to get to the trail require four-wheel drive and high ground clearance. But if you can get there, you can wander for miles along the rim of the Yakima Canyon between Ellensburg and Selah.

For the Umtanum Canyon Trailhead, take exit 109 off I-90 near Ellensburg. Go right onto Canyon Road. Soon you'll be driving through the Yakima Canyon alongside the river, a beautiful trip in its own right. Park on the right at the Umptanum Creek Recreation Area, 12 miles from the interstate. Walk across the suspension bridge over the Yakima, cross the railroad tracks, and find the trail leading into the brush.

S Frenchman Coulee

This coulee isn't as hiker-friendly as Ancient Lakes coulee, but it has some of the most interesting basalt formations in the state. The mighty, free-standing columns of basalt known as The Feathers and other walls in the area are popular rock-climbing destinations. From the bottom of the coulee, an old jeep track leads 2 miles to a waterfall that spills over a 400-foot basalt cliff to the floor of the coulee. The downside to this hike is that you can see nearly all of it, including the waterfall at the end, from the road. Even so, the coulee and the area on top of it are worth exploring for the breathtaking views and spires of rock. Don't miss the views into the Columbia River either.

From Ellensburg drive east for 33 miles on I-90 to exit 143. After exiting, turn left and go under the interstate. In less than 1 mile, turn left onto Vantage Road. Drive 2.7 miles to the small parking area on the right, at the bottom of the coulee.

T Ginkgo Petrified Forest State Park Backcountry

In addition to a 1.5-mile paved trail leading to samples of petrified wood, this state park has some deserted trails that climb high-desert bluffs over the Columbia River.

An old jeep track and roughly 5 miles of trail lead up the ridge, but you don't need a trail to explore the open shrub-steppe. Views over the cliffs and into the massive river are excellent, as are the wildflowers.

From Ellensburg drive 26 miles east on I-90 to exit 136 toward Vantage, Turn left onto Vantage Highway, drive 1 mile, and then turn right onto Recreation Road. In 0.5 mile park on the left side of the road at the trailhead by the old jeep track, or continue to the end of the road to park and walk back uphill to the trailhead.

U Badger Mountain

Badger Mountain is a short but scenic hike just minutes from Richland. The trail to the top gains more than 800 feet of elevation on the way to a broad summit with views of the Tri-Cities. Like many desert high points near cities, it's a popular training hike for locals. You can do a 3.6-mile loop by ascending the trail on the northeast side of the mountain and taking the more gradual trail down the southeast slope.

From eastbound I-82, take exit 3 for Queensgate Drive. Turn right onto Queensgate Drive and head south. In 0.5 mile take the second left onto Keene Road. In 0.6 mile turn right onto Shockley Road, which becomes Queensgate Drive in 0.5 mile. Park in the lot near White Bluffs Street, just after the road begins going uphill.

V Juniper Dunes Wilderness

There's nothing else like the Juniper Dunes Wilderness—at least not in Washington. It's the state's only non-forested wilderness area and the only Bureau of Land Management managed wilderness. Juniper trees grow in places, but mainly the area is covered in rolling white dunes. Naked wilderness. A variety of desert plants and flowers temporarily hold the dunes in place, but the landscape is constantly shifting. The wilderness is waterless, and the only trails are animal tracks. It's easy to get lost wandering among the sage, sand dock, deer and bird tracks, and cactus. The 7,100-acre wilderness has no trails, so bring a compass or GPS while you wander the dunes; it's easy to get disoriented. The hike is best in spring, when wildflowers are blooming. Unfortunately, the wilderness is currently hard to access.

The road to the official trailhead parallels private property and several No Trespassing signs and ends in an impassible road miles from the entrance to the wilderness. A farmer on the north side of the wilderness allows access across his property in March, April, and May. As of winter 2014, the BLM is working on securing public access to the Juniper Dunes. To get to the Juniper Dunes's northern access (open from March to May) from US 12 in Pasco, go northeast on Pasco-Kahlotus Road for 24 miles. Turn left onto Snake River Road and in 3.5 miles turn left again onto E. Blackman Ridge Road. In 2.4 miles turn left onto Joy Road and follow it 2 miles to a deadend at Juniper Dunes Ranch. Respect the rules at the trailhead and the generous farmer who allows access across his land.

The Olympic Peninsula

T he Olympic Peninsula, with its mass of jumbled mountains and more than 1,500 square miles of protected space, is probably the best hiking destination in the state for fans of pristine landscapes. Rain forest valleys with ancient trees and rugged, glaciated mountains fill the heart of Olympic National Park in the center of the peninsula. Around the park, a doughnut of wilderness areas protect even more forest and wildlife habitat, allowing some animals to migrate around the heart of the wilderness at lower elevations.

The peninsula has the longest stretch of undeveloped shoreline in the lower 48. It's a mix of long, sandy beaches and dangerous rocky headlands. Sea stacks hundreds of feet tall, topped with gnarled trees and windswept grass, stand like sentinels along the coast.

The expanse of unbroken wilderness in the park is a haven for wildlife. Hikers frequently see bears and mountain goats in the Olympic high country, and multitudes of elk migrate between the alpine meadows and lowland river valleys.

The Olympic Mountains aren't a linear mountain range but a sprawling mass of mountains and valleys with subranges in every direction. The mountains started as ocean floor and uplifted as the Juan De Fuca Plate subducted beneath the North American Plate. The resulting mountains aren't as high as the Cascades—Mount Olympus is the tallest point at 7,979 feet. But they begin near the ocean shore, and the incredible depth of the river valleys make them seem plenty high.

The mountains here are, for the most part, not as jagged as much of the Cascades. Several areas of hard, glaciated basalt are the exceptions. The Sawtooth Range near Flapjack Lakes and the Needles west of Marmot Pass are both composed of this erosion-resistant basalt, which is much harder than the sandstone and shale that make up much of the rest of the range. The upside to the range's softer rock is that you can traverse many of the tall, prominent ridges on easy trails.

Major rivers spiral out from the center of the wilderness. Due to the rain, trees in these valleys grow incredibly tall. Some of the biggest and oldest trees of their kind grow in the temperate rain forest valleys on the peninsula's west side. Like the Cascades, the Olympics also shield their east slopes from rain. While 200 inches of precipitation fall near Mount Olympus (mostly in the form of snow), Sequim, in its rain shadow, gets just 17 inches of rain annually.

Flower gardens in Grand Valley (hike 47).

44 Flapjack Lakes

Sometimes in the Olympic Mountains it takes a while to get to your destination. The trailhead to Flapjack Lakes—two emerald-green lakes below Sawtooth Ridge—starts way down in the Skokomish River Valley amid some of the biggest trees on the east side of the peninsula. You'll be tired when you finally emerge at the sublime lakes, but the cold blue water and jagged skyline peaks will wash away memories of the long journey.

Start: Trailhead next to the Staircase Ranger Station
Distance: 15 miles out and back
Hiking time: About 8 to 10 hours
Difficulty: Difficult due to length and elevation gain
Trail surface: Wide gravel and dirt trail that becomes a narrower dirt trail at the junction for Flapjack Lakes
Elevation gain: 2,850 feet
Land status: National park
Nearest town: Hoodsport
Best season: Mid-June to Oct

Other trail users: None
Canine compatibility: No dogs allowed
Fees and permits: Olympic National Park entry fee
Maps: *Green Trails Custom Correct Mount Skokomish-Lake Cushman; Green Trails no. 167, Mt. Steel*
Trail contacts: Olympic National Park Wilderness Information Center, Port Angeles; (360) 565-3100; nps.gov/olym
Other: Camping is limited by quota between May 1 and Sept 30.

Finding the trailhead: From Hoodsport turn left onto WA 119. It's on the north end of town, right next to Hoodsport Hamburger and Ice Cream. Follow WA 119 for 9.2 miles to a T junction with FR 24. Turn left and drive for 5.4 miles (pavement ends at 1.7 miles). Turn right at a junction, following signs for the Staircase Ranger Station, and continue 1.2 miles to the trailhead parking lot on the right side of the road, across from the campground. GPS: N47 30.95' / W123 19.67'

The Hike

It's a long lowland march to see these twin lakes deep in the southwestern Olympics. The steep climb to the lakes basin is hard after the long, flat first half of the hike. But the view of the emerald-green lakes at the foot of perhaps the barest, most jagged rock ridge in the Olympics is enough to melt your fatigue away.

Sawtooth Ridge is composed of some of the hardest rock on the peninsula. The ridge started as a series of underwater volcanic mountains in the Pacific Ocean. As the Juan de Fuca Plate moved westward, it pushed these mountains skyward for thousands of feet, resulting in an arc of basalt peaks that are mostly on the eastern edge of the Olympic Mountains. The rock is pillow basalt, which is formed when lava flows into the water. The dark rock looks bubbly—almost like a series of drip castles made from wet sand. This makes it easy to imagine the alpine peaks forming underwater.

Upper Flapjack Lake and Mount Lincoln

These basalt peaks are much harder than the rest of the rock in the Olympics, which is mostly sandstone, shale, and slate. In this glaciated landscape, they protrude like spines from the softer rock.

The trail to the lakes used to be about 3.0 miles shorter, but a section of the access road kept washing out and is now part of the trail. The trail begins on this road-returned-to-trail. The first section is flat, but it's not boring. The old-growth forest along the Skokomish River is some of the biggest and most diverse on the eastern side of the Olympics. Alaskan yellow cedar, hemlock, and Douglas fir trees reach hundreds of feet into the air. Their thousands of needles grasp at the sun above a forest that's home to a rich array of insects, fungi, and mammals. On the way through these ancient forests, you'll cross Slate Creek 0.5 mile from the parking lot. All the while, the North Fork Skokomish gushes by.

At 1.8 miles you'll pass a sign marking the 1985 Beaver Fire. Spare patches of huge trees survived the blaze. In between them, young trees are quickly growing up amid big domes of pillow basalt.

The trail to the lakes begins with a right turn onto the Flapjack Lakes Trail in 3.6 miles. It begins climbing a slope covered in huckleberries. Rangers say bears are frequently seen here and at the meadows south of Flapjack Lakes. Watch and listen for them to come crashing through the brush on their way to a meal of berries.

After some switchbacks in the first 1.0 mile of the Flapjack Lakes Trail, the path flattens out and crosses some marshy areas on boardwalks. The trail stays flat or climbs gently until the final 1.0 mile to the lake, where it's plain steep.

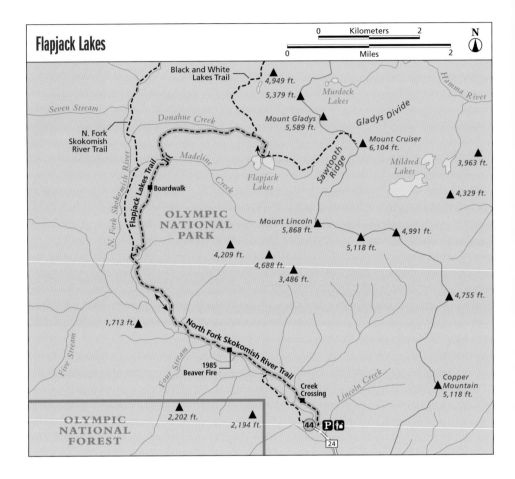

The finger of land between the lakes is closed for revegetation, but there are several campsites around the two lakes. If you're not content to admire the view from the forested shores of the Flapjack Lakes, take the 1.4-mile trail from the lakes to Gladys Divide and get more intimate with Sawtooth Ridge. The divide is a gap between the rugged range and a high round hump called Mount Gladys. Exquisite wildflower meadows grow along the way, and icy snowfields draped around the shoulders of the basalt peaks extend nearly to the trail below the divide.

Miles and Directions

0.0 Start at the parking lot/trailhead for the North Fork Skokomish River Trail.

0.5 Cross Slate Creek on a log bridge or hop across on rocks.

0.8 Cross a creek.

1.0 Continue straight at a junction with the Rapids Loop Bridge Trail.

1.8 Pass a sign marking the 1985 Beaver Fire.

3.6 Turn right onto the Flapjack Lakes Trail.

5.0 Hike across wet sections of the trail on an elevated boardwalk.

5.2 Cross Madeline Creek on a sturdy bridge over a small canyon.

6.9 Turn right at a junction with the trail to Black and White Lakes.

7.5 Reach Flapjack Lakes. Return the way you came.

15.0 Arrive back at the trailhead.

Option

From Flapjack Lakes, continue east on the trail for 1.4 miles to Gladys Divide.

Hike Information

Lodging

Olympic National Park Staircase Campground, at the trailhead, Staircase Ranger Station; (360) 877-5560

Glen Ayr Resort, 25381 N. US 101, Hoodsport; (360) 877-9522; glenayr.com

Restaurants

Hoodsport Hamburger & Ice Cream, 2440 N. Lake Cushman Rd., Hoodsport; (360) 877-6122

OLYMPIC BACKCOUNTRY SHELTERS

In 1932 more than one hundred backcountry shelters protected travelers in Olympic National Park and Forest from the elements. Shelter construction started in 1912, according to a 2008 report the national park published on historic structures in the park. At that time, the USDA Forest Service thought a network of trails throughout the area was essential for fire prevention. Shelters were built to store equipment and provide protection for fire crews and patrol personnel.

By 1920 more and more people were coming to the park to hike and backpack, and the forest service recognized the recreational value of their backcountry shelters. Before the advent of modern tents, a dry, sturdy shelter a full day's walk from the nearest road was a cherished part of the wilderness experience for many hikers. The last shelters were built in the 1960s. Few shelters remain in the national park, and many of those still standing are in disrepair.

45 Mount Ellinor

A short but very steep staircase of a trail leads to the top of Mount Ellinor. This classic peak on the southeast corner of the Olympic Mountains has incredible views of Lake Cushman, Hood Canal, and the Olympic interior. It's a treat to be at the edge of the Olympic Mountains, where you can see so much water surrounding alpine mountains.

Start: Trailhead at the end of FR 2419-014

Distance: 3.4 miles out and back

Hiking time: About 3 hours

Difficulty: Moderate due to steep sections of trail and elevation gain

Trail surface: Dirt, gravel, and rock trail

Elevation gain: 2,400 feet

Land status: National forest, federal wilderness area

Nearest town: Hoodsport

Best season: July through Oct

Other trail users: None

Canine compatibility: Leashed dogs allowed

Fees and permits: Northwest Forest Pass required to park at trailhead

Map: *Green Trails Custom Correct Mount Skokomish–Lake Cushman*

Trail contacts: Olympic National Forest, Hood Canal Ranger District; (360) 956-2402; www.fs.usda.gov/recarea/olympic

Finding the trailhead: Turn west onto WA 119 in Hoodsport, following signs for the Hood Canal Ranger District. Continue 9 miles to a T junction and turn right onto FR 24. In 1.6 miles turn left onto FR 2419. Continue 6.2 miles (you'll pass the lower trailhead parking area on the right in 4.8 miles) to a junction, and turn left onto FR 2419-014. Continue 1 mile to the upper trailhead and parking area. GPS: N47 30.61' / W123 14.87'

The Hike

Among short hikes to long views, Mount Ellinor is queen. Less than 2.0 miles of trail climax at a panorama spanning views of Lake Cushman and Hood Canal, the majority of the Cascade Range, and the heart of the Olympics. The views, combined with the fact that this is one of the easiest parts of the Olympic Mountains to reach from Puget Sound metropolises, make this a popular hike.

But don't get the wrong idea—it's not easy to get to the summit. In just 1.7 miles the Mount Ellinor Trail climbs 2,400 feet. Most of the way, the trail is a staircase of rocks, roots, and logs; it's as steep as they come. The trail is well built, though, and can handle the volume it gets.

From the upper lot, the hike stays on top of a steep ridge covered in mature trees. It's steep right from the get-go, and it only gets steeper and rougher. (**Option:** A lower trail winds through old-growth forest for 1.5 miles before connecting with the upper trail 0.3 mile from the parking lot. Adding the lower trail to the hike to Mount Ellinor creates a 6.6-mile out and back hike.)

Lake Cushman and the steep trail up Mount Ellinor

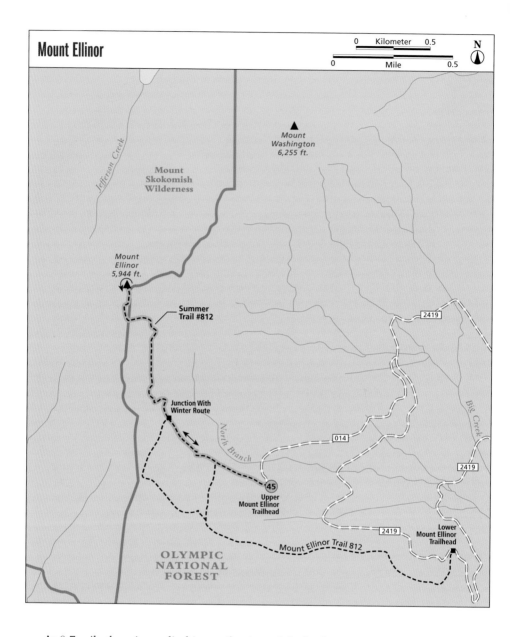

0   Kilometer   0.5

0   Mile   0.5

N

Mount
Washington
6,255 ft.

Mount
Skokomish
Wilderness

Jefferson Creek

Mount
Ellinor
5,944 ft.

Summer
Trail #812

2419

Junction With
Winter Route

North Branch

Big Creek

014

2419

45

Upper
Mount Ellinor
Trailhead

2419

Lower
Mount Ellinor
Trailhead

Mount Ellinor Trail 812

OLYMPIC
NATIONAL
FOREST

At 0.7 mile the winter climbing trail swings right, leading to a snowy gully below the summit. Bear left and you'll soon be rewarded with the first views. Through gaps in the clumps of subalpine firs, you can see west to Hood Canal and the Cascades. Gentians, lupine, and paintbrush grow in between blocky boulders. Even though you're less than 1.0 mile from the trailhead, you'll be tempted to take a water break and admire the view from the flat top of one of these boulders.

Near the top, the trail enters the Mount Skokomish Wilderness Area. The 13,015-acre wilderness is one of five wilderness areas that form a doughnut of protected land around Olympic National Park. Just below the summit, the trail leaves the boulder gardens behind and switchbacks up bare rock slopes speckled with green patches of vegetation and wildflowers. After a final steep scramble, the trail tops out on Ellinor's rocky summit. Here you're surrounded by the deep greens and blues of two mountain ranges, Lake Cushman, and Hood Canal. Mount Washington is the tall summit to the northeast. To the north, Mounts Pershing and Stone sit next to the rugged Sawtooth Range to their west. Beyond is the rest of the Olympic Mountains, which, from this southeast corner, extend about 40 miles to the northwest.

Miles and Directions

- **0.0** Start at the upper trailhead.
- **0.3** Bear right at a junction with the lower trailhead; continue up the steep ridge.
- **0.7** Continue straight, following signs for the summer trail, at a junction with a faint trail leading right (east).
- **1.7** Reach the rocky summit of Mount Ellinor. Return the way you came.
- **3.4** Arrive back at the upper trailhead.

Hike Information

Lodging
Olympic National Park Staircase Campground, Staircase Ranger Station; (360) 877-5560
Glen Ayr Resort, 25381 N. US 101, Hoodsport; (360) 877-9522; glenayr.com

Restaurants
Hoodsport Hamburger & Ice Cream, 2440 N. Lake Cushman Rd., Hoodsport; (360) 877-6122

46 Marmot Pass

You may not hear the whistling of the Olympic Peninsula's endemic marmots from this high notch, but the view into the rugged heart of Olympic National Park won't let you down. Craggy basalt peaks—some of the hardest and sharpest in the Olympics—spread across the horizon on one side of the divide. In the other direction, the Pacific Ocean completes the panorama.

Start: Big Quilcene Trail 833, on FR 2750
Distance: 10.6 miles out and back
Hiking time: About 6 hours
Difficulty: Difficult due to length and elevation gain
Trail surface: Dirt trail
Elevation gain: 3,450 feet
Land status: Federal wilderness area
Nearest town: Quilcene

Best season: Mid-July to Oct
Other trail users: None
Canine compatibility: No dogs allowed
Fees and permits: Northwest Forest Pass required to park at trailhead
Map: *Green Trails Custom Correct Buckhorn Wilderness*
Trail contacts: USDA Forest Service, Quilcene Ranger District; (360) 765-2200

Finding the trailhead: From Olympia drive 70 miles on US 101 N. About 1 mile south of Quilcene, turn left (west) onto Penny Creek Road. In 1.4 miles turn left onto Big Quilcene River Road. Continue on Big Quilcene River Road, bearing right in 3.1 miles. Reach FR 2750, 9.4 miles after turning onto Big Quilcene River Road. Follow this road up and down for 4.5 miles until you reach the parking area next to Big Quilcene Trail 833, 15.3 miles from US 101. GPS: N47 49.67' / W123 02.47'

The Hike

Marmot Pass is one of the prettiest alpine viewpoints in the Olympics. The Mount Constance and Warrior Peak group nearby are some of the tallest, craggiest peaks on the dry side of the Olympic Range, and an assortment of other peaks line the horizon. Several paths lead to this high pass. The classic route along the Big Quilcene River described here is the shortest. It leads through deep forests alongside misty pools and logjams in the river and up through flower-filled meadows past several campsites to a final push to a gap between mountains.

At the pass, you can look back the way you came at meadows and Puget Sound in the distance. Marmot Pass is near some of the tallest mountains in the Olympics. The peaks demonstrate the rain shadow effect of the western Olympic Mountains. Mount Constance, at 7,756, feet is barely lower than 7,979-foot-tall Mount Olympus, yet it has a fraction of the snow and glaciers. That's because Mount Olympus is directly west of Mount Constance and collects the storms blowing off the Pacific Ocean. Much less water and snow make it farther east to Mount Constance and the east side of the Olympics.

Wildflowers and basalt crags on the way to Marmot Pass

The trail begins deep in a mosaic of green surrounding the foaming Big Quilcene River. Big trees grow out of a low carpet of moss. The meandering trail occasionally nears the cool stream that plunges and pools between snarls of downed trees and mossy boulders. As the trail climbs, the low mat of understory moss is slowly joined by taller groundcover plants like Oregon grape and salal.

Several small creeks flow from beneath barren basalt piles on the tall northern slopes and into the creek. The streamside zones are thick with berries and some patches of spiny devil's club. Elderberries and thimbleberries reach for the sun, and the moisture feeds salmonberries the size—and sometimes color—of strawberries.

The trail switches back at 1.7 miles and then switchbacks again shortly after and drops beneath a waterfall that fans out over volcanic rock. The trail begins climbing in earnest after the falls. The path climbs away from the creek and skirts beneath craggy rock spires on the southern slopes of Buckhorn and Iron Mountains. Small clumps of Alaskan yellow cedars and subalpine fir grow along the trail. A variety of flowers sprout in talus crevices. Arnicas and asters add color to the dark mountains in the background. About a dozen wildflowers are endemic to the Olympic Peninsula, and at least a couple of them grow along the trail to Marmot Pass. Look for purple

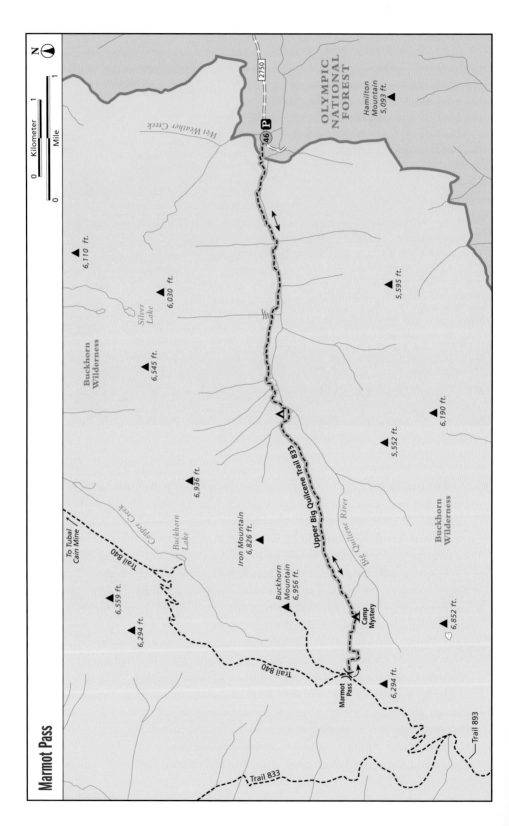

Marmot Pass

N

| 0 | Kilometer | 1 |
| 0 | Mile | 1 |

OLYMPIC NATIONAL FOREST

Hamilton Mountain
5,093 ft. ▲

5,595 ft. ▲

6,110 ft. ▲

6,030 ft. ▲

Silver Lake

6,545 ft. ▲

6,190 ft. ▲

5,552 ft. ▲

Buckhorn Wilderness

Wet Weather Creek

2750

46

6,936 ft. ▲

Upper Big Quilcene Trail 833

Big Quilcene River

Buckhorn Wilderness

6,852 ft. ▲

To Tubal Cain Mine

Trail 840

Copper Creek

Buckhorn Lake

Iron Mountain
6,826 ft. ▲

Buckhorn Mountain
6,956 ft. ▲

Camp Mystery

6,559 ft. ▲

6,294 ft. ▲

Marmot Pass

Trail 840

6,294 ft. ▲

Trail 833

Trail 893

Piper's bellflower and Olympic violets. Smatterings of much more common paint-brush, lupine, and Queen Anne's lace also grow in gardens along the trail.

The wildflowers keep getting better until you reach Camp Mystery, a flat spot with established camps near a creek at 5.0 miles. From here, hike up a few final switchbacks toward Marmot Pass. The view behind you swells all the time, until at last Puget Sound appears. Once you reach the crest of Marmot Pass, a whole new world of wilderness appears. Gaze west into the heart of Olympic National Park. Mount Mystery, Mount Deception, and a line of rugged points called the Needles crown the top of a tall ridge. Between Marmot Pass and this row of mountains, the headwaters of the Dungeness River drain a deep green gulf.

Options: From the pass, walk on the trail south to the top of a knoll for even better views, or climb the loose trail to the top of Mount Buckhorn for 360-degree views of the rugged mountains and Puget Sound.

Miles and Directions

0.0 Start at the Upper Big Quilcene 833 trailhead on FR 2750.

1.9 Pass a fan-shaped waterfall on the right side of the trail. Shortly after, cross another small stream; the trail begins climbing in earnest.

3.2 Pass several campsites along the Big Quilcene River.

5.0 Pass Camp Mystery—several campsites scattered around water trickling off snow near Marmot Pass.

5.3 Reach Marmot Pass. Return the way you came.

10.6 Arrive back at the trailhead.

Hike Information

Lodging

USDA Forest Service Falls View Campground, 3.5 miles south of Quilcene on US 101; (360) 756-3368

Restaurants

The Olympic Timberhouse Restaurant, 295534 US 101, Quilcene; (360) 765-0129

OLYMPIC MOUNTAIN GOATS

Mountain goats are native to the Cascades and British Columbia Coast Range, but they never made it to the Olympic Peninsula on their own. In the 1920s mountain goats were introduced to the Olympics, probably by hunters. Today the snow-white ungulates thrive in the Olympics, scrambling over cliffs and feasting on the high alpine plants.

President Franklin Roosevelt signed the act establishing Olympic National Park in 1938, protecting the Olympic mountain goats from hunting. In comparison, mountain goats in the Cascades were overhunted between 1950 and the late 1980s.

Soon the Olympic goat population outnumbered their relatives in the Cascades, and since they weren't hunted, they became increasingly bold.

Olympic National Forest officials closed the Mount Ellinor Trail in 2012 after several hiking parties reported encountering aggressive mountain goats. The mountain goats had learned that humans have food and expel salty urine and had begun pursuing hikers in hopes of handouts. So forest service officials set out to change the goats' opinion of humans. They yelled at goats, blew air horns, and threw rocks at them.

To keep the Olympic goats wild, stay away from them. If you must urinate in the wilderness, do it on rocks away from the trail. This way, goats won't kill vegetation while digging to get at the salt and minerals found in human urine.

Another challenge with the Olympic mountain goats is that since they're nonnative, they have caused a lot of damage to the dozen or so plant species endemic to the Olympics. In the 1980s parks officials captured as many goats as they could and relocated them to the Cascades. Wildlife officials are considering relocating additional Olympic mountain goats, but the process of tranquilizing and transporting mountain goats is expensive.

47 Grand Valley

The hike to Grand Valley is backwards—you start from one of the highest trailheads in the Olympics, roam through the sky on a ridge of flowery alpine tundra, and then descend to a lake-filled valley. The valley is grand, and so are the lakes and the view of Mount Olympus from the hike's high points.

Start: Lillian Ridge Trailhead at the Obstruction Point parking lot

Distance: 7.6 miles out and back

Hiking time: About 5 hours

Difficulty: Moderate due to elevation gain on the return trip

Trail surface: Dirt trail and broken rock that is loose in places

Elevation gain: 1,400 feet on the return trip from Grand Valley; 2,000 feet on the Badger Valley Loop

Land status: National park

Nearest town: Port Angeles

Best season: Late July through Oct

Other trail users: None

Canine compatibility: No dogs allowed

Fees and permits: Olympic National Park entry fee. Camping is limited between May 1 and September 30; 50 percent of campsites can be reserved.

Maps: *Green Trails no. 134S, Elwha North–Hurricane Ridge; Green Trails Custom Correct Hurricane Ridge*

Trail contacts: Olympic National Park Wilderness Information Center, Port Angeles; (360) 565-3100; nps.gopv/olym

Other: Camping is limited between May 1 and Sept 30; 50 percent of campsites can be reserved.

Finding the trailhead: From Port Angeles go south on Race Street, which becomes Hurricane Ridge Road. Pass the Wilderness Information Center and the entry station to the park, where the park fee is collected. Continue on Hurricane Ridge Road for 17.5 miles from Port Angeles. Turn left onto Obstruction Point Road, a gravel road, just before the Hurricane Ridge Visitor Center's parking lot. Drive 7.7 miles to a parking lot at the end of the road. GPS: N47 55.09' / W123 22.93'

The Hike

In 1788 English explorer John Meares named Mount Olympus because he thought it looked like a suitable dwelling for the gods. Just north of Mount Olympus, this trail along Lillian Ridge to Grand Valley seems a suitable walk for the gods.

From Obstruction Point, one of the most beautiful spots you can drive to in the state, there are several interesting options for day hiking and backpacking. The trail through the sky along Lillian Ridge eventually leads down to Grand Valley, where after exploring several lakes you can retrace your steps to the parking lot or take the long route back via the gladed meadows of Badger Valley.

The hike begins high up in cool mountain air. From the Obstruction Point parking lot, wander out into the clouds on the Lillian Ridge Trail. The ridge is a lofty spine that reaches toward the center of the Olympics, surrounded by deep drainages

A marmot on the trail

on both sides, flowing away more than 4,000 feet to streams fed by the lingering snow, carving their channels ever deeper.

The ridge runs roughly parallel to the Bailey Range, which includes Mount Olympus and several others of the highest, snowiest peaks in the Olympics. On the other side of the trail, ash-black ridges of crumbling volcanic talus rise and fall on their way to Deer Park and other destinations.

The first 2.0 miles of trail along Lillian Ridge make a great short hike, with views starting at the parking lot and minimal elevation change. After that, follow the trail as it winds around the ridge and begin descending 1,200 feet toward Grand Valley. You'll leave Mount Olympus behind as you turn the corner and begin walking toward Puget Sound, the San Juan Islands, and Mount Baker.

The surroundings slowly change as the dusty trail switchbacks downhill. Only the hardiest subalpine plants and flowers suck nutrients from beneath the shards of loose rock at the top of the descent. Slightly lower, islands of stunted subalpine fir grow outwards instead of up. Farther down, the trees get thicker and the space between them fills with meadows of grass and flowers.

Grand Lake is the first lake you come to, and the most popular for camping. The lakes are exquisite. Trails wind around them, and you can find plenty of private nooks amid the water and flowers.

Either explore the valley and return the way you came, or head north on the trail above Grand Lake toward Badger Valley. Most hikers return on the trail to Lillian Ridge rather than making the loop, because the trail to Badger Valley descends nearly 900 feet before climbing back to Obstruction Point. On the way to Badger Valley, the trail passes several streams with roaring waterfalls hidden by the forest. From the bottom of the valley, the trail climbs through open glades and flowery meadows bursting with lupines, paintbrush, and monkey flower. Finally, switchbacks lead up a slope of loose, broken basalt to the Deer Park Trail. Round the bend and you'll see Mount Olympus again, just before arriving back at the trailhead.

Miles and Directions

0.0 Start on the Lillian Ridge Trail from the Obstruction Point parking lot and trailhead.

1.0 Descend from the crest of Lillian Ridge on rock steps.

1.4 Return briefly to the top of Lillian Ridge.

2.0 Round the side of Lillian Ridge, leaving views of Mount Olympus and the Bailey Range behind, and begin descending toward Grand Valley.

3.6 Turn left at a junction with the trail to Grand Lake and Badger Valley.

3.8 Reach the shore of Grand Lake. There are several campsites along the right (south) side of the lake. Turn around to return the way you came.

7.6 Arrive back at Obstruction Point.

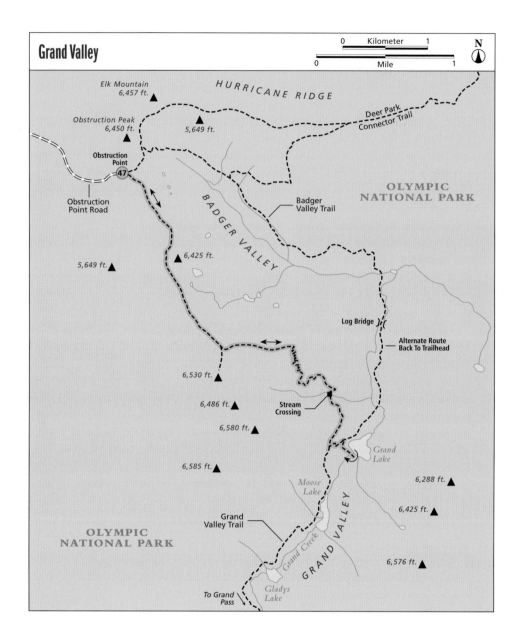

0   Kilometer   1

0   Mile   1

N

Elk Mountain
6,457 ft.

HURRICANE RIDGE

Deer Park
Connector Trail

Obstruction Peak
6,450 ft.

5,649 ft.

Obstruction
Point

47

Obstruction
Point Road

BADGER VALLEY

Badger
Valley Trail

**OLYMPIC
NATIONAL PARK**

5,649 ft.

6,425 ft.

Log Bridge

Alternate Route
Back To Trailhead

6,530 ft.

6,486 ft.

Stream
Crossing

6,580 ft.

*Grand
Lake*

6,585 ft.

6,288 ft.

*Moose
Lake*

6,425 ft.

**OLYMPIC
NATIONAL PARK**

Grand
Valley Trail

Grand Creek

GRAND VALLEY

6,576 ft.

To Grand
Pass

*Gladys
Lake*

Option

From Grand Lake, continue north on the Badger Valley Trail, which descends about 900 feet before climbing back up. In 4.7 miles, turn left at a junction with the Deer Park Trail. From here, it's 0.2 mile to Obstruction Point, making a 9.7-mile loop.

Grand Lake

Hike Information

Local Events
Dungeness Crab and Seafood Festival, Port Angeles; (360) 452-6300; crabfestival.org

Lodging
Olympic National Park Heart O' The Hills Campground, Olympic National Park Wilderness Information Center, Port Angeles; 6 miles south of Port Angeles on Hurricane Ridge Rd.; (360) 565-3100; nps.gov/olym

Restaurants
Smuggler's Landing Restaurant and Lounge, 115 E. Railroad Ave., Ste. 101, Port Angeles; (360) 452-9292

Organizations
Klahhane Hiking Club; klahhaneclub.org

48 High Divide Loop

The 19-mile High Divide Loop journeys deep into the Olympics. The climax of the trip is roaming in the shadows of Mount Olympus on the High Divide. But there's plenty more to this loop, including bears, elk, a rocky basin crowded with pristine lakes, an ancient rain forest valley, and several wooded lakes.

Start: Trailhead at Sol Duc
Distance: 19.5-mile loop
Hiking time: About 10 to 12 hours
Difficulty: Difficult due to length and elevation gain
Trail surface: Dirt trail
Elevation gain: 3,400 feet
Land status: National park
Nearest town: Forks
Best season: July to Oct
Other trail users: Stock allowed, except in the Seven Lakes basin
Canine compatibility: No dogs allowed

Fees and permits: Park entrance fee required
Map: *Green Trails Custom Correct Seven Lakes Basin–Hoh*
Trail contacts: Olympic National Park Wilderness Information Center, Port Angeles; (360) 565-3100; nps.gov/olym
Special considerations: Bear canisters are required and can be rented from the park service.
Other: Overnight camping permits are required for camping; minimal cost per person, per night.

Finding the trailhead: From Port Angeles continue west on US 101 for 28 miles. Turn left (south) onto Sol Duc Road, signed SOL DUC HOT SPRINGS ROAD, 2.1 miles past the end of Lake Crescent. Or get to this point by driving east 27.6 miles on US 101 from Forks. Follow this road for 13 miles to the parking lot and trailhead at its end. GPS: N47 57.29' / W123 50.08'

The Hike

Meadows and berry fields on the High Divide Loop offer a late summer banquet to some of the biggest megafauna in Olympic National Park. For hikers, the lake basin and high ridgeline offer a banquet of views. The High Divide straddles two worlds. On one side is a basin with dozens of alpine lakes swaddled in rocky meadows. On the other, Mount Olympus and the Bailey Range—the white crown of the Olympics—rise above the Hoh River's 4,000-foot-deep valley.

The High Divide Loop is good in either direction, but this description is for the counterclockwise trip. From the Sol Duc Trailhead, a wide gravel trail descends gently toward the river. In 0.9 mile you'll reach a fork at the Canyon Creek Shelter. The loop begins here. Turn right and cross a wooden bridge over Sol Duc Falls, where the river spills in several separate streams and lands in a deep canyon. After several more miles of climbing through forest, you'll reach Deer Lake, a calm pool in a forested basin. Deer Lake is worth exploring, and parties who hike the loop in three or more days (which is recommended) often spend the first night at Deer Lake.

Sol Duc Falls

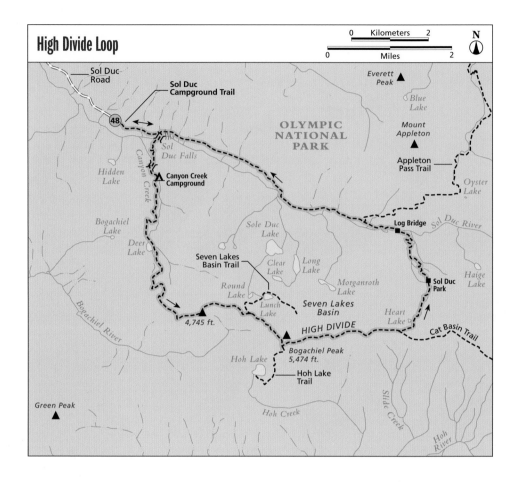

0   Kilometers   2

0   Miles   2

N

Sol Duc Road

Sol Duc Campground Trail

Everett Peak

Blue Lake

OLYMPIC NATIONAL PARK

Mount Appleton

48

Sol Duc Falls

Appleton Pass Trail

Hidden Lake

Canyon Creek

Canyon Creek Campground

Oyster Lake

Bogachiel Lake

Sole Duc Lake

Log Bridge

Sol Duc River

Deer Lake

Seven Lakes Basin Trail

Clear Lake

Long Lake

Morganroth Lake

Sol Duc Park

Haige Lake

Round Lake

Lunch Lake

Seven Lakes Basin

Heart Lake

Bogachiel River

4,745 ft.

HIGH DIVIDE

Cat Basin Trail

Hoh Lake

Bogachiel Peak 5,474 ft.

Hoh Lake Trail

Green Peak

Hoh Creek

Slide Creek

Hoh River

Just beyond Deer Lake, the trail climbs a ridge toward open meadows dotted with reflective ponds. The trail slowly climbs higher and higher until you can see the Pacific Ocean beneath the mountains and valleys in the blue distance. At about 4,800 feet, a trail snakes through a notch in the ridge and descends toward Seven Lakes Basin. First the path leads to Round and Lunch Lakes, both large lakes are at the bottom of flowery slopes. Below these two lakes are several larger, more forested lakes. Above Lunch Lake are nearly a dozen smaller lakes and ponds. These lakes, which drain into Lunch Lake, are treeless, with boulders spilling into them.

The lakes are a pleasure to wander around. A basin full of lakes is a rare treat in the Olympic Mountains, where water and snowmelt tend to flow uninterrupted down steep, steady slopes to river valleys far below.

East of the Seven Lakes Basin cutoff trail, the High Divide Loop crosses to the other side of the steep ridge. Here you'll traverse steep slopes at the head of the Bogachiel River valley. After several tight switchbacks, the trail passes under Bogachiel Peak and onto the High Divide, where you can see Seven Lakes Basin far below and the entire long, complicated Bailey Range. Summits protrude through the ice in a long arcing chain from Mount Carrie east of the High Divide to Mount Tom west of Mount Olympus. For the best views, take the 0.1-mile trail to the top of Bogachiel Peak.

The High Divide dips slowly up and down on a high ridge for almost 2.0 miles before descending to Heart Lake. For the next 3.0 miles, the trail descends through parklike meadows to the Sol Duc River. At the river, a thick canopy of trees once again crowds the sky, turning your gaze to the colors and textures immediately in front of you. It's a long slog out along the river, but ancient trees and a slight downhill grade will pull you back to Sol Duc Falls and the junction with the trail you hiked in on.

Camping on the High Divide Loop is popular and strictly controlled by the park service. It's difficult to get a permit. But the area has several good options for long day hikes. Go to Heart Lake for parklands and meadows or to the Seven Lakes Basin to see shimmering water in an alpine setting. Bogachiel Peak has the best views. Some hikers prefer to do the High Divide Loop in one day, leaving little impact and forgoing the permit process altogether.

Miles and Directions

0.0 Start at the Sol Duc Trailhead.
0.1 Pass a trail that leads to the Sol Duc Campground.
0.9 Reach the Canyon Creek Shelter and, shortly after, a bridge over Sol Duc Falls.
4.0 Arrive at Deer Lake.
7.7 Arrive at a junction with the trail to Seven Lakes Basin.
8.6 Bear right at a junction with a trail to Hoh Lake.
8.8 Pass a short trail to the top of Bogachiel Peak on the left.
8.9 Arrive at the High Divide, a long ridge above Seven Lakes Basin.
10.9 Reach the junction with the Cat Basin Trail. Turn left toward Heart Lake.
11.4 Arrive at Heart Lake.
12.3 Hike through Sol Duc Park, a meadowy area with several campsites.
13.8 Cross the Sol Duc River on a log bridge.
14.6 Pass a trail to Appleton Pass, on the right (north) side of the trail.
18.6 Pass the Canyon Creek Shelter again.
19.5 Arrive back at the trailhead.

Hike Information

Lodging
Olympic National Park Sol Duc Hot Springs and Sol Duc Campground, Olympic National Park Wilderness Information Center, 3002 Mount Angeles Road, Port Angeles; (360) 565-3100; nps.gov/olym

Other Resources
The Final Forest: Big Trees, Forks, and the Pacific Northwest, by William Dietrich

49 Pete's Creek to Colonel Bob Peak

In the southwest corner of the Olympics, Colonel Bob Peak bulges over Lake Quinault, providing hikers with superb views of the lake, the ocean, and the sharp but small peaks in the Colonel Bob Wilderness. The peak is only 4,510-feet high, but it's a long climb to the top. On the way you'll pass fruitful berry bushes and a meadow cradled by mountains.

Start: Pete's Creek Trailhead at the north side of FR 2204
Distance: 8.0 miles out and back
Hiking time: About 4 hours
Difficulty: Difficult due to length and serious elevation gain
Trail surface: Dirt trail
Elevation gain: 3,400 feet
Land status: Federal wilderness area
Nearest town: Hoquiam
Best season: June to Oct

Other trail users: Equestrians allowed from the trailhead to Moonshine Flats between July 1 and Nov 30
Canine compatibility: Leashed dogs allowed
Fees and permits: Northwest Forest Pass required to park at trailhead
Map: Green Trails no. 198, Grisdale
Trail contacts: USDA Forest Service, Pacific Ranger District, Quinault; (360) 288 2525; www.fs.usda.gov/recarea/olympic

Finding the trailhead: From Aberdeen drive north on US 101 for 24 miles and turn right (east) onto Donkey Creek Road. In 8.7 miles turn left onto FR 2204, following signs for Pete Creek Trail. In 3.3 miles—12 miles from US 101—the pavement ends. Continue 8 more miles (20.1 miles total from US 101) to Pete's Creek Trailhead, which is on the left side of the road. Parking and a privy are on the right. GPS: N47 27.44' / W123 43.89'

The Hike

Don't judge a mountain by its height. At 4,510 feet in elevation, Colonel Bob Peak isn't exactly scraping the clouds, but with the Quinalt and Humptulips Rivers cutting deep valleys on either side, the highest point in the Colonel Bob Wilderness towers over its surroundings. After the 3,500-foot climb to the top, your quads will think Colonel Bob Peak is a worthy mountain.

The small Colonel Bob Wilderness Area, at the southwestern edge of the Olympic Mountains, is composed of small, craggy peaks and dark forest valleys. Blueberries

▶ **Who was Colonel Bob?** According to *Washington's Wilderness Areas: The Complete Guide,* by Kai Huschke, Colonel Bob Peak and Colonel Bob Wilderness were named for Robert Ingersoll, a lawyer, political activist, vocal agnostic, and colonel and commanding officer of the 11th Illinois Volunteer Cavalry during the Civil War. Apparently, an Ingersoll admirer named the mountain for him. Colonel Bob never set foot on the mountain or wilderness area bearing his name.

Steep switchbacks on the trail to Colonel Bob

and huckleberries blanket the wilderness, and the bushes along the trail to Colonel Bob Peak are as productive as can be. You won't be the only one enjoying the berries, as the bear scat along the trail attests. Somehow the berries seem to ripen from near the beginning of the trail all the way to the summit, all at once.

One mile into the trail, you must cross 1-foot-deep Pete's Creek. It should be easy to cross on rocks or logs but may need to be forded. At 1.5 miles the trail begins switchbacking. Tight switchbacks lead to an open slope and through jungles of salmonberry, thimbleberry, and a variety of ferns. All along, the trail passes patches of blueberries and huckleberries, but they're especially concentrated here.

After traversing the open slopes and low jungles west of Gibson Peak, the trail passes through a notch between Gibson and Colonel Bob Peaks and enters the Moonshine Flats. Mountains hem in this gem of a meadow on all sides. Heather, huckleberries, and wildflowers mingle with groves of Alaskan yellow cedar, subalpine firs, and hemlocks that creep down from steep slopes. Moonshine Flats has several established campsites and is a good destination on its own.

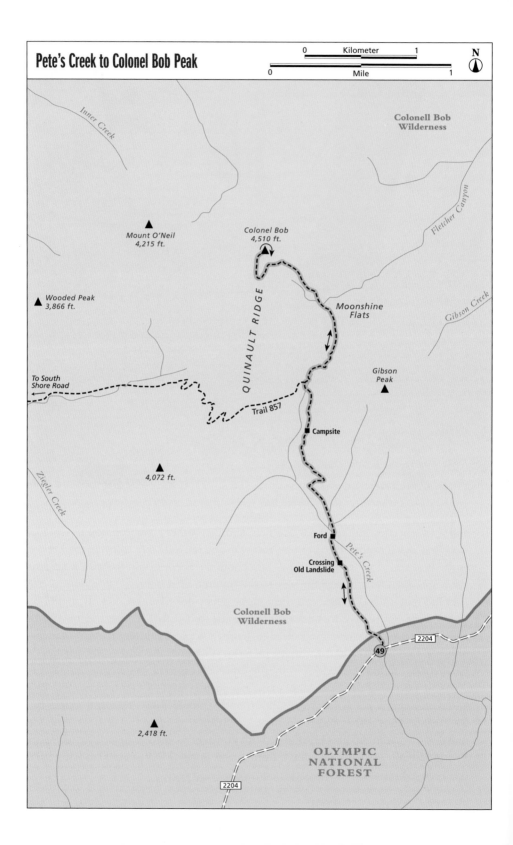

Pete's Creek to Colonel Bob Peak

0 Kilometer 1

0 Mile 1

N

Colonell Bob Wilderness

Inner Creek

Fletcher Canyon

Mount O'Neil 4,215 ft.

Colonel Bob 4,510 ft.

Moonshine Flats

Gibson Creek

Wooded Peak 3,866 ft.

QUINAULT RIDGE

Gibson Peak

To South Shore Road

Trail 857

Campsite

4,072 ft.

Ziegler Creek

Ford

Pete's Creek

Crossing Old Landslide

Colonell Bob Wilderness

2204

49

2,418 ft.

OLYMPIC NATIONAL FOREST

2204

Past the flats, the trail gets much steeper for the last 1.0 mile and 1,000 vertical feet to the top of Colonel Bob Peak. The trail gains a high ridge south of the peak before traversing beneath volcanic cliffs to the peak's mellower east face.

A nice flat spot on the west edge of the ridge of volcanic rock at the summit affords a fine vantage toward Lake Quinalt and the Quinalt River, the Pacific Ocean, and the ample peaks in the Colonel Bob Wilderness Area. The river is slowing on its way through a broad alluvial fan upstream of the lake. Luckily, there's plenty of room on the summit to spread out and rest after the hard climb to the top.

A frog in Moonshine Flats

Miles and Directions

0.0 Start from the trailhead at the north side of FR 2204.

0.7 Hike across the rocky rubble of an old landslide.

1.0 Cross Pete's Creek on a log, or ford the ankle-deep water.

1.9 Pass a campsite near Pete's Creek.

2.5 Bear right at a junction with Trail 857, which comes from South Shore Road.

3.0 Pass several streams, pools, and campsites at Moonshine Flats.

4.0 Reach the summit of Colonel Bob Peak. Return the way you came.

8.0 Arrive back at the trailhead.

Hike Information

Lodging
Yurt rentals at USDA Forest Service Coho Campground on Wynoochee Lake, Pacific Ranger District, Quinault; (360) 288-2525; www.fs.usda.gov/recarea/olympic

Restaurants
Al's Hum Dinger, 104 Lincoln St., Hoquiam; (360) 533-2754

50 Queets River Trail

A walk along the jungly rain forest of the Queets River. This hike combines two rare elements: protected lowland wilderness and solitude in a national park. The solitude comes because you have to ford a waist-deep river to get to the trailhead. This hike should only be attempted in late summer, and watch the weather forecast—a rainstorm will almost immediately spike the water level.

Start: Trailhead across the river from the Queets River Campground. The thigh- to waist-deep river must be forded to reach the trailhead.

Distance: 10 miles out and back

Hiking time: About 5 hours

Difficulty: Easy trail due to gentle terrain and little elevation gain, but difficult due to the river ford

Trail surface: Dirt trail

Elevation gain: 150 feet

Land status: National park

Nearest town: Hoquiam

Best season: Late July through Oct, depending on the height of the river

Other trail users: None

Canine compatibility: No dogs allowed

Fees and permits: National park permits required for camping; no reservations required

Map: *Green Trails Custom Correct Queets Valley; Green Trails no. 165, Kloochman Rock*

Trail contacts: USDA Forest Service, Pacific Ranger District, Quinalt; (360) 288-2525; www .fs.usda.gov/recarea/olympic

Finding the trailhead: From US 101 in Aberdeen, go north for 49 miles and turn right (east) onto FR 21. In 8.5 miles turn left onto FR 2180, following signs for Upper Queets Valley. In 1.3 miles turn left again onto Queets River Road. Continue for 4.9 miles, bearing right at a small junction in 0.7 mile and continuing to the parking lot at the end of the road, just past the Queets River Campground. GPS: N47 37.48' / W124 00.85'

The Hike

What's the fastest way to leave behind the hordes of Olympic National Park hikers and tourists to find solitude in a rain forest? You could start by fording a deep, swift river. That's how the Queets River Trail starts, leaving happy campers behind at the campground.

Like the Hoh River valley, the Queets River valley is one of the park's true temperate rain forests, with ancient trees and shag carpets of moss in every texture and color. Thanks to the river crossing, which can be thigh or waist deep in summer and much deeper the rest of the year, visitors to the Queets won't find tourists from all over the planet like they would in the Hoh valley. If you're intimidated by the crossing, go farther north and hike in the Bogachiel or Hoh River valley. The Sams River Trail loop, which is right next to the Queets Campground, is a great short alternative that doesn't require crossing the current.

Mossy maples in the Queets Valley

The crossing looks intimidating but is relatively easy and safe with trekking poles or a solid walking stick or two. Just plant your stick, move your feet, plant your stick, move your feet, and repeat, as the water rushes by. Be sure to wear an old pair of shoes or some sturdy sandals.

Once across the river, the hard part is over and a ribbon of trail leads into one of the wildest, most scenic and least-visited rain forest valleys on the peninsula. Huge trees and dense growth crowd the trail. Plants, animals, and fungi grow together in every nook. Young spruce trees grow on top of the 30-foot-tall stumps of toppled old-growth trees. Oyster mushrooms push through the bark of recently fallen trees. Head-high nurse logs feed rows of huckleberries, cedars, and firs. Stands of ancient conifers alternate with parklike groups of deciduous trees. Ancient maples wearing gowns of lichen tower over flats of sword fern.

Queets River Trail

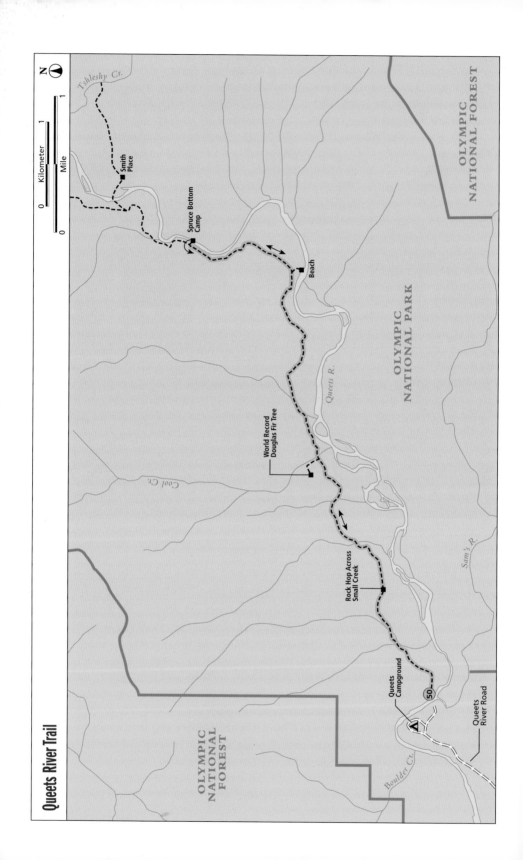

Tshleshy Cr.

Smith Place

Spruce Bottom Camp

Beach

Queets R.

World Record Douglas Fir Tree

Cool Cr.

Rock Hop Across Small Creek

Sam's R.

Queets Campground

50

Queets River Road

Boulder Cr.

OLYMPIC NATIONAL FOREST

OLYMPIC NATIONAL PARK

OLYMPIC NATIONAL FOREST

N

0   Kilometer   1

0   Mile   1

Deer and Roosevelt elk also roam the valley and can often be seen
the day in the clearing at Andrews Field, the site of an old homestead 2.0
the trailhead. Mergansers, kingfishers, and herons frequent the river's edge.

A faint path 2.4 miles from the trailhead, just west of Coal Creek, leads to o
the largest Douglas firs in the world. The rarely visited tower of bark and paltry lin
is 221 feet tall and 17 feet in diameter.

After the short side trip to see the tree, cross Coal Creek and continue east along
the river. At 4.2 miles from the trailhead, you'll come to another junction. The trail
to the right leads to a long, rocky beach. If you bear left to continue on the Queets
River Trail, you'll reach Spruce Bottom in just over 0.5 mile. Spruce Bottom is a big
camp at the base of several ancient trees. It's right next to a rocky beach. You can also
bushwhack to several smaller beaches in this stretch of trail along the river.

The beach at Spruce Bottom or the beach before it at the junction are good
destinations for a day hike. Camps here are good bases for more walking farther up
the river. The trail peters out nearly 14 miles past Spruce Bottom at the Pelton Creek
Shelter.

Miles and Directions

0.0 Start from the Queets River Trailhead on the north side of the Queets River, across the river
from the campground.

1.0 Step on stones across a small creek.

2.4 Go right at a junction. A 0.2-mile trail to the left leads to a record Douglas fir tree.

4.2 Turn left at another junction. The trail to the right leads to a long rocky beach.

5.0 Reach the Spruce Bottom Camp, at the base of several giant trees next to the river. Return
the way you came.

10.0 Arrive back at the trailhead.

Hike Information

Lodging
Queets Campground at the trailhead and yurt rentals at USDA Forest Service Coho
Campground on Wynoochee Lake, Pacific Ranger District, Quinault; (360) 288-
2525; www.fs.usda.gov/recarea/olympic

Restaurants
Al's Hum Dinger, 104 Lincoln St., Hoquiam; (360) 533-2754

Other Resources
Forest Giants of the Pacific Northwest, by Robert Van Pelt

to Hole-in-the-Wall

ful beach leads to Hole-in-the-Wall, a dramatic doorway
rrounded by tide pools. This is a crowded hike, but there's
t the beach. Consider this an introduction course to the
ness coastline.

Start: Rialto Beach parking lot at the end of Mora Road
Distance: 3.6 miles out and back
Hiking time: 2 hours
Difficulty: Easy
Trail surface: Sandy and pebbly beach; rocky tide pools and boulders at the arch
Elevation gain: None
Land status: National park
Nearest town: Forks
Best season: Year-round; weather best in summer

Other trail users: None
Canine compatibility: Dogs allowed on the beach only to Ellen Creek, about halfway to Hole in the Wall
Fees and permits: National park permit required for camping
Maps: *Green Trails no. 130S, Ozette; Green Trails Custom Correct North Olympic Coast*
Trail contacts: Olympic National Park Forks Office, 551 S. Forks Ave. (US 101); (360) 374-7566; nps.gov/olym/index.htm

Finding the trailhead: From Forks, drive 1.5 miles north on US 101 out of town. Turn left (west) onto La Push Road (WA 110). In 7.8 miles turn right onto Mora Road to continue on WA 110. Continue on Mora Road for 5 miles, passing the Mora Campground, and arrive at the parking lot at the end of the road. GPS: N47 55.19' / W124 38.28'

The Hike

The walk from Rialto Beach to Hole-in-the-Wall is a perennial favorite beach day hike. Rialto is a fantastic stretch of beach—long and sandy in places and covered in perfect skipping stones in others. Waves roll in from the Pacific and crash on the shores. Their slow power over time has excavated a hole in a wall of solid rock 1.5 miles down the beach from the parking lot.

The waves crash into the shore endlessly, with the power and determination of a glacier creeping down a mountain, carving and polishing stone on its journey. When the waves are good, surfers flock to Rialto Beach to ride the cold barrels toward the pebbly shore.

From the base of Hole in the Wall, rocky reefs filled with tide pools spread out in all directions. The cove north of Rialto Beach especially is covered in tide pools. The hike from Rialto Beach to Hole in the Wall, like most hikes on this wild stretch of coastline, is better at low tide. In fact, you won't be able to get through and beyond the Hole-in-the-Wall if the tide is high.

The hike starts on a gentle section of the beach covered in perfectly rounded skipping stones. Massive driftwood logs line the beach. The bigger ones have a

Hole-in-the-Wall

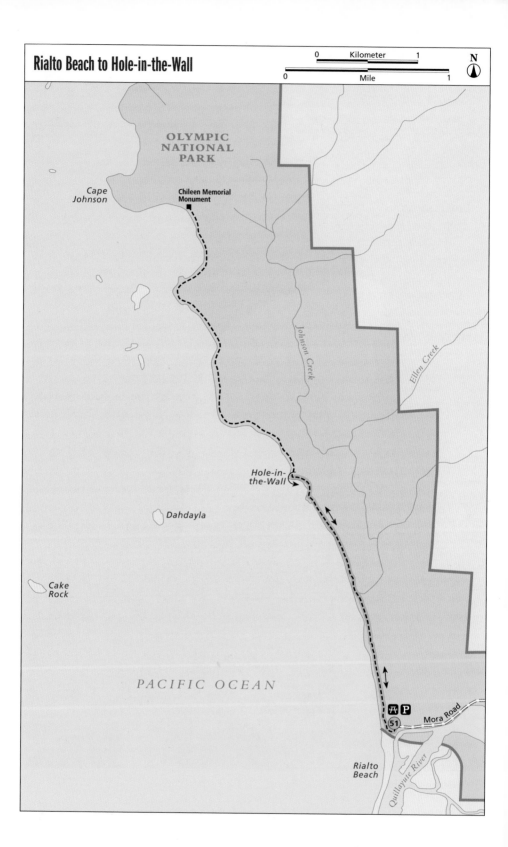

Kilometer

Mile

N

OLYMPIC
NATIONAL
PARK

Cape
Johnson

Chileen Memorial
Monument

Johnson Creek

Ellen Creek

Hole-in-
the-Wall

Dahdayla

Cake
Rock

PACIFIC OCEAN

51

Mora Road

Rialto
Beach

Quillayute River

6-foot-diameter and root-balls that reach far overhead. These logs started out in the Olympic Peninsula's rain forests. Storms toppled them and flushed them out to the ocean, where wind and waves eventually pushed them ashore.

At 0.9 mile cross Ellen Creek. Camping is allowed past Ellen Creek, and the creek is the first freshwater along the way. Ellen Creek, like most creeks on the Olympic Coast, is a brownish, tea color because of dissolved tannins from roots and organic matter brewing in the water. It's safe to drink if treated.

Just before the Hole-in-the-Wall are several incredible sea stacks. The huge sandstone teeth rise directly out of the sandy beach, and the tallest one is about 80 feet high. Scraggly trees grow around their pointed summits.

Hole-in-the-Wall is just beyond the sea stacks. The arch at the union of earth and water solicits wonder and exploration. At low tide, tide pools surround Hole in the Wall. It's a quick and easy day hike, and most tourists stop there. If you venture farther north, the coastline gets more rugged and lonely. A popular longer trip is the 23-mile journey from Rialto Beach to Cape Alava and Lake Ozette. The section of the beach is called the Shipwreck Coast, and long-distance hikers pass a Chilean shipwreck memorial 1.0 mile north of Hole-in-the-Wall and a Norwegian memorial 5.0 miles farther.

The beach gets more rugged directly past Hole in the wall. Wave-carved boulders and shallow rock reefs harbor tide pools big and small. Explore the beach and you'll probably come across massive, rusted parts of old shipwrecks. The mariners who sailed the vessels off this coast knew it as some of the most treacherous waters. To hikers and tide poolers, on the other hand, the wild coast and towering sea stacks are paradise.

Miles and Directions

0.0 Start hiking north on the beach from the day-use or backpacker parking lot at Rialto Beach.

0.9 Cross Ellen Creek, a small stream running through the sand. Camping is allowed north of here.

1.8 Reach several immense sea stacks and Hole-in-the-Wall. Return the way you came.

3.6 Arrive back at the parking lot.

Hike Information

Local Information
Quileute Nation; www.quileutenation.org

Lodging
USDA Forest Service Mora Campground, Olympic National Park Forks Office, 551 S. Forks Ave. (US 101); (360) 374-7566; nps.gov/olym/index.htm

Other Resources
The Final Forest: Big Trees, Forks, and the Pacific Northwest, by William Dietrich

52 Shi Shi Beach–Point of the Arches

After crashing through forest on a muddy road, you'll descend to a long, sandy beach. At the far end, some of the most spectacular arches, sea stacks, and tide pools on Washington's wild coastline protrude 0.5 mile into the Pacific Ocean. Try to get there at low tide—the tide pools are amazing.

Start: Trailhead at the day-use parking lot on Tsoo-Yess Beach Road
Distance: 8.8 miles out and back
Hiking time: About 5 hours
Difficulty: Moderate due to length and steep descent to the beach upon entering the national park
Trail surface: Dirt trail, muddy roadbed, sandy beach
Elevation gain: 200 feet
Land status: Makah Indian Reservation, Olympic National Park
Nearest town: Neah Bay

Best season: Year-round; first 2 miles of trail muddy year-round
Other trail users: None
Canine compatibility: No dogs allowed
Fees and permits: Makah Recreation Pass, Olympic National Park permit required for camping; fee to park at private overnight lots
Maps: *Green Trails no. 98S, Cape Flattery; Green Trails Custom Correct North Olympic Coast*
Trail contacts: Olympic National Park Forks Office, 551 S. Forks Ave. (US 101); (360) 374-7566; nps.gov/olym/index.htm

Finding the trailhead: From Port Angeles go west on US 101 for 5 miles, and turn right onto WA 112 (Strait of Juan de Fuca Highway). Continue 64 miles to Neah Bay. (Alternately, reach Neah Bay from Forks by driving north on US 101 for 12.3 miles to a junction with SR 113. Turn left [north] onto Route 113 and continue for 10 miles to the junction with WA 112. Turn left [west] and drive 26 miles to Neah Bay.) From Neah Bay continue west on Bayview Avenue. Makah Recreation Passes are available at Washburn General Store and several other places in Neah Bay. At the west end of town, turn left onto Fort Street; take the third right onto Third Avenue and then the second left onto Cape Flattery Road. Follow signs for Cape Flattery and Hobuck Beach Resort through this section. Continue 2.4 miles on Cape Flattery Road. Turn left onto Hobuck Road and drive over the Waatch River, following signs for the fish hatchery. Continue on this road, which becomes Tsoo-Yess Beach Road, for 4 miles to the day-use parking area and trailhead. If you are camping, unload packs here and drive back to the last residence and pay the parking fee. GPS: N48 17.63' / W124 39.94'

The Hike

The longest stretch of wild coastline in the lower 48 has many amazing beaches, tide pools, and sea stacks. An entire breed of backpackers devote themselves to wandering this rugged coast, eschewing the high mountain glaciers and views. Instead, beach hikers count the surf as their constant companion and look for migrating whales beyond the breakers. The coast's beaches and camp spots invite long days of wandering barefoot in the sand, watching the sun sink into the empty horizon, brightening a new day in Japan.

The Point of the Arches on Shi Shi Beach

Shi Shi Beach (pronounced "shy shy") and Point of the Arches are as good a spot as any on the Olympic Peninsula's rugged coast. With the required national park camping permit, the Makah Recreation Pass, and the cost for overnight parking, it can be expensive to camp at Shi Shi Beach, although day hikers get around much of that cost.

When you descend from the seaside jungle and arrive at Shi Shi Beach and see the arches and sea stacks at the other end of the beach's sandy arc, you'll forget the cost and the long drive. The beach is well worth the admission price.

The first of the 100-foot-tall sea stacks at Point of the Arches towers above the sand, and the broken line of arches continues more than 0.5 mile into the Pacific. Yet the entire length of the beach is sandy, from Point of the Arches to the rocky coves 2.4 miles north.

Viewed from a campsite at the north end of the beach, the stacks are tall and majestic. Up close, they're full of life, with rich tide pools under their cavernous arches and tunnels. At low tide (the lower the better) you can explore these tide pools. At extremely low tides, the maze of pools and rock walls seems to go on forever. Around each bend is a new wall of orange starfish hanging onto the edge of a deep tide pool, or a tunnel covered in barnacles and sea anemone.

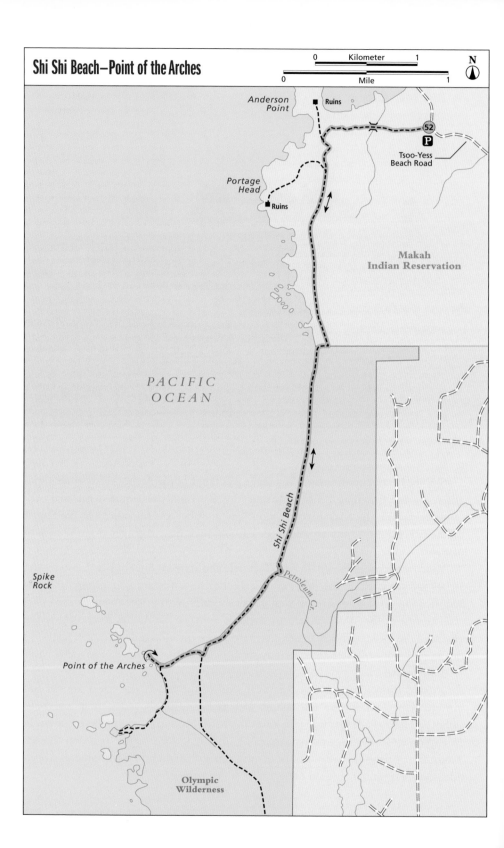

Shi Shi Beach–Point of the Arches

Kilometer
0 1

Mile
0 1

N

Anderson Point

Ruins

52

P

Tsoo-Yess Beach Road

Portage Head

Ruins

Makah Indian Reservation

PACIFIC OCEAN

Shi Shi Beach

Spike Rock

Petroleum Cr.

Point of the Arches

Olympic Wilderness

But time is of the essence. Let your camera feast on the sites, and explore the tide pools quickly. Then make sure to scamper back before the tide gets too high.

From the trailhead, boardwalks and bridges climb a moist hill to an old roadbed on a plateau. At this point, slightly less than 1.0 mile from the parking lot, the trail gets muddy; it's nice to have tall hiking boots to keep your feet dry. You never know when your foot will squelch up to your ankle in deep mud through the boggy sections of trail. In 2.0 miles, just past a view overlooking the ocean, the trail reaches the border of Olympic National Park and begins a quick descent to Shi Shi Beach. The trail switchbacks across roots and steep dirt. Ropes tied to trees provide an extra handle in the steeper parts.

Then you arrive on the beach. Hiking on the beach is easiest when the tide is low. That way, you can walk in the firm wet sand without having to leap for dry sand every time a wave comes up to lap at your muddy feet.

People camp all along the beach by the hundreds on sunny weekends. The first reliable water source is at Petroleum Creek, 1.3 miles down the beach. To avoid the parking and camping fees, and the required use of bear canisters for storing your food overnight, you can day-hike to Shi Shi and Point of the Arches. Try to plan your trip to the arches at low tide so that you can thoroughly explore the point.

Miles and Directions

0.0 Start from the trailhead at the Shi Shi Beach day-use parking lot.

0.3 Cross a creek on Cantilever Bridge, a tall wooden A-frame bridge.

0.7 Begin a section of trail that crosses over and around dozens of large mud holes.

2.0 Cross into Olympic National Park and begin descending to Shi Shi Beach.

3.3 Cross Petroleum Creek after 1.3 miles of hiking along the beach. In summer, this is the first source of freshwater on the beach.

4.4 Arrive at the Point of the Arches, which can be explored at low tide. Return the way you came.

8.8 Arrive back at the trailhead.

Hike Information

Local Events/Attractions
Makah Museum, Neah Bay; makah.com; (360) 645-2711

Lodging
Hobuck Beach Resort, 2726 Makah Passage, Neah Bay; (360) 645-2330; hobuckbeachresort.com

Other Resources
The Northwest Coast: Or, Three Years' Residence in Washington Territory, by James Swan and Norman Clark

Honorable Mentions

W Hoh River to Glacier Meadows

The hike up the Hoh River is one of the most popular hikes in Olympic National Park; it's certainly the most popular rain forest hike. It begins in a forest of giant, ancient trees draped in moss. Elk graze in the valley. Walk the paved Hall of Mosses Trail for 0.2 mile to marvel at the colossal trees, or continue 17.5 miles to Glacier Meadows beneath Mount Olympus's Blue Glacier—a curving expanse of ice that extends for thousands of feet beneath Olympus's summit.

From Forks go south on US 101 for 13 miles (or north 90 miles from Aberdeen) to Upper Hoh Road. Go east on Upper Hoh Road for 18 miles to a large parking lot and visitor center at the trailhead.

X Enchanted Valley

To properly experience the wild valley on the Upper Quinalt River in the Olympic Peninsula, you have to spend a night or two. The Enchanted Valley Chalet, in a cirque below Anderson Pass, is 13 miles from the trailhead. Continues 12 more miles to alpine gardens surrounding Lake La Crosse. Required permits are limited, especially on weekends. In this magical valley, you'll find milky glacial water rushing past ancient trees and possibly elk and black bears. Snowcapped mountains surround Enchanted Valley, but for most of the trail it's hard to see beyond the towering trees. From the Enchanted Valley Chalet, you can turn around and retrace your tracks, climb south to O'Neill Pass and a lake-filled alpine basin, or climb up and over Anderson Pass to the east and hike to the other side of the Olympics in the Dosewallips River valley.

Drive to the South Shore Road/Lake Quinalt Road on US 101 (40 miles north of Aberdeen). Continue past the lake for 18 miles to Graves Creek Campground. At the campground, the South Shore Road narrows and continues for 0.5 mile to the trailhead.

Y Silver Lake

For an easy-to-access wilderness getaway, hike the 5.5-mile trail to Silver Lake, a small alpine lake tucked below Welch Peak and Mount Townsend. Part of Silver Lake's appeal is its tranquility and solitude. The crowds head to nearby Mount Townsend and Marmot Pass. Silver Lake doesn't have the 360-degree views of those destinations, but it's a peaceful spot to absorb the sunshine and surrounding peaks.

From Olympia drive 70 miles on US 101 N. About 1 mile south of Quilcene, turn left (west) onto Penny Creek Road. In 1.4 miles turn left onto Big Quilcene River Road. Continue on Big Quilcene River Road, bearing right in 3.1 miles at a junction with Road 2740, until you reach FR 27-190, 9.4 miles after turning onto Big Quilcene River Road. Follow this road up to the trailhead in 0.8 mile.

Hike Index

HM = Honorable Mention

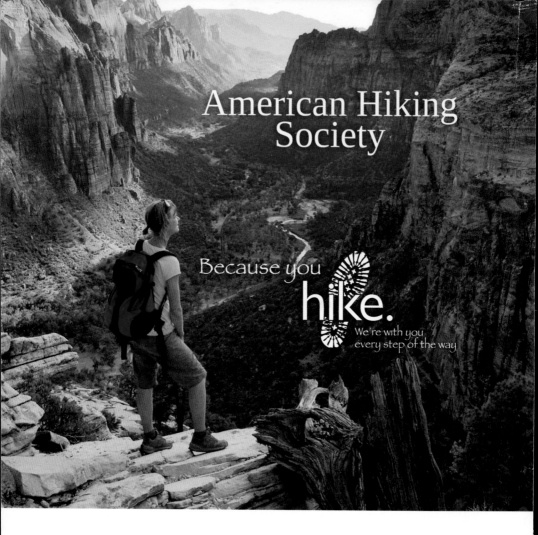

American Hiking Society

Because you
hike.
We're with you
every step of the way

As a national voice for hikers, **American Hiking Society** works every day:

- Building and maintaining hiking trails
- Educating and supporting hikers by providing information and resources
- Supporting hiking and trail organizations nationwide
- Speaking for hikers in the halls of Congress and with federal land managers

Whether you're a casual hiker or a seasoned backpacker, become a member of American Hiking Society and join the national hiking community! You'll enjoy great member benefits and help preserve the nation's hiking trails, so tomorrow's hike is even better than today's. We invite you to join us now!

American Hiking Society

www.AmericanHiking.org • info@AmericanHiking.org